Strategy and Security in U.S.–Mexican Relations beyond the Cold War

U.S.–MEXICO CONTEMPORARY PERSPECTIVES SERIES, 9
CENTER FOR U.S.–MEXICAN STUDIES
UNIVERSITY OF CALIFORNIA, SAN DIEGO

Contributors

Sergio Aguayo Quezada
John Bailey
John A. Cope
Michael J. Dziedzic
Guadalupe González González
Luis Herrera-Lasso
David R. Mares
Jorge E. Tello Peón
Manuel Villa Aguilera

Strategy and Security in U.S.–Mexican Relations beyond the Cold War

Edited by

JOHN BAILEY
AND
SERGIO AGUAYO QUEZADA

CENTER FOR U.S.–MEXICAN STUDIES
UNIVERSITY OF CALIFORNIA, SAN DIEGO

Printed in the United States of America

Library of Congress Cataloging-in-Publication Data

Strategy and security in U.S.–Mexican relations beyond the Cold War / edited by John Bailey and Sergio Aguayo.

p. cm.

Includes bibliographical references.

ISBN 1-878367-32-3 (pbk.)

1. United States—Relations—Mexico. 2. Mexico—Relations—United States. 3. National security—United States. 4. National security—Mexico. I. Bailey, John, 1944 Nov. 30– II. Aguayo, Sergio. III. Series.

E183.8.M6S88 1996

303.48′273072—dc20 96-21807

CIP

Contents

Civil and Military Responses

Acknowledgments

The editors are especially grateful for generous financial support from the John D. and Catherine T. MacArthur Foundation and for Foundation officials' patience and cooperation at various stages of the project. Also, we thank Wayne Cornelius, formerly Director of the Center for U.S.–Mexican Studies of the University of California, San Diego, and Arturo Valenzuela, Director (on leave) of the Center for Latin American Studies at Georgetown University, as well as Ilán Bizberg, Director of the Center for International Studies, and Gustavo Vega, Director of the U.S.–Canada Program, both of El Colegio de México, for hosting meetings of the Study Group. Tim Goodman of Georgetown University's Department of Government did an excellent job in routing multiple drafts among several authors and keeping track of it all, while also turning out timely and accurate translations.

1

Strategy and Security in U.S.–Mexican Relations

John Bailey and Sergio Aguayo Quezada

The guerrilla insurrection that burst forth on January 1, 1994, in Chiapas, the southernmost state in Mexico, illustrates well the significance of the end of the cold war. If, ten years earlier, more than a thousand armed and masked insurgents had marched out of the jungles bordering Guatemala, the reaction in Washington would have verged on panic. A guerrilla uprising in the United States' southern neighbor would have realized the worst nightmares of security policy makers: spillover of Central America's civil wars into Mexico's most impoverished region. In 1994, however, official Washington was concerned but remained calm and deliberately avoided involvement in an internal Mexican problem. The end of superpower rivalry had created a markedly different context. The Chiapas events were seen not as a nostalgic throwback to the 1960s and 1970s, but rather as a radical form of protest growing out of the "lost decade" of the 1980s and the wrenching consequences of the economic stabilization and structural adjustment policies of the 1990s. The U.S. government's response to the uprising was to support continued liberalization of the Mexican political system.

National Interests in the Bilateral Relationship

The end of the cold war has prompted a general reconsideration of strategic and security interests among scholars and interested publics throughout the world. Alliances and rivalries fostered by nearly four decades of a stable bipolar system are being reexamined in a new light. Such is the case with the United States and Mexico, two neighbors that bring different, and often conflicting, interpretations of their national interests to the formulation of national security policies. As a result, policies adopted by each government can become a source of discord and tension with the other, since they are often formulated without due consideration of the other country's interpretation of its own national interests.

For more than forty years, anticommunism and containment, along with promotion of democracy and market economies, formed the core of U.S. security thinking. Much effort was devoted to articulating these views and their supporting strategies both at home and abroad. The Mexican government, however, avoided public discussion of national security or the formulation of an explicit national security doctrine, fearing that such action might provide an opening for the United States to impose its own security priorities on Mexico. Historically, U.S. security policy toward Latin America has tended to stress military defense against conventional external aggression and the neutralization of domestic leftist movements seen as threats to the internal stability of friendly governments. Mexico has been vigilant in opposing any U.S. effort to promote the more interventionist manifestations of the U.S. security agenda in the region—for example, with respect to Central America in the 1980s.

Recent developments at both the regional and global levels have impelled both governments to reconsider the concept of national security and the bilateral security agenda. Since the late 1980s, and as part of a fundamental restatement of its national development project, the Mexican government has discussed national security issues more extensively and publicly than it had done previously. In this context, the government has publicly identified new security threats (such as drug trafficking) and recognized an increasing number of joint U.S.–Mexican security interests. For its part, the U.S. government has also reconsidered the concept of national security and its applications, in light of the potential rise of regional commercial blocs and the emergence of new threats such as transnational organized crime, terrorism, regional conflicts, failed states, and uncontrolled flows of refugees.

The U.S.–Mexican relationship is unique in the world. Only here do the developed and developing worlds meet along such a long (nearly 2,000–mile) border. The relationship is distinguished by what Thorup (1992: 1) has called "extreme interdependence," a concept used "to underscore the unique depth, breadth, and long history of this very intense relationship. The concept also gives special emphasis to the transnationalization of civic participation and growing societal interdependency between the United States and Mexico." Relations between the two countries should be seen as "intermestic" in the sense that they combine both domestic and international dynamics, as is the case, for example, with trade and investment, organized crime, undocumented migration, public health and environment, and so on. Three recent trends are especially important. First, the bilateral relationship has become even more extensive and intensive in the post–cold war period, reinforced by closer economic and social integration and technological innovation in travel and communications. Second, both societies are experiencing increasing rates of crime and social distress. Third, the United States seeks to impose its own legal concepts and policy preferences on other countries generally and on Mexico specifically.[1]

There is little reason, however, to expect a natural convergence of thinking about strategy and security between the United States and Mexico. The bilateral redefinition of strategic and security interests will likely engender new tensions and conflicts, as well as new opportunities for cooperation. Possible future points of bilateral tension include:

- heightened control, even militarization, of the border region arising from antidrug and anti-immigration policy;

- "interventionist" methods of promoting democracy and defense of human rights, as exemplified by the United States in Haiti;

- military involvement in the antidrug struggle, as was seen in Panama; and

- Mexican perceptions of a persistent U.S. tendency toward unilateralism.

The Bilateral Project on Strategy and Security

Beginning in 1991, and supported by generous funding from the John D. and Catherine T. MacArthur Foundation, the Georgetown University Project on Strategy and Security in U.S.–Mexican Relations in

[1] Admittedly quite vague, our use of "social distress" refers not only to crime but also to broader ills in both countries, such as structural poverty and unemployment, homelessness, and personal insecurity. Some U.S. experts suggest that crime rates in the United States have not increased significantly; rather, the news media have tended to sensationalize specific crimes and thus portray a worsening situation. Even so, inviting reflection is a recent report to the effect that the number of persons presently subject to the U.S. prison system (behind bars, on parole, and the like) will soon surpass the number of persons in four-year colleges and universities. The best general discussion linking U.S. foreign policy with law enforcement is Nadelmann 1993.

the Post–Cold War Era has reflected on these issues. The study group was made up of distinguished scholars from both countries. Also, officials from security and foreign policy agencies participated in discussions, and several contributed memoranda or papers. The core group met for extended discussions in La Jolla, California (February 1992), Tepoztlán, Morelos (October 1992), Washington, D.C. (June 1993), and Mexico City (August 1995). Additional guests were invited to participate in each of these meetings.

We should underline the novelty, even uniqueness, of the project. The scholarship on U.S.–Mexico relations has focused extensively on commercial, economic, cultural, demographic, and political themes. An exception is the edited volume by Bagley and Aguayo (1993), which focused largely on concepts and theory. By and large, however, issues of strategy and security, especially at the organizational and operational levels, were largely considered "out of bounds" for scholars, as was dialogue with security policy makers. U.S. researchers were leery of topics freighted with "cold war" overtones and involving the defense and intelligence establishments. Mexican scholars were concerned not only about this U.S. dimension but also about the possibility that their scholarly involvement might lend legitimacy to the Mexican security apparatus, long associated with internal repression. Furthermore, Mexican officials were reluctant to address practical issues of security, even in Mexican public circles.

These deeply ingrained prejudices were tested by the end of the cold war. Our belief that questions of security must be reconsidered in light of a changed global setting coincided with a new willingness by Mexicans—both academics and public officials—to engage in dialogue. What Sergio Aguayo has called a "quiet revolution" in the professionalization of Mexican security agencies was reflected in an unprecedented willingness to discuss issues previously considered taboo. Thus the project was unique in bringing together scholars and officials drawn from both countries to consider at length the sensitive and crucial topic of strategy and security in the bilateral relationship.

Clearly, the post–cold war relaxation of tensions and prospects for a successful conclusion to the NAFTA negotiations fostered cooperation, which was especially important with respect to the Salinas administration's willingness to allow Mexican officials to participate in the project. But there remained some reservations. Objections were also signaled by the U.S. Embassy in Mexico City, which was similarly committed to a successful NAFTA negotiation. Had some unfortunate event occurred, or if the negotiations had soured, our project might have been placed "off limits" with respect to official cooperation.

Therefore, ours was a fragile undertaking, and some taboos were respected. Active-duty Mexican military officers did not participate. By general agreement, we excluded participation of the Central Intelligence Agency. Also, we deliberately chose to avoid making recommendations as a group or project, although various authors have offered policy advice and virtually all of the chapters contain policy-relevant analyses. We were more than satisfied to convene the meetings, promote dialogue, and thereby move issues of strategy and security out of the offices of "specialized bureaucracies" and closer to the mainstream discussion.

We anticipated that the discussions would be complex and perhaps difficult, especially since the convocation of both scholars and policy makers was breaking new ground. In fact, this proved to be the case. We were not prepared, however, for the extraordinary political volatility that beset both countries and the bilateral relationship between 1991 and 1995, forcing repeated delays in bringing our deliberations to closure. As a group, we lived through the surprising collapse of the Bush administration and the election of Bill Clinton in 1992. Then came the drama of the NAFTA debates and the treaty's passage by the U.S. Congress in November 1993. For Mexico, 1994 proved to be an eventful, traumatic year, beginning with the Chiapas rebellion and followed by horrific, high-profile assassinations and a dramatic presidential election in August. Just as events appeared to return to something like normalcy, the peso collapsed in December 1995 and Mexico once again entered a phase of extreme uncertainty.

This volatility brought personal adjustments as well. Sally Shelton, one of the original project codirectors, accepted an appointment in the Clinton administration with the Agency for International Development; Sergio Aguayo became deeply engaged in Mexico's presidential elections as one of the national coordinators of Alianza Cívica, an umbrella organization of some four hundred pro-democracy groups; and Arturo Valenzuela, the project's patron from the outset, joined the Clinton administration in the Department of State, which resulted in John Bailey's appointment as interim director of Georgetown's Center for Latin American Studies. In addition, several other members of the original core group moved along—and arguably up—their respective career tracks. While these adjustments slowed the project, we are convinced that they improved the product. We shudder to think how irrelevant conclusions reached in 1993 would be in light of subsequent developments. And we recognize that the pace of change will likely not slow in the coming months and years. Even so, we are better prepared to report our findings.

Overview of Findings

Several broad questions structured our discussions. How do Mexico and the United States each understand the concepts of national strategy and security? What issues does each government regard as proper strategic and security concerns? Do the two countries have common strategic and security interests? What might these be? What impact does each country's interpretation of strategy and security have on the other? How do the changes wrought since the end of the cold war (regional economic integration, intensified antidrug operations, and political liberalization, among others) affect strategic and security considerations? What might be sources of future bilateral tensions and conflicts about strategy and security, and how might these tensions be mitigated? How appropriate is bilateral or multilateral resolution of security problems, given concerns about national sovereignty, self-determination, and interventionism?

An initial framework and assignment of topics rather quickly proved to be inadequate, as discussions and events forced us to think in new ways. We have grouped the chapters that grew out of our discussions under three broad categories, recognizing that the themes overlap in a number of ways. We begin with a broad overview of new strategic and security interests; from this we proceed to chapters whose central concerns involve a bilateral perspective. The final section focuses on civilian and military agency–level responses to new security issues.

In "Strategic Interests in the U.S.–Mexican Relationship," David Mares uses the concept "grand strategy" to analyze how Mexico and the United States identify their respective strategic interests and adopt policies to defend those interests. He argues that until the 1980s, both countries had a relatively stable threat assessment. Mexico viewed potential U.S. domination as its only significant state-based security threat, while the United States viewed direct or indirect Soviet aggression as the only real threat to its security interests. Mares argues that these traditional grand strategies are no longer adequate to address the new issues and challenges that will dominate the bilateral agenda in the post–cold war era, such as fighting the drug trade and promoting regional economic integration and global commercial competitiveness. Because these new bilateral issues are generally not susceptible to resolution by unilateral or military means, Mares warns against defining them as "security interests," given that security matters almost by definition demand unilateral resolution. To define economic competitiveness as a "security interest," for instance, might generate pressures for trade protectionism and thus undermine economic liberalization. Mares also warns against defining democratization as a security interest or challenges to democracy as security threats since, he suggests, authoritarian regimes pose no inherent threat to democracies. He criticizes efforts to promote democracy through interventionist means as fraught with problems and rarely successful.

In "Mexico in the Sphere of Hemispheric Security," Luis Herrera-Lasso gives us a detailed examination of the various organizations that together constituted the cold war hemispheric security framework, and especially of those through which the United States and friendly Latin American governments cooperated in defeating the security threats of that era. Herrera-Lasso differs with Mares, however, in including democratization and human rights among the new security interests common to the United States and Latin American nations, although he agrees with Mares that these interests must not be secured through interventionism or the use of force. Even though Mexico opposes such tactics, Herrera-Lasso believes that other Latin American nations are increasingly receptive to external intervention in the domestic affairs of sovereign states, provided both that the motive is worthy—for example, promotion of democracy or human rights—and that the interventions are conducted multilaterally, preferably under the aegis of the United Nations or the Organization of American States. Herrera-Lasso underlines Mexico's deep reservations about external and aggressive forms of intervention into the internal affairs of sovereign nations, even for laudable and widely supported ends. Such interventions create troubling precedents that can lead to counterproductive actions in the future.

Moving toward a more bilateral perspective, Michael Dziedzic and Manuel Villa Aguilera paint interesting contrasts of perspectives on strategy and security held by governing elites. In "Mexico and U.S. Grand Strategy: The Geo-strategic Linchpin to Security and Prosperity," Dziedzic characterizes the geo-strategic relevance of Mexico for the United States. Mexico's strategic significance has evolved along with changes in the global order. During the cold war, and long before, Mexico was prized as a geopolitical fulcrum. On the southern flank of the United States, it was cultivated as a source of leverage to distract U.S. energies away from other vital pursuits. In the post–cold war period, Mexico's geoeconomic importance has become much more salient. Mexico's efforts to move toward an open economy (whether successful or not) will heavily influence the viability of the U.S. government's strategy of enlargement. Concurrently, Dziedzic suggests, Mexico has also become a choke point for an array of what he terms "geosocial" or transnational afflictions that respect no national boundaries. Thus Mexico will play a key role in the emerging struggle to ward off the direct consequences of what pessimists refer to as the "new world disorder." If Mexico succumbs, the United States can scarcely expect to avoid the full and direct consequences of what Robert Kaplan (1994) has called "the coming anarchy." Thus Mexico has been, and will continue to be, pivotal to the success of U.S. grand strategy.

In contrast to both Herrera-Lasso and Dziedzic, Manuel Villa ("Mexico's National Security Policies and Institutions in the Post–Cold War Era") underlines points of divergence between the United States and Mexico. He warns that future tensions between Mexico and the United States are most likely to result from mutual insensitivity to each other's national priorities and from the failure to communicate clearly. Villa rejects the contention of the volume's editors that Mexico failed to articulate a national security doctrine during the cold war era because it feared subordination to the United States. The absence of doctrine resulted instead from Mexico's distinctiveness in formulating a clear national project that created sufficient political space for labor and the Left, in contrast to most other Latin American countries. Further, Villa argues that failure to communicate clearly helps to explain why the United States tends to project its own priorities onto Mexico. (The reverse also happens, but to a much lesser extent.) Villa also warns that the U.S. tendency toward unilateralism in Latin America remains a threat, as illustrated by its militaristic and coercive methods in fighting the hemisphere-wide drug trade. He advises the U.S. government to rely less on military operations and diplomatic pressures against Latin American countries to restrict local supply, and more on fighting the poverty and ignorance upon which drug traffickers feed. Finally, Villa regards the U.S. insistence on global promotion of its own conception of democracy not only as inconsistent with Mexico's interests but also as an implicit threat to Mexico's own security. Villa anticipates that Mexico will have to formulate a more explicit and active doctrine of national security in order to keep from acquiescing in U.S. initiatives that contradict its own interests.

In "Challenges of Unfinished Modernization: Stability, Democracy, and National Security in Mexico," Guadalupe González undertakes the daunting task of characterizing Mexico's transition away from authoritarianism and linking this to concerns about security. Unlike Manuel Villa, González regards the Mexican regime as a source of instability and insecurity, not as the country's main protection against insecurity. She expands the definition of national security to include the nation's capacity for economic, social, and political progress. González urges us to consider the domestic factors that shape national security threats facing "peripheral" countries such as Mexico. These include domestic social conflict, ethnic diversity, poverty, economic underdevelopment, population growth, and weak state and political institutions, as well as the resources and strategies for dealing with those threats. She notes that domestic social conflicts can become security problems when they are resolved through force, outside of established political and legal channels.

González's analysis of the formulation of national security policy highlights "political" variables—including political support coalitions, state institutions, state strength, and internal sociopolitical cohesion and consensus. State institutions is the most important of these variables, since weak sociopolitical cohesion can undermine both the regime's political legitimacy and the prevailing consensus regarding basic national values. This in turn conduces to violence and domestic instability which can undermine national security. Further, she believes that inadequate social and political integration—insufficient democratization—is the chief security challenge facing Mexico today. During the 1980s, the nationalist project inherited from the Mexican Revolution underwent a fundamental transformation, as the desire for democracy came to overshadow the imperative of maintaining national unity against perceived external threats. Only democracy, González insists, can give the country enduring stability and internal peace. Genuine democratization requires not just clean and fair elections but also effective administration of justice and decentralization of power. The major contrast between the administrations of Carlos Salinas and Ernesto Zedillo, she suggests, is the latter's emphasis on governing within legal institutions. The dilemma, however, is that while stressing legality reinforces trends toward democratization, it weakens the presidency's short-term ability to deal with authoritarian political bosses and conservative elements in the ruling party.

In "Controlling Drugs: Strategic Operations and U.S. and Mexican National Interests," Jorge Tello Peón provides a useful bridge from broader global and bilateral issues to our interest in operational matters of policy making and institutions. Tello Peón views the struggle against the international drug trade as an opportunity for closer U.S.–Mexican cooperation. He explains that drug trafficking has become increasingly both a hemisphere-wide concern and a bilateral security challenge. It is a many-sided problem that requires an "integral" solution—that is, one that uses a variety of means to attack simultaneously all of its various manifestations. Since the causes and impacts of the drug problem are global in scope and implications, so must be its solution. Tello Peón explains that the drug trade has come to pose a direct national security threat to Mexico, even though the country has traditionally served only as a transit point for drug shipments, and even though it does not share the cultural weaknesses that have allowed drug traffickers to penetrate the United States so easily. Nevertheless, drug trafficking has steadily undermined Mexico's territorial integrity, domestic political stability, and atmosphere of legality.

Consistent with his emphasis on "integrality," Tello argues that multinational cooperation is essential to defeating the international drug trade. He provides useful descriptions of the Mexican government's various bureaucratic innovations to assist in fighting drug trafficking, especially in the areas of information sharing, demand reduction, and crop eradication. He warns, however, that such cooperation must always eschew interventionism and violations of each nation's right to self-determination.

Sergio Aguayo Quezada asserts in "Intelligence Services and the Transition to Democracy in Mexico" that our complete ignorance about Mexico's intelligence services is not only absurd but dangerous, since the role of these services in Mexico's political transition has tremendous importance. Aguayo makes a twofold contribution: he carefully analyzes the functions of intelligence services in democratic polities, and he describes the origins and recent evolution of Mexico's security services in the postwar period, and especially from the mid-1980s to the present. He maintains that democratic polities need effective intelligence and security services but that special arrangements must be made to subject these services to democratic controls, especially through popularly elected legislatures. He identifies several requirements that must be met in order to reconcile the efficiency of intelligence services with respect for democracy and human rights. These include legislative control, especially through oversight and budgets; the separation of intelligence gathering from security operations; the separation of foreign from domestic intelligence; effective interagency coordination; the creation of career personnel systems; and some means for legal self-defense against security agencies' operations. He recognizes that security services by their nature pose permanent problems for democracies, but the collective experience of various countries offers valuable insights of use to the Mexican case.

Aguayo describes the founding of Mexico's Federal Security Directorate (DFS) in 1947 and the varieties of problems incurred from the outset. President Miguel Alemán created the agency by decree, without consulting congress. The DFS acted thereafter as a virtually unrestrained presidential instrument. It operated without professional personnel, mixed intelligence gathering with operations, and used violence with impunity in its main task of controlling the population. Aguayo suggests that the broad freedom of operation granted to the DFS in its campaign against urban guerrillas in the 1970s contributed to the agency's degradation. He describes how in the area around the state of Jalisco a convergence of right-wing social and governmental groups, including death squads, became intermixed over time with elements from the DFS and with drug traffickers, and facilitated the arrival of the international drug trade to Guadalajara. Complicity between the DFS and drug traffickers festered until 1985, when the murder of DEA agent Enrique Camarena and his Mexican pilot precipitated a complex crisis within Mexico and in the bilateral relationship with the United States. Out of that crisis came the impetus to reform the intelligence services, thus launching a period of transition in which their character and mission began to be reconsidered. Aguayo traces the steps that led to the formation of the Center for Investigation and National Security (CISEN) and describes some of the agency's shortcomings in the mid-1980s. Rather than bemoaning CISEN's lack of effectiveness, he suggests that the admixture of impunity and efficiency could have been devastating for Mexico's democratic transition. By stressing important changes in civil society and some progress in the professionalization of the agency, Aguayo leaves us with a basis for cautious optimism.

In "Law Enforcement and Intelligence in the Bilateral Security Context: U.S. Bureaucratic Dynamics," John Bailey focuses on bureaucratic dynamics of U.S. agencies, emphasizing aspects of agency structure and culture. He notes that security takes on effective meaning in agency behavior at the policy implementation phase. The decentralized, pluralistic nature of U.S. politics allows ample space for government agencies to develop clients, purposes, and tasks, all of which comprises the institutional basis for bureaucratic politics. This level of analysis is important to the overall security relationship due to a mix of institutional and conjunctural factors. These include the weakness of the Clinton presidency, due to underlying structural causes (such as continuing party dealignment and fiscal deficits) and erratic performance; the Republican resurgence in Congress after the November 1994 elections, which further weakened presidential leadership over the bureaucracy; and the inclusion of Mexico-related issues in mainstream U.S. policy debates and thence into bureaucratic maneuvering. Finally, the most salient foreign policy concerns in U.S. public opinion in 1994–95 involved Mexico (including drugs, migration, employment, energy, and trade), and domestic concerns focused on crime and violence, all of which suggest that security will occupy a high priority in the agenda with Mexico.

Bailey describes how constituent agencies within certain bureaucracies—especially the Departments of State, Justice, and Defense, and the Central Intelligence Agency—appear to be redefining their missions in the bilateral relationship. He describes how organizational structures and cultures affect interagency conflict and cooperation, especially between general-purpose security agencies, such as CIA and Defense, with those whose main mission is law enforcement, such as the Federal Bureau of Investigation and the Drug Enforcement Administration. He notes how agencies such as Defense and CIA are undergoing role expansion as they adjust their missions in the post–cold war period. His discussion highlights the rather erratic efforts of the Clinton administration to link national security to broader concerns about law enforcement, democracy, and human rights, and he describes the comparatively high levels of controversy and instability that U.S. security agencies are experiencing. Bailey concludes that some aspects of bureaucratic politics will, by the institutional nature of U.S. politics, continue into the future. This is the case, for example, with problems of control and coordination. In contrast, some significant adjustments in behavior should be expected as the defense and intelligence communities shift from their cold war orientations toward greater attention to issues of law enforcement.

John Cope's "In Search of Convergence: U.S.–Mexican Military Relations into the Twenty-first Century" seeks to dispel some of the mystery surrounding the little-studied nature of U.S.–Mexican military relations, whose current state and future potential are far more important than they seemed in the past. He suggests that the frame of reference for military dialogue and cooperation provides a rare analytic window for observing aspects of Mexican strategic thinking about national defense and cooperative security. Cope describes the origins of the Joint Mexican–United States Defense Commission (JMUSDC), which continues to be one of the main structures for military diplomacy between the two countries and a means for signaling government positions or intentions. The JMUSDC also offers a means for rough measurement of the effectiveness of international and bilateral security- and confidence-building programs. Military diplomacy through JMUSDC, Cope suggests, provides a case study of how change can occur within corresponding national institutions in neighboring countries when both are affected by a common compelling influence, such as the development of a free trade agreement. The experiences of the U.S. and Mexican defense establishments stemming from NAFTA may hold lessons from which other government institutions may benefit.

Cope finds that the U.S. military sought improved relations with their Mexican counterparts more actively after 1988. What followed was a pattern of proactive U.S. proposals and reluctant Mexican responses. The intensity and cordiality of contacts increased, especially at the higher ranks. By and large, improvements in relations among naval forces has advanced farther than those between the armies. Still, efforts to strengthen institutional ties, especially through JMUSDC, have not lived up to expectations. It became increasingly apparent in 1993 and 1994 that Mexican military leaders did not want to broaden the commission's mandate and were particularly opposed to its assuming an operational role. Even so, Cope recommends continuation of U.S. initiatives, within a careful respect for Mexico's unique balance of civilian-military relations. He warns that difficulties could arise if the U.S. government should begin to tempt the Mexican armed forces with visions of high-cost, high-tech equipment or urge Mexican officials to reform their system of civil-military relations along more democratic lines. Overall, the Mexican model of civil-military relations, with its emphasis on unquestioned and unfettered civilian control, has worked well for the country. The creation of a powerful, autonomous corporate identity with its own ideas could spell trouble in the context of a complex political transition.

Directions for Future Research

One of the most useful results of the project is that we have a clearer idea about the kinds of topics that will most likely receive attention in the future. A recurring theme in the chapters that follow is the relationship between democratization and security in Mexico, and the possible roles that should or should not be played by the United States. The democratization-security link is a consequence of a reality that has "overdetermined" several aspects of the bilateral relationship: Mexico and the United States have quite different, and in some respects incompatible, political systems. Mexico is one of the oldest authoritarian regimes in the world; the United States is one of the oldest and most deeply rooted liberal democracies. This asymmetry in the nature of the political systems will receive growing attention in the future (in part because of the growing interaction among societies) and will raise delicate problems about the right to "intervene" versus the right to self-determination.

Democracy will also be linked to security because of the possibility that the economic crisis, touched off by the peso devaluation of December 1994 and continuing throughout 1995 and well into 1996, will accentuate social conflicts, even to the point of violence in some regions. There is evidence that the conflict in Chiapas will not be resolved without significant progress toward broader democratization of the political system and of national institutions.

To this point the Clinton administration and its congressional allies have identified U.S. national interests with the government of Ernesto Zedillo and its agenda of gradualist reform. The long-established consensus to support Mexican authoritarianism, however, is coming under severe challenge due both to economic mismanagement by the Mexican government in 1994 and 1995 and to doubts that the reformist political agenda will result in significant change. Are there circumstances under which the U.S. government might push for more rapid reform?

Mexico's ongoing crisis will fuel a number of other problems that will continue to receive attention as part of the strategic and security agenda. Drugs and immigration are the two most important. Mexico will continue to be a major transit route, producer, and even consumer of illegal drugs, with all the economic, political, and security risks that this implies. How will the drug problem expand and deepen relations between the intelligence and law enforcement agencies of the two countries? Is there on the horizon the possibility of an expanded military relationship?

In the matter of illegal immigration there are also new developments. One of the most important, and least understood, is that the U.S. government may gradually be "regaining control" of its southern border and may be better able to block illegal immigration. This alteration of the status quo will have important implications because the U.S. economy continues to attract cheap, unskilled labor. As Mexico will be incapable of creating the necessary jobs for the foreseeable future, the conditions are being created for an agreement similar to the "Bracero" programs of old.

Yet another issue that is raised obliquely in several of the chapters is the security relevance of police, law enforcement, and the criminal justice systems of the two countries. Personal insecurity and the priority given to law enforcement in opinion surveys in both countries signal the growing attention that these issues will receive. High-profile crimes such as murders, assassinations, kidnappings, and the like have seriously complicated bilateral relations since the mid-1980s. The penetration by criminal organizations of security agencies and key services such as transportation and communications (air traffic control, for example) is cause for profound concern. That we could not find a single systematic, empirically based, academic study of the Mexican police underlines the enormous gap to be addressed. Further, the patent inability of the police to deal effectively with crime has led Mexican authorities to involve military forces on a growing scale in civilian law enforcement. Although some of our contributors will disagree, we believe the inevitable problems of corruption and politicization that accompany such involvement will complicate civil-military relations in the near term.

These various problems need to be considered in the context of the enormous power asymmetry between the two countries. This implies that U.S. conceptualizations of its security interests have global implications, whereas those of Mexico are limited to the region and the bilateral relationship. It is not enough to recommend that Washington take into account Mexico City's perspectives. Most likely, the U.S. government will continue to act unilaterally when it deems this to be convenient. Yet there are dangers in unilateralism. The current Mexican financial and economic crisis reminds us of the interdependence between the two countries and the vulnerability of the United States.

We believe there are grounds for optimism, however. The most important result of the project and book is that there has been progress in willingness to discuss openly the several problems faced by the two countries, and these discussions helped to advance our knowledge of the issues. Many gaps remain, and we have underlined the need to know more about police and intelligence activities of both countries and the ways in which these are—or are not—coordinated. The most useful contribution we can make, under these circumstances, is to create conditions to promote continued open discussion about and systematic research on issues of strategy and security.

References

Bagley, Bruce M., and Sergio Aguayo Quezada, eds. 1993. *Mexico: In Search of Security*. Coral Gables, Fl.: North-South Center, University of Miami/Transaction Publishers.

Kaplan, Robert. 1994. "The Coming Anarchy," *Atlantic Monthly* 273 (2): 44–76.

Nadelmann, Ethan Avram. 1993. *Cops across Borders: The Internationalization of U.S. Criminal Law Enforcement*. University Park, Penn.: Pennsylvania State University Press.

Thorup, Cathryn L. 1992. "Managing Extreme Interdependence: Alternative Institutional Arrangements of U.S. Policymaking toward Mexico, 1976–1988." Ph.D. dissertation, Harvard University.

New Security Interests?

2

Strategic Interests in the U.S.–Mexican Relationship

David R. Mares

All states have "strategic interests"—the core interests that states cannot adequately defend or pursue without considering the interests of other states. These strategic interests are both objective (such as territorial integrity and political sovereignty) and subjective (the maintenance of certain political institutions, for example). The U.S.–Mexican relationship has been characterized at different historical moments by disagreement, tension, and cooperation over various of these core interests.

This chapter uses the concept of "grand strategy" to analyze the international determinants of the strategic interests that affect the U.S.–Mexican relationship. I offer five core observations. First, the most common strategic interest—security from military threats—has been irrelevant to the bilateral relationship ever since the end of World War II. Second, both Mexicans and Americans should resist the temptation to define nonmilitary core interests as security interests. Although states can legitimately use unilateral and military means to pursue their security interests if cooperative efforts fail, this sort of action cannot resolve most of the new bilateral issues. Third, the bilateral strategic interests of Mexico and the United States are becoming more congruous, although not identical. Fourth, domestic forces often try to build grand strategies that mold international influences to meet domestic interests. Fifth, these international influences remain too powerful for either the United States or Mexico to resist, except at the cost of their prosperity.

This analysis is organized in three sections. I first discuss the notion of grand strategy and its usefulness in explaining the strategic interests that undergird the U.S.–Mexican relationship. Second, I consider arguments claiming that the international context of the U.S.–Mexican relationship has undergone significant change. And finally, I examine the contemporary grand strategies that have brought Mexico and the United States closer together without merging them into one.

The Utility of a Grand Strategy Focus

The concept of grand strategy can help us to understand the logic underlying a state's efforts to defend its core interests in both war and peace (Kennedy 1991). This strategy might be either an explicit policy, such as the U.S. National Security Act of 1947, or an implicit one, as in the Roman Empire.[1] Grand strategy has three components: the identification of threats; the elaboration of economic, military, and other means to oppose those threats; and the relative ranking of these means (Posen 1984: 13).

The authority to decide what constitutes a threat and how to address it is a fundamental attribute of sovereignty. Strategic interaction, however, implies that one state cannot adequately assess threats or adopt appropriate policies without taking into consideration the interests of other states whose behavior might affect those core interests. Sovereignty, therefore, cannot be absolute in any international system.

The various means that a state chooses to defend its sovereignty, and the priority ranking it assigns to those means, depend upon how it characterizes the threat or threats. That is, the nature of the threat will both determine the range of appropriate means and contribute to their rank ordering. We might group potential sources of threat in the U.S.–Mexican relationship into five categories: (1) the two countries themselves, (2) great power rivals of the United States (at various times, Britain, Germany, Japan, and the Soviet Union), (3) neighbors in Central America and the Caribbean, (4) transnational economic forces, and (5) domestic rivals of the governing coalition.

The international relations literature regards the first three sources of threat as the most common. Both power (either its presence or absence—that is, a power vacuum) and proximity compel states to evaluate whether or not a neighboring state or distant great power poses a threat at any given time.[2] Although transnational forces can

[1] Luttwak (1976) argues that the strategy was implicit.

[2] For Mexican perceptions of the United States as a threat to national sovereignty, see Cope, this volume. For a discussion of how political weakness in Central America

be economic or ideological, this chapter emphasizes the former, which can be either impersonal market forces (such as currency markets) or international institutions (like the International Monetary Fund). Transnational corporations can also be considered transnational forces if they respond to international markets rather than to home government policies.[3] These transnational forces constitute a potential threat to the nation's core interests. The scale of threat depends upon the degree of interdependence between the threatened country and the actors that could intervene in the market to alter the impact of international market forces.[4]

States can also confront serious internal challenges to their constituted governments. In these cases, besieged elites will normally regard their domestic rivals as threats to the nation. Since those elites control government allocation of resources, they are likely to modify the nation's grand strategy in order to divert attention and resources to the internal threat.

The first four threats can arise at any given time from purely international factors, purely domestic factors, or some combination of the two. If strictly international factors generate the threat—for instance, if a state is militarily attacked—they will be so perceived by whoever holds power. The international context becomes irrelevant, however, when the threat arises from purely domestic sources, as when a government faces a homegrown insurgency. When domestic and international forces interact to produce a threat, the coalition of domestic forces governing the country perceives specific international conditions or forces as threats to the coalition's core interests.

Just as states do not exist in isolation from each other, their grand strategies are also interrelated. It is theoretically and empirically useful to identify four different relationships between the grand strategies of states: competitive, coincident, parallel, and subordinate. A competitive relationship exists when one state poses the chief security threat to another. Two states have coincident grand strategies when they independently identify the same threat to their security. A parallel relationship occurs when two countries independently identify distinct and noncompeting threats to their security. A subordinate relationship exists when one country poses the principal threat to the

has increased Mexico's concerns about its vulnerability to the United States, see Mares 1988.

[3] Traditionally, Latin Americanists perceived U.S.–based transnational corporations as instruments of U.S. foreign policy. For a similar view of Japanese TNCs, see Ozawa 1979.

[4] For a general view of interdependence, see Keohane and Nye 1977. International currency markets illustrate the differences between Mexican and U.S. vulnerabilities. When the Mexican peso depreciates, fewer G-7 countries intervene to support it than when the U.S. dollar, the Japanese yen, or the German deutsche mark declines to an extent that the country of issue sees as disadvantageous.

other's sovereignty but is not considered as such in the latter's grand strategy.

Threat perception constitutes only the initial step in understanding a state's grand strategy. Once threats have been identified, remedies must be devised. Those policies can be military, diplomatic, economic, legal, social, or some combination of these. Military doctrine represents the integration of military means with military strategy to address the threat. Diplomatic defense indicates that the state has entered into political agreements (alliances, ententes, or politically determined economic integration schemes) with other states as a way to confront a threat. Macroeconomic policy constitutes a domestic economic response, while criminalization of the threat turns it into a legal problem. Social laissez-faire (emigration or immigration, for example) represents a nongovernmental response by social forces.

A country's grand strategy will explicitly or implicitly integrate multiple threats and policy responses. Like all other government outputs, it results from a political process in which various actors struggle to advance their own interests and values. Unless the international threat is unambiguous and pressing, this political process will govern the identification of the threat and the choice of responses (Posen 1984).

Mexican and U.S. Grand Strategies, 1945–1980

From the end of World War II until the early 1980s, the grand strategies of Mexico and the United States had numerous parallel and coincident elements, with strong competitive elements as well from the Mexican point of view. The relationship between the two grand strategies was also asymmetrical, since Mexico's grand strategy focused on the United States, while the United States virtually ignored Mexico. By the 1980s, however, both countries found their traditional grand strategies increasingly inadequate in addressing new security challenges.

Although Mexican foreign policy took U.S. interests into consideration during these years, it responded to indigenous definitions of the Mexican national interest (Ojeda 1976; Mares 1988). The interests of the U.S. and Mexican governments regarding the political opposition in Mexico have coincided ever since 1938, when President Lázaro Cárdenas began to consolidate the gains of the Mexican Revolution. The strategy of the ruling Institutional Revolutionary Party (PRI) for managing its domestic opponents ("ignore when possible, corrupt when necessary and repress only as a last resort" [Domínguez 1982]) responded not to any U.S. interest but rather to the PRI's own interest in staying in power.

Mexico's identification of threats has remained consistent over time, largely because of the country's status as an underdeveloped, one-party state bordering a great power with no local rivals. The U.S. security umbrella protects Mexico from any great power rival of the United States but not from U.S. threats. The Central American and Caribbean countries pose no direct threat to Mexico; until the late 1980s their ongoing domestic turmoil produced ripples of immigration which Mexico could easily assimilate. Consequently, only one foreign state—the United States—has posed a threat to Mexico, although the country's underdeveloped status makes it vulnerable to other threats from transnational economic forces. Finally, the authoritarian nature of Mexico's political system has turned sustained domestic opposition into a threat to the governing elite.[5]

The United States also maintained a consistent threat assessment from World War II until the early 1980s. In the bipolar cold war context, the Soviet Union posed the only serious threat to the United States. Buoyed by the U.S.–fostered liberal international economic order (LIEO), the U.S. economy faced no major challenge from transnational economic forces until the early 1970s. As soon as the U.S. government perceived the threat posed by these forces, it undertook dramatic unilateral actions (such as abandoning the gold standard in 1971 and raising interest rates in 1979, thereby provoking a recession) that underscored its continuing independence of action. With U.S. democratic institutions secure (the 1960s civil rights and antiwar movements demonstrated their vitality in a polity unaccustomed to grassroots democracy on a national scale), the government's domestic opponents either played by the rules or were marginalized.

While Mexico's grand strategy has focused on its northern neighbor, the United States has only sporadically viewed Mexico as relevant to its grand strategy. During the early 1970s, first the drug trade and then political instability in Mexico stirred minor U.S. interest in rethinking the relationship with Mexico. That interest increased during the late 1970s, as Mexico's oil and gas industries boomed, international energy markets tightened, and the Central American foreign policies of the two countries increasingly diverged. Whether in energy markets or in Central America, however, Mexico remained a relatively minor irritant to a U.S. government more concerned about challenges from the oil producers' cartel (of which Mexico was not a member), the Soviet Union, Cuba, Nicaragua, El Salvador, and the U.S. Congress.

Throughout the postwar period, Mexico and the United States have addressed their threat perceptions in various ways. During that

---

[5]For a general introduction to Mexico's political economy, see Hansen 1971; Reyna and Weinert 1977.

time, military means of resolving the threats posed by each country to the other have been "subrationally unthinkable."[6] In strictly military terms, the United States and Mexico have constituted a "pluralistic security community" (Holsti 1988: 423–37). Bilateral diplomatic arrangements to defend the core interests of Mexico and the United States have also played a minor role during the postwar period. Prior to the North American Free Trade Agreement (NAFTA), Mexico and the United States had entered into only two significant formal agreements: a very short-lived trade agreement and a guest worker (bracero) program terminated in the 1960s. Each side sought to limit the other's influence rather than to defend its strategic interests in a complementary way. Mexico did so because it feared that its relative political and economic weakness would jeopardize its interests, while the United States believed that the same disparity gave it license to act unilaterally when necessary.

Mexico's grand strategy between 1948 and 1982 consisted in unilateral and multilateral policies to neutralize threats to its core interests. The government adopted import-substituting industrialization (ISI) in the 1930s in order to shield Mexico from transnational economic forces that it identified with U.S. interests. Mexico feared that these forces would undermine its ability to industrialize and thus threaten its economic security and prosperity (Villarreal 1976). Although the PRI/government offered some concessions to its domestic opponents, it also resorted to repression of workers in 1948, peasants in 1958, and students in 1968, and it practiced systematic electoral fraud while blocking significant political liberalization. Internationally, Mexico refused to join the U.S.–backed General Agreement on Tariffs and Trade (GATT), affiliating instead with the Third World–oriented United Nations Conference on Trade and Development (UNCTAD) and later supporting the creation of a new international economic order (NIEO) (Mares 1985).

By 1982 both the PRI and Mexico at large realized that this grand strategy had failed to protect core interests. Fatally wounded by internal disagreement and by U.S. unwillingness to take it seriously, the UNCTAD/NIEO agenda was never implemented (Rothstein 1979). ISI brought Mexico not economic security and prosperity but technologically backward and high-cost industries, a ruined agricultural sector, soaring underemployment, balance of payments crises, and a huge public debt. Ironically, in defending its core interests Mexico had gambled its future on the performance of two international markets (energy and finance) in which it could only be a price taker.

---

[6] The phrase is John Mueller's, who uses it to describe the relationship among the advanced industrialized countries (1989: 240–44).

When those markets collapsed, the government's ability to manage its domestic rivals was severely strained.

U.S. grand strategy underwent a similar but less traumatic evolution from "rollback" to "containment" of the military and ideological threat posed by the Soviet Union. Liberal international financial institutions (the International Monetary Fund), trade associations (GATT), and development agencies (the International Bank for Reconstruction and Development, that is, the World Bank) would underpin the country's economic security and prosperity. Thus strengthened, U.S. democratic institutions could be reformed to incorporate new actors (such as ethnic and racial minorities) while withstanding the violent assaults of such fringe groups as the Weathermen.

U.S. grand strategy confronted new challenges during the 1970s. The continued viability of containment came into question as the USSR achieved nuclear parity, détente became discredited, and Western Europe moved toward an accommodation with Soviet power (Hoffmann 1978). The energy crisis of the late 1970s also challenged U.S. grand strategy. By the mid-1980s, however, a more fundamental challenge had emerged. As its liberal international economic order took root, the United States became increasingly wary of the economic recovery of Japan and Western Europe and of the rise of the newly industrializing countries (NICs), including Mexico. This sensitivity found popular and therefore political expression in accusations of foul play directed against U.S. trading partners.

Initially the United States offered its trading partners increased market access in return for adjustments that would decrease U.S.–perceived vulnerability. The U.S. Trade Act of 1974 gave the president, "for the first time in history, the authority to harmonize, reduce, or eliminate all barriers to free trade,"[7] including nontariff barriers. This legislation sought to induce developing nations to join the LIEO by offering them trade benefits under the Generalized System of Preferences. It also tightened the definitions of purported unfair trade practices, strengthened the corresponding sanctions, and loosened the criteria by which U.S. producers could qualify for protection via the "escape clause."

At the Tokyo Round of GATT talks, the United States urged the adoption of a number of performance codes to liberalize trade, of which two have particular interest. The government procurement code was designed to open such purchases to competitive bidding, although 85 percent of U.S. purchases were effectively excluded from the code. The subsidies code was inconsistent with GATT rules requiring an injury test before countervailing duties are imposed. In

[7]Pastor 1980: 137. This discussion also draws on Block 1977; Lande and VanGrasstek 1986.

both cases the United States broke with GATT policy by eliminating unconditional most-favored-nation treatment for nonsignatories of the codes. The U.S. Trade Agreements Act of 1979 basically followed this same formula.

The United States also threatened to "graduate" the NICs from the Generalized System of Preferences so that they would not benefit from advantages granted to less developed countries. Major exporters to the United States continued to face "voluntary" export restraints and other nontariff barriers. The United States also began to make overtures to Canada and Mexico concerning some type of joint partnership (initially with Canada and Mexico providing energy to fuel the U.S. industrial complex) to confront the increasingly competitive international market.[8]

The success of the new grand strategy was short lived. A military buildup unprecedented in peacetime helped to drive the Soviet Union into collapse by the middle 1980s, but it also imposed a severe strain on the U.S. economy. The recession of the early 1980s was followed by a debt-led expansion that turned the United States into the world's largest debtor nation. Canada and the United States reached agreement on liberalized trade rules for automobiles, which later evolved into a broader free trade agreement. Mexico, however, formally rejected all efforts to tie its fate to the United States. By the middle 1980s the vulnerability—to say nothing of the sensitivity—of U.S. core interests to international influences had reached an all-time high.

Since the early 1980s the grand strategies of both the United States and Mexico have dramatically shifted, becoming more coincident than at any time since World War II, when both countries were allies. Before we examine those changes, we should investigate the international context that stimulated them.

A Changing International Context?

The end of the cold war brought international politics to a unique turning point: a peaceful transition to a new world order, however we define that term.[9] Every significant change in the international context affects the United States as a great power. Only some of those inter-

[8]Regarding the controversial natural gas agreement between the United States and Mexico, see Fagen and Nau 1979. During the 1980 U.S. presidential campaign, both Ronald Reagan and Jerry Brown advocated the establishment of free trade zones with Mexico and Canada. Canada began to consider the idea seriously in 1983, the MacDonald Commission advocated this dramatic change in grand strategy in 1985, and three years later Canada signed a free trade agreement with the United States. See Winham 1988.

[9]For a discussion of international issues surrounding the end of the cold war, see Lynn-Jones 1991; Kegley 1991; Jervis 1991/92.

national changes will affect Mexico either directly or indirectly, since it plays only a minor international role. In this section I will examine those international changes that can potentially affect the U.S.–Mexican relationship.

Two basic concepts of contemporary world politics can help us to address this subject. The nation-state and sovereignty are the traditional concepts that have informed the study of international politics since the Peace of Westphalia in 1648. The idea of the nation-state retains widespread relevance and appeal, as clearly attested by peoples' ongoing willingness to fight for their country and by the current realignment of national loyalties following the collapse of the Soviet empire. Poorly comprehended but deeply felt, sovereignty—understood as the right to decide how one will respond to international opportunities and constraints—gives identity to the nation.

Nevertheless, the concepts of nation-state and sovereignty now appear to be undergoing fundamental redefinition. Many observers believe that the West European process of economic and political integration will produce a new type of political unit in which economic integration coexists with political diversity. Many analysts believe that these new political, economic, and juridical modes of interaction will provide a model for other regions, including Latin America. The formation of the Southern Cone Common Market (also known as Mercosur) by Argentina, Brazil, Paraguay, and Uruguay was undoubtedly influenced by the perceived success of Western European integration. The North American Free Trade Agreement certainly cannot be understood in isolation from the history of the European Community.

Not only is the basic political-economic unit of international politics supposedly experiencing significant change, the meaning of sovereignty in today's interdependent world is also being reformulated in a dramatically new way. Although sovereignty has never been regarded as absolute in any practical sense, both citizens and statesmen have found the intellectual and legal fiction of absolute sovereignty useful. For today's analysts of international interdependence, however, the notion of sovereignty as the ability to decide for oneself is so riddled with exceptions that it has become a misleading and even dangerous way to think about a people's aspirations and international role.

Some analysts stress the dangers that have arisen in the wake of the de facto creation of a global community, particularly the mass movements of economic and political refugees from the developing world to the advanced industrialized countries. One implication of this "shrinking world," according to these analysts, is that the industrialized countries have an interest in preventing the underdeveloped countries from sinking into regional war, civil war, and economic disaster. President Clinton's speech to the nation justifying U.S. military participation in the Bosnian peace plan noted not only the moral imperative facing the United States but also our national interest in limiting regional conflict before it spreads (Bahr 1985: 31–36; Stark 1992; Mitchell 1995).

Other analysts stress the costs of staying out of the new international groupings that have developed following the end of the cold war. The end of the struggle for global domination has caused some underdeveloped regions of the world to lose their attractiveness and relevance to the advanced industrialized countries. One variant of this thesis holds that trading blocs will form the nucleus of new regional groupings, and another variant predicts a reformulated North-South division, with political and economic stability a requisite for affiliation with the North (MacFarlane 1991; David 1992/93).

Have the concepts of the nation-state and sovereignty really undergone significant change? At least until mid-1992, Western Europe appeared to be experiencing such a transformation (although the ongoing U.S. military presence there might also account for some of the region's conviviality) (see Mearsheimer 1990). Nevertheless, several recent developments—France's narrow approval of the Maastricht treaty, Danish approval of a significantly modified treaty, and the decisions of Great Britain and Italy to withdraw their currencies from the European exchange rate mechanism (ERM)—advise caution in evaluating the degree to which these fundamental concepts have changed even in Western Europe.

While Western Europe's interpretation of these two concepts remains undefined, the rest of the world shows even less evidence of such change. Demands for nationhood and sovereignty have overshadowed the desire for economic viability and the benefits of interdependence among the new nations of the former Soviet empire. Economic interdependence is proceeding in Asia, but without posing the institutional challenges to the traditional nation-state that one finds in Western Europe.

In North America, the rhetoric of the 1992 U.S. presidential campaign and growing anti-immigration sentiment, as evidenced by Senator Alan Simpson's bill to further limit immigration, suggest the continuing vitality of an "us versus them" mentality of nationalism.[10] The United States–Canada free trade agreement has not mitigated

---

[10] President Bush, clearly the most internationalist of the three candidates in 1992, claimed that only by remaining active on the world stage could the United States stay economically competitive with other nations. This stance contrasts with another that emphasizes a greater sense of world community akin to "the common Europe home." Note President Clinton's emphasis that U.S. troops in the Bosnian multilateral peacekeeping force would serve under an American commander (Mitchell 1995). On Simpson, see Branigin 1995.

nationalistic feelings in either country, as shown by the strength of Canadian concerns over the economic cost of the trade pact. Canadian diplomats also express concern over potential threats to their cultural security.[11] President Salinas has stated repeatedly that his program of reducing state involvement in the economy sought ultimately to strengthen the state's capacity to guide the development of the nation (Salinas 1992: 1069). The Zedillo administration is pursuing the same goal of strengthening the state's rectoral capacity, but by decentralizing it, strengthening the judiciary (he named a member of the opposition party as attorney general), and making policy making more transparent.[12]

It is also unlikely that the world will divide into three large trading blocs, as some observers have predicted. Although the European Union is expanding, U.S. capital, goods, and services continue to penetrate it. The United States is unlikely to be shut out of Asia, due to its growing relationship with the People's Republic of China and the fear of Japanese hegemony on the part of virtually every country in the region. Moreover, Japan already has significant investments in the United States, and NAFTA will likely stimulate additional Japanese, Korean, and Taiwanese investment in Canada and Mexico (*Japan Economic Institute Report* 39A [October 18, 1991]).

More likely than the rise of exclusive regional trading blocs is the prospect of a new North-South divide that does not radically redefine the concepts of sovereignty and the nation-state. With the end of the cold war, simply being anticommunist is no longer enough. Zones of strategic concern have been redrawn, leaving many Third World countries out. The new path to partnership with the North is economic. In order to participate fully on the Northern side in the world market, partners from the South will need to contribute tangible benefits. Countries must increasingly have a broad-based consumer society, a quiescent labor force for export production, and preferably both. These attributes require a level of capital formation and economic growth that is unlikely to be present in countries lacking political stability, adequate infrastructure, and market-based rather than political criteria for allocating economic resources. Mexico should be well placed to prosper in this new economic context.

---

[11] Remarks made at a workshop entitled "North American Security in the Time of NAFTA," held at the National Defense University, Washington, D.C., in September 1994.

[12] The Zedillo administration is followed closely in *Sourcemex*, published by the Latin American Data Bank, University of New Mexico.

Reconceptualizing Security and Democracy?

Linked to the question of the nation-state's potential eclipse is that of the meaning of "security." The traditional definition of security stressed the integrity of physical borders and government independence from external dictation. Security analysts studied not only intentional aggression but also inadvertent conflict resulting from the "security dilemma" (which holds that under conditions of anarchy, one country's efforts to achieve security provoke another's insecurity) (Jervis 1978).

Dramatic changes in international life since the middle 1970s have prompted a rethinking of definitions of security that stress physical borders, political sovereignty, and military defense.[13] Military conflict between the United States and Mexico, for instance, has been virtually unthinkable ever since World War II. The proliferation of new definitions of security calls for a reexamination of the advantages and disadvantages of a broad or narrow definition of the concept. Security as a political concept in international relations is an empowering device. To label an issue as a security matter is to raise its relative standing on a country's agenda, expand the resources devoted to it, and increase both the risks and the costs that one is willing to incur in formulating appropriate policies. Perhaps most importantly for students of international politics, the security label can legitimize state actions that might otherwise face condemnation.

The utility of this concept in generating vast resources and concentrating the attention of policy makers leads even those analysts who disdain the traditional militarized definitions of security to frame the new issues in the politicized terms of "security." By categorizing the new issues that affect U.S.–Mexican relations as security issues, however, one might hinder rather than promote their mutually beneficial resolution.

Despite the short-term advantage of attracting increased resources, such broadening of the definition of security carries a significant risk. Security interests may legitimately be defended unilaterally if cooperative efforts fail, yet most of the new bilateral issues are not susceptible to unilateral resolution. If the U.S. government were to classify drug trafficking, for instance, as a security threat similar to those posed by Nazism or communism, the U.S. public would demand that its leaders answer the threat unilaterally, since cooperation with the Mexican government has clearly "failed." Since U.S. drug consumption is at least as much a matter of demand as of supply, any effort to force Mexico to increase dramatically the effectiveness of its

[13] See Jervis 1991/92 for a summary of the debate on this issue.

antidrug policies would cause severe turmoil in that country while bringing just marginal benefits to the United States (Mares 1992).

By redefining security in economic rather than military terms, one does not necessarily promote peaceful inter-state relations. Economic interdependence has two general implications, one conducive to and the other destructive of international stability. Those who believe that sovereignty is compatible with economic interdependence will tend to define security in terms of success in the global market. Many leaders of developing countries and the successor states of the former Soviet Union seem to follow this approach. The major OECD countries, however, seem increasingly to be modifying their acceptance of interdependence with qualifications about "level playing fields" and "strategic trade theory" that come uncomfortably close to neomercantilism.[14] As the vulnerability of domestic political economic bargains increases, the former defenders of economic liberalization are facing increased pressure to ensure that their own citizens share its benefits.[15]

For similar reasons, threats to democracy should not be regarded as security threats. Many analysts draw a correlation between democracy and the absence of war,[16] concluding that the defense of democracy should constitute a fundamental component of contemporary security policy. The use of this empirical relationship to design a security policy for the U.S.–Mexican relationship raises a number of problems. Although democracy can be defined in various ways, few analysts would call Mexico a democracy.[17] Even if one objected to including Mexico in the broader category of "liberal republics" and emphasized instead its authoritarianism, it would not pose a traditional security threat. Most authoritarian governments do not engage

---

[14] This literature is reviewed in Sylan 1981 and Richardson 1990. Any observer of Latin American history and politics between 1950 and 1980 cannot help but notice the similarity between the argument that "strategic industries" must be defended because of their links to the next generation of economic growth and the justifications for Latin American strategies of import-substituting industrialization. The concern over "level playing fields" is also reminiscent of Latin America's objections to the unfair advantages enjoyed by multinational corporations vis-à-vis national entrepreneurs.

[15] For the classic analysis of this domestic side of liberal foreign economic policy, see Ruggie 1982.

[16] Rummel 1983. See also Chan 1984; Doyle 1986. Although democratic states have experienced serious conflicts and engaged in military skirmishes, these disputes have all been resolved with fewer than one thousand battlefield deaths. See Maoz and Abdolali 1989.

[17] The original arguments behind the Pacific Union proposition (Kant's Liberal Peace and Doyle's resurrection of him) focus on "Liberal Republics," a term that is broader than "democracy"; hence Doyle legitimately includes Mexico after 1928 (see Doyle 1986: 1164). The policy debate in Washington and the popular perception are not oriented around such fine distinctions, however. Whether or not Mexico is "democratic" (rather than just "liberal") can thus become an important security issue.

in inter-state war, and Mexico in particular has maintained peaceful relations with all of its neighbors ever since the revolution.

Even if it could be proven that nondemocratic regimes pose inherent threats to international peace, intervention to install liberal democratic governments creates its own problems. Success requires more than will and capability on the part of the intervening power. Liberal democracy also requires certain socioeconomic conditions that are still not clearly understood. Past U.S. efforts to create democratic governments in Latin America have invariably fallen victim to U.S. global concerns such as fighting communism or to political rivalries within the target country.

Security is intimately related to our definitions of sovereignty and the nation-state. If the definition of political community is not extended beyond the nation-state and toward a global community, broadening the definition of security to include new elements will increase the severity of disagreements between countries. To label an issue a "security issue" gives it priority and attracts resources—even military resources—and justifies behavior (such as covert destabilization) that would not be acceptable under other conditions. Hence, countries will perceive themselves to be less secure even as the military threats of the cold war recede.

In summary, it is at best premature to conclude that international relations have undergone a sea change. States have fundamentally altered their behavior only in trying to become economically more competitive with each other. The new structural economic issues that affect the U.S.–Mexican relationship are likely to alter radically the grand strategies of each country and the interaction between them. The possibility that a debate over democracy could have a major impact on the two countries depends more on domestic factors than on international politics.

Contemporary Grand Strategies

The first section of this chapter argued that the grand strategies of both Mexico and the United States had become inadequate to defend the strategic interests of each country. The second section suggested that changes in the international economic environment would affect the transition from historical to contemporary grand strategies. The current section argues that Mexico's grand strategy has now suddenly and dramatically collapsed, while that of the United States has merely become more vulnerable. As a result, the coincident elements in their grand strategies have significantly increased. Nevertheless, competitive strains remain in the relationship due to U.S. unilateralism. Because U.S. unilateral action responds more to domestic concerns than to any particular action Mexico might undertake, Mexico cannot assume that any bilateral understanding (including NAFTA) is sufficient to resolve a given issue. Virtually overnight the United States can violate either the spirit or letter of an agreement, thus creating serious complications for any partner who has come to rely on a specific agreement with that country.[18]

Mexican grand strategy was fundamentally revised between 1985 and 1990. Although it continued to view the United States, transnational economic forces, and domestic rivals as the chief sources of threats, Mexico also came to recognize that transnational economic forces are not simply manipulated by the United States but instead have their own dynamic. The government's recognition that these two threats are mutually independent has allowed it to devise new policies to confront them. Contemporary Mexican grand strategy thus seeks both to use the international market to get a better deal with the United States and to use its relationship with the United States to benefit more from the international economy. Mexico offers the United States cheap labor and markets for its goods and services. In return, Mexico expects increased employment, better access to the U.S. market for its own goods, and help from U.S. entrepreneurs in modernizing its economy. At the same time, Mexican access to the U.S. market is expected to draw increased foreign investment into Mexico (especially from Asia), since these investors hope to use Mexico as a point of entry into the increasingly protectionist U.S. market.

The Mexican political elite's recognition of this new dynamic in the bilateral relationship has helped it to accept more easily the de facto integration of the two economies. The technocratic elite affiliated with Presidents de la Madrid and Salinas has chosen not to ignore or resist this integration, as Mexican governments did from the revolution until the debt crisis of the 1980s, but instead to formalize the bilateral relationship in order to gain the benefits deriving from Mexico's comparative economic advantage and the political interest of the United States in a domestically stable Mexico.

Initially, Mexico resisted joining the United States and Canada in a free trade zone. Its goal remained trade diversification; to this end Mexico acceded to the GATT in 1986. In the 1980s, however, economic crisis and the resultant need to boost exports forced Mexico to modify its economic relationship with the United States. The two countries entered into several bilateral agreements intended to alleviate short-term problems as negotiators from each side worked to resolve them or as trade diversification diminished their impact.[19] (These agreements included a 1985 accord in which Mexico received

[18] For a discussion of U.S. unilateralism in the trade arena, see Bayard and Elliott 1994.

[19] For an analysis of Mexican trade policy during this period, see Mares 1991, 1987.

the benefit of an injury test in dumping cases in return for a commitment to phase out subsidies, and a 1987 framework agreement for bilateral trade negotiations and dispute settlement.) The success of the short-term agreements and the continued failure of efforts to diversify trade, however, strengthened the pull of the U.S. economy on Mexico. In addition, the U.S.–Canada free trade agreement posed new challenges to Mexico's strategy by suggesting that Canada's new terms of access to the U.S. market might allow Canada to increase its market share at Mexico's expense (del Castillo 1988; Vega Cánovas 1988).

By 1990 the foundations had been lain for a dramatic formal shift in Mexico's grand strategy. President Salinas precipitated the shift by traveling that year to Western Europe in search of financial support for Mexico's new outward-oriented development strategy. Salinas discovered that European leaders were too preoccupied with Eastern Europe to provide significant aid to Latin America. Upon returning to Mexico, the president opened discussions with the United States on a free trade agreement.

Mexico's new grand strategy confronts many challenges. U.S. domestic politics, for instance, have raised formidable obstacles to the degree and type of integration that Mexico's new elite wants to see between Mexico and the United States. In mid-1993 Mexico's new grand strategy was held hostage to the domestic political debates surrounding changes in U.S. grand strategy. Even after Mexico accepted side agreements concerning issues not originally included in NAFTA, it had to endure a barrage of insults in the U.S. Congress and the press as well as uncertainty about NAFTA's acceptance until the final vote in Congress was taken.

NAFTA has the potential to be a watershed-type event in the formation of a deeper and broader economic relationship among Canada, the United States, and Mexico. The politicized environment in which NAFTA was negotiated led both its advocates and detractors to overemphasize the short-term results that would follow its implementation. Not only did these promises raise expectations once the agreement was signed, but they also linked NAFTA to the economic collapse Mexico suffered as a result of economic mismanagement during the presidential transition period. As a result, both Mexicans and Americans are taking new and harder looks at the interdependence furthered by NAFTA, with some analysts and politicians calling for renegotiation. But the central governments of both countries remain committed to NAFTA.

The United States is reformulating its grand strategy, which has failed both to guarantee U.S. hegemony and to limit U.S. vulnerability in a post–cold war world inhabited by one military superpower and many economic powers. Mexico's role in the new U.S. grand strategy is not yet clear. The United States can enhance its economic competitiveness by gaining greater access to Mexican labor and consumer markets. That increased access, however, would disadvantage certain politically powerful U.S. interest groups that consequently oppose increased U.S.–Mexican integration. Although Mexico has succeeded in reformulating its grand strategy, the United States has not yet done so.

The United States responded to the economic and military changes of the 1980s by taking increasingly unilateral positions in multilateral forums and by adopting new bilateral initiatives such as section 301 legislation in trade and the U.S.–Canadian free trade agreement.[20] These measures represent continued efforts to maintain U.S. leadership in both the security[21] and economic realms, while shifting more of the cost to allies.

As previously noted, economic concerns have become far more central than military concerns in the U.S.–Mexican relationship. The United States has shown its reluctance to break cleanly with a unilateralist grand strategy in its behavior regarding GATT and NAFTA. In the first case, U.S. unilateralism threatens the very liberal international economic order that the United States regards as fundamental to its prosperity, while in the second case it might significantly reduce the benefits of NAFTA to both countries.

The Uruguay Round of GATT negotiations was opened at Punta del Este in 1986. The talks covered numerous issues in international trade (*GATT Focus* 1986). Because the United States enjoyed a comparative advantage in many agricultural products, however, it linked progress on other GATT issues to liberalization of trade rules for grains and oilseeds (*GATT Focus* 1992a). First scheduled for 1990, the conclusion of the Uruguay Round was later postponed to 1991. Negotiations were broken off in December of that year, when the European Community rejected the U.S. position on domestic subsidies. Although oilseed subsidies were technically separate from the round, the United States insisted that resolution of the oilseeds controversy had to precede GATT negotiations on reductions in European grain production.

The agricultural dispute alone cannot explain the U.S. willingness to hold up trade negotiations vital to the world's economic recovery (*GATT Focus* 1992b). The difference between the U.S. and EC positions was not great: the United States demanded a 22 percent reduc-

---

[20] For section 301 legislation, see Bayard and Elliott 1994. On the Canadian pact, see Winham 1988.

[21] The Pentagon's draft document for defense planning in the post–cold war era emphasized that the United States had to maintain world military preeminence in order both to protect U.S. interests, especially if "collective security" failed to do so, and to "convince potential competitors that they need not aspire to a greater role or pursue a more aggressive posture to protect their legitimate interest" (Tyler 1992).

tion in EC-subsidized grain exports, while the EC offered a 21 percent reduction, a difference of just 80,000 tons of grain (Redburn 1992).

The U.S. position should be understood in the context of a general concern among U.S. analysts and policy makers that the world's three major economic powers (the United States, the European Union, and Japan) could not coordinate their leadership of the liberal international economic order.[22] The United States believed that its continued leadership was essential for preserving a liberal international economic order that benefited all participants, and thus that U.S. leadership was in the general interest. Having won an apparent victory on agricultural subsidies, the United States then threatened to exert unilateral pressure in a similar way on services. As in a game of "chicken," it faced the challenge of deciding when to surrender in order to keep the game going.

The United States must become more economically competitive, especially as it continues to take the lead among industrialized countries in pushing for greater economic openness through institutions like the new World Trade Organization. Enlarging the domestic market and using less expensive Mexican labor can contribute to this international competitiveness, as presidential candidates Jerry Brown and Ronald Reagan recognized in 1980 by welcoming the prospect of a North American common market, and as the Bush administration recognized in 1990 by welcoming President Salinas's NAFTA proposal. A grand strategy for international competitiveness animates the defenders of NAFTA in the U.S. government and the private sector. Fear of the social, economic, and ecological costs of regaining international competitiveness, though, temporarily slowed the move toward U.S.–Mexico free trade.

In short, Mexico has already designed, proposed, and largely implemented its new grand strategy. The elements of that strategy that are relevant to the United States, though, are only now coming to fruition, since the United States is still debating how to respond to its new international challenges. The NAFTA side agreements on environmental and labor conditions promise both to raise the costs to Mexico and to reduce the benefits beyond those initially contemplated by the Salinas administration.

This situation is doubly ironic. First, although Mexico came to seek a grand strategy significantly more coincident with that of the United States than at any time since World War II, the United States held up

---

[22] By 1982 one-third of the U.S. market for manufactures was regulated by nontariff barriers. The corresponding figure for Japan was 7 percent, for West Germany 20 percent, and for France 32 percent. These figures are weighted by each sector's share of total manufacturing consumption. See Cline 1983. The debate about leadership and cooperation in the liberal international economic order is reviewed in Keohane 1987. For an argument that the United States remains hegemonic, see Strange 1987.

the bargain and at the last minute bullied Mexico into accepting significant changes in what had already been negotiated. Second, the United States anticipated that the NAFTA side agreements would reduce the social and political costs to it of formally integrating an undeveloped with a developed economy. It may be necessary for the United States to pay higher costs in order to remain competitive in a liberal international economic order that favors the most efficient producer without discounting for unfair labor practices and bad environmental policy.

Conclusion

Mexico and the United States are very different countries. Their core interests are dissimilar except in a vague, long-term sense of promoting peace and development. Instead, their interests will coincide and diverge to a greater or lesser degree. Both countries should work to reinforce the convergences and accept divergence without damaging their overall relationship, as has occurred in the past. The need to defend core interests in an increasingly competitive world economy has brought Mexico and the United States closer together. Mexicans have learned from the failures of the 1970s and 1980s that they need the United States. If the United States can evaluate its own failures and come to a similar conclusion, the relationship built in times of adversity might prosper even as international constraints loosen.

References

Bahr, E. 1985. "Observations on the Principle of Common Security." In *Policies for Common Security*, edited by the Stockholm International Peace Research Institute. London: Taylor and Francis.

Bayard, Thomas O., and Kimberly Ann Elliott. 1994. *Reciprocity and Retaliation in U.S. Trade Policy*. Washington, D.C.: Institute for International Economics.

Block, Fred L. 1977. *The Origins of International Monetary Disorder*. Berkeley: University of California Press.

Branigin, William. 1995. "Sen. Simpson Offers Overhaul of Legal, Illegal Immigration," *Washington Post*, November 4.

Chan, Steve. 1984. "Mirror, Mirror on the Wall. Are the Freer Countries More Pacific?" *Journal of Conflict Resolution* 28 (4): 617–48.

Cline, William 1983. "Exports of Manufactures from Developing Countries: Performance and Prospects for Market Access." As cited in Robert Reich, "Beyond Free Trade," *Foreign Affairs* 61 (4): 773–804.

David, Steven R. 1992/93. "Why the Third World Still Matters," *International Security* 17 (3): 127–59.

del Castillo V., Gustavo. 1988. "Relaciones continentales en Norteamérica: un análisis de las relaciones tripartitas México–Estados Unidos–Canadá," *Foro Internacional* 28 (3): 367–86.

Domínguez, Jorge I. 1982. "International Reverberations of a Dynamic Political Economy." In *Mexico's Political Economy*, edited by J. Domínguez. Beverly Hills, Calif.: Sage.

Doyle, Michael W. 1986. "Liberalism and World Politics," *American Political Science Review* 80 (4): 1151–69.

Fagen, Richard R., and Henry R. Nau. 1979. "Mexican Gas: The Northern Connection." In *Capitalism and the State in U.S.–Latin American Relations*, edited by R. Fagen. Stanford, Calif.: Stanford University Press.

GATT Focus. 1986. "Ministerial Declaration on the Uruguay Round," no. 41 (October).

———. 1992a. "Uruguay Round Link Hampers Settlement of Disputes," no. 91 (July).

———. 1992b. "Round Package Needed to Spur World Economic Recovery," no. 95 (November–December).

Hansen, Roger D. 1971. *The Politics of Mexican Development*. Baltimore, Md.: Johns Hopkins University Press.

Hoffmann, Stanley. 1978. *Primacy or World Order*. New York: McGraw-Hill.

Holsti, K.J. 1988. *International Politics*. Englewood Cliffs, N.J.: Prentice Hall.

Jervis, Robert. 1978. "Cooperation under the Security Dilemma," *World Politics* 30 (January): 167–214.

———. 1991/92. "The Future of World Politics: Will It Resemble the Past?" *International Security* 16 (3): 39–73.

Kegley, Charles W., Jr., ed. 1991. *The Long Postwar Peace: Contending Explanations and Projections*. New York: Harper-Collins.

Kennedy, Paul. 1991. *Grand Strategies in War and Peace*. New Haven, Conn.: Yale University Press.

Keohane, Robert O. 1987. *After Hegemony*. Princeton, N.J.: Princeton University Press.

Keohane, Robert O., and Joseph S. Nye. 1977. *Power and Interdependence*. Boston, Mass.: Little, Brown.

Lande, Stephen L., and Craig VanGrasstek. 1986. *The Trade and Tariff Act of 1984*. Lexington, Mass.: Lexington Books.

Luttwak, Edward. 1976. *The Grand Strategy of the Roman Empire*. Baltimore, Md.: Johns Hopkins University Press.

Lynn-Jones, Sean M. 1991. *The Cold War and After: Prospects for Peace*. Cambridge, Mass.: MIT Press.

MacFarlane, S. Neil. 1991. "The Impact of Superpower Collaboration on the Third World." In *Third World Security in the Post–Cold War Era*, edited by Thomas G. Weiss and Meryl A. Kessler. Boulder, Colo.: Lynne Rienner.

Maoz, Zeev, and Nasrin Abdolali. 1989. "Regime Types and International Conflict, 1816–1976," *Journal of Conflict Resolution* 33 (1): 24–26.

Mares, David R. 1985. "Explaining Choice of Development Strategies: Suggestions from Mexico, 1970–1982," *International Organization* 39 (4): 667–98.

———. 1987. "Mexico's Challenges: Sovereignty and National Autonomy under Interdependence," *Third World Quarterly* 9 (3): 788–803.

———. 1988. "Mexico's Foreign Policy as a Middle Power: The Nicaraguan Connection, 1884–1982," *Latin American Research Review* 23 (3): 81–107.

———. 1991. "U.S. Trade in Mexican Economic Restructuring: Bilateralism under a Multilateral Guise." In *Mexico's Second Revolution?* edited by Michael Howard and Douglas Ross. Burnaby, British Columbia: Center for International Studies, Simon Fraser University.

———. 1992. "The Logic of Inter-American Cooperation on Drugs." In *Drug Policy in the Americas*, edited by Peter H. Smith. Boulder, Colo.: Westview.

Mearsheimer, John. 1990. "Back to the Future: Instability in Europe after the Cold War," *International Security* 15 (1): 5–56.

Mitchell, Alison. 1995. "Clinton Lays Out His Case for U.S. Troops in Balkans; 'We Must Do What We Can,' " *New York Times*, November 28.

Mueller, John. 1989. *Retreat from Doomsday*. New York: Basic Books.

Ojeda G., Mario. 1976. *Alcances y límites de la política exterior de México*. México, D.F.: El Colegio de México.

Ozawa, Terutomo. 1979. *Multinationalism, Japanese Style*. Princeton, N.J.: Princeton University Press.

Pastor, Robert. 1980. *Congress and the Politics of U.S. Foreign Economic Policy, 1929–1976*. Berkeley: University of California Press.

Posen, Barry. 1984. *The Sources of Military Doctrine*. Ithaca, N.Y.: Cornell University Press.

Redburn, Tom. 1992. "Farm Deal within Reach," *International Herald Tribune*, November 11.

Reyna, José Luis, and Richard S. Weinert. 1977. *Authoritarianism in Mexico*. Philadelphia: Institute for the Study of Human Issues.

Richardson, J. David. 1990. "The Political Economy of Strategic Trade Policy," *International Politics* 44 (1): 107–35.

Rothstein, Robert R. 1979. *Global Bargaining*. Princeton, N.J.: Princeton University Press.

Ruggie, John Gerard. 1982. "International Regimes, Transactions, and Change: Embedded Liberalism in the Postwar Economic Order," *International Organization* 36 (2): 379–418.

Rummel, R. J. 1983. "Libertarianism and International Violence," *Journal of Conflict Resolution* 27 (1): 27–71.

Salinas de Gortari, Carlos. 1992. "Cuarto Informe de Gobierno," *Comercio Exterior* 42 (11): 1068–97.

Stark, Jeffrey. 1992. "Rethinking Security in the Americas," *North-South Issues on Democratization*, September.

Strange, Susan. 1987. "The Persistent Myth of Lost Hegemony," *International Organization* 41 (4): 551–74.

Sylan, David J. 1981. "The Newest Neo-Mercantilism," *International Organization* 35 (2): 375–93.

Tyler, Patrick E. 1992. "U.S. Strategy Plan Calls for Insuring No Rivals Develop," *New York Times*, March 8.

Vega Cánovas, Gustavo. 1988. "El acuerdo bilateral de libre comercio entre Canadá y Estados Unidos: implicaciones para México y los países en desarrollo," *Foro Internacional* 28 (3): 387–403.

Villarreal, René. 1976. *El desequilibrio externo en la industrialización de México, 1929–1975*. México, D.F.: Fondo de Cultura Económica.

Winham, Gilbert R. 1988. *Trading with Canada*. New York: Priority Press.

3

Mexico in the Sphere of Hemispheric Security

Luis Herrera-Lasso

Evolution of the Hemispheric Security System

The end of the cold war had important consequences for the Western Hemisphere. Perhaps the most important of these was the rapid disappearance of the menace that for decades had loomed from the other pole of the East-West conflict. The communist threat spurred the development during the 1940s of a hemispheric defense strategy and a collective defense system that for more than four decades extended a security umbrella over the hemisphere.

As the hemisphere's main combatant in the East-West struggle, the United States played the decisive role in designing and implementing this hemispheric security system. This responsibility vastly expanded the scope of U.S. presence and influence throughout Latin America and the Caribbean. U.S. policy found expression in support for friendly governments as they fought against any political movement posing an actual or potential threat to their interests, defined in terms of the struggle with the Soviet Union and its allies. This array of menaces ranged from avowedly communist or socialist parties or other organizations to intellectuals, progressives, leftist parties, and labor unions, all of which were regarded as threats to the ruling regimes. The most crucial factor influencing U.S. foreign policy toward these favored governments was not their democratic credentials but their support for what were perceived as U.S. national interests in the region. This coincidence of interests led the United States, in more than one instance, to lend its support to military regimes.

For nearly forty years the United States provided military assistance to these "friendly" Latin American governments, supported their counterinsurgency campaigns, and made use of multilateral instruments such as the Organization of American States to "contain communism" in the region. These policies helped to produce the Guatemalan revolution of 1954, the hemispheric ostracism of revolutionary Cuba (especially between 1961 and 1964), the Dominican incursion of 1965, the 1973 military coup in Chile, and the Grenada invasion of 1983.

Economic and social concerns received less attention than did those of a strategic or military character. The Alliance for Progress of the early 1960s, and to a lesser extent the 1983 Caribbean Basin Initiative, together represented the most ambitious U.S. efforts to use social and economic programs to check unfavorable political tendencies in the region. These programs, however, in no way diminished the preeminence of strategic and military policies as the pivot point of U.S. relations with the Latin American countries.

The most important organizations that together constituted the cold war hemispheric security framework were the Organization of American States (founded in 1949), the Inter-American Treaty of Reciprocal Assistance (popularly known as the Rio Treaty, established in 1947), the Inter-American Defense Board (established in 1942), and the Inter-American Defense College (created in 1963). Each of these organizations had a distinct purpose. The OAS provided the political framework for the hemispheric security system. The Rio Treaty committed member states to aid each other in repelling aggression from outside the hemisphere. The Inter-American Defense Board was established as a consultative mechanism for developing hemispheric defense plans. The Inter-American Defense College, headquartered in Washington, D.C., and statutorily headed by an American, was responsible for fostering communication among the various armed forces and for schooling Latin American military officers in U.S. strategic doctrine.

Until the middle 1970s this security structure worked more or less as intended. During that decade, however, the inter-American system began to show signs of weakness. The Panamanian government's declaration that it intended to negotiate Panamanian sovereignty over the canal sparked the first serious discord within the system. In 1977, Panamanian president Omar Torrijos enlisted the support of Colombia, Mexico, Venezuela, and other Latin American countries in negotiating the terms of the Panama Canal treaties with the U.S. administration of Jimmy Carter. The U.S. "concession" of eventual Panamanian sovereignty over the canal zone was harshly criticized by conservatives and especially by Republican candidate Ronald Reagan during the 1980 presidential campaign.

The first important breach in the internal unity of the OAS appeared in June 1979, when most of the organization's member states refused to support a U.S.–backed initiative advanced by the Nicaraguan government to create a multinational force that would prevent Sandinista insurgents from taking control of Managua. The opposition to the initiative contributed significantly to the Somoza regime's downfall, and it marked an important break in the long-standing OAS consensus behind U.S.–led military action as the preferred solution to regional crises. The 1982 Malvinas-Falklands war between Argentina and Great Britain went much further to weaken the inter-American system. Available evidence indicates that the Argentine high command expected the United States to support its invasion of the islands. The U.S. government tried to mediate the conflict between its two treaty allies in order to reach a negotiated solution that would preclude British use of force. Once these efforts failed and armed hostilities had begun, however, the United States chose to assist its strategic ally—Great Britain—against its hemispheric "ally"—Argentina. Arguing that it had fallen victim to aggression from an extraregional power, the Argentine government invoked the mutual defense guarantees of the Rio Treaty—an initiative which the United States blocked.

The Malvinas-Falklands matter underscored the incapacity of the OAS to achieve political and military objectives. The United States subsequently paid little heed to the organization and for several years even refused to pay its share of the OAS budget. This active neglect slowly pushed the organization into a state of virtual political and financial collapse.

Between 1983 and 1989 an interesting and unprecedented situation obtained in the region. The OAS, having lost its long-standing central role in the resolution of regional conflicts, was effectively replaced by a purely Latin American mechanism for conflict resolution, one in which the United States played no role. In January 1983 Colombia, Mexico, Panama, and Venezuela formed the so-called Contadora Group to push for negotiated political settlements of civil conflicts then under way in several Central American countries. In 1986 Argentina, Brazil, Peru, and Uruguay joined this political effort as the Contadora Support Group (also known as the Rio Group).

The Contadora Group's efforts drew support from most other interested countries and international organizations, including the weakened OAS. The United States, meanwhile, was acting unilaterally in Central America, but its almost complete diplomatic isolation did not prevent U.S. policy from determining the course of political developments in the subregion. In 1983 U.S. marines invaded Grenada in response to a request from the Association of Eastern Caribbean States. This action showed the clear political determination of the U.S. government to maintain recourse to military force as the touchstone of its foreign policy toward Latin America, despite the absence of legitimizing sanction from the OAS. The Grenada operation succeeded brilliantly in military terms and helped to revitalize the "hard-line" tendency in U.S. strategic doctrine that had been in retreat for nearly ten years. The disastrous U.S. experience in Vietnam had seriously weakened this hard-line position, not because it had forever delegitimized direct U.S. military intervention in regional conflicts, but rather because of the counterproductive way in which that intervention had been conducted.

New Approaches to Hemispheric Security

The closing years of the 1980s brought stunning political changes at both the global and hemispheric levels. In the first place, the policies inaugurated in 1985 by Soviet leader Mikhail Gorbachev produced a relaxation of East-West tensions that culminated in the end of the cold war. Simultaneously, the foreign debt crisis brought home to most Latin American nations the need for better relations with the United States, which was bound to influence heavily the foreign policies adopted by these countries. These years also witnessed the gradual return of democracy as the political norm for most Latin American countries.

The end of the cold war transformed the situation in Central America as well. Soviet-bloc involvement in the region's domestic conflicts rapidly declined to the point that Washington no longer saw it as a security threat. By 1989, one could no longer point to the communist presence in Latin America as a justification for intervening in the domestic affairs of these countries.

At least in the Western Hemisphere, the end of the cold war signaled the indisputable triumph of democracy and freedom, values which for forty years had served the United States as sword and shield in its struggle with the Soviet Union. Although this triumph might have appeared rather less indisputable in other parts of the world, it was total in the Western Hemisphere, the "backyard" of the United States and a region in which the very idea of security had traditionally been fused to U.S. national security doctrine.

In this transformed atmosphere, the United States sought in mid-1989 to revitalize the OAS as a multilateral instrument for achieving U.S. national objectives in Panama. Most Latin American governments had assiduously avoided conflict with the United States during the 1980s while working to improve their relations with it—especially in economic matters. Despite this positive trend, the OAS had remained largely inactive as a cooperative means of conflict resolution during these years.

However, when it failed to win OAS support for the November 1989 Panama intervention, the United States was forced to conduct the operation unilaterally. As a result, the invasion planners had to concoct a new political rationale for the operation, one that the U.S. public would find both credible and compelling. The old rhetoric about fighting communism had become obsolete, and drug trafficking had become the hot-button subject on the hemispheric security agenda. Noriega's alleged drug running thus became the central legal justification for the U.S. invasion.

From the U.S. perspective, drug trafficking had all the necessary elements of a priority security issue. It posed a genuine threat to U.S. interests and elicited universal moral condemnation, since its ravages touched all of society in one way or another. As a result, any antidrug operation enjoyed the presumption of legitimacy. Drug trafficking also loomed large in hemispheric relations, especially on the supply side, since narcotics of Latin American origin filled a large part of U.S. domestic demand. Consequently, any effective antidrug campaign required concerted action at the hemispheric level. Underlying all of these arguments was the U.S. strategic interest in preserving a military presence in Panama, an ultimate goal that lay hidden beneath the crush of other rationales animating the antidrug crusade.

The deft use of military force contributed to the Panama operation's success. The United States scored a rapid victory with little U.S. loss of life, the apparent achievement of all political objectives, and total control of the news media. This last point is significant because in Panama, as in Grenada in 1983, only one version of events—that of the U.S. government—became known in Latin America and indeed throughout the world. Orthodox U.S. strategic doctrine held that it was precisely the absence of such news management that contributed to the American disaster in Vietnam.

The Panama operation is comprehensible only in light of the profound changes that were then occurring at the global level. For the first time in four decades the United States could act freely in the Western Hemisphere without regard to reactions from the Soviet Union or its allies. Additionally, the rapid dissipation of the East-West conflict encouraged a general sense that the United States was the undisputed victor in the cold war. This perception clearly obtained among those who saw the East-West conflict as a clash of philosophies and the Iron Curtain as the frontier of civilization. This situation would engender the founding principles of a new security doctrine for the Western Hemisphere.

Although the OAS member states neither endorsed direct military intervention in Panama nor participated in the U.S. invasion, their silence betokened indirect complicity in the operation. The Panama invasion marked the dawn of a new era in hemispheric relations. Some Latin American governments even began to suggest the need for a new understanding of national sovereignty. Under certain conditions foreign intervention might be not only justifiable but obligatory, especially when democracy had to be restored or strengthened and when human rights—including political rights—had come under constant assault. These arguments would be repeated later within the councils of the Rio Group, especially regarding the Cuban and Haitian cases.

Most Latin American countries have taken a position—described by some as realistic, by others as pragmatic—that in its essence implies the slow acceptance of new principles intended to legitimate various forms of intervention. This new openness to intervention has a variety of sources. Many newly established democratic governments, still weak and subject to overthrow by the armed forces, see the prospect of supranational action against de facto military regimes as a deterrent against any interruption of constitutional norms and as a means to widen their own maneuvering room.

As has been mentioned, the widespread desire for better economic relations with the United States has also served to lessen resistance among Latin American countries to interventionism and other violations of national sovereignty, provided these are clothed in the mantle of defending democracy. Final approval in late 1993 of the North American Free Trade Agreement (NAFTA) intensified both the desire for closer economic ties with the United States and the corresponding fear of being shut out of the new trade association.

Political developments in other parts of the world have strengthened these tendencies. The United Nations–led military operation against the Iraqi regime of Saddam Hussein in 1991 heralded a new era of military interventions that would enjoy the legitimizing sanction and political support of the foremost multilateral organization responsible for peace and international security.[1] As in Panama in December 1989, the U.S.–led military operation in the Persian Gulf ran like clockwork, producing a swift victory with minimal allied loss of life (we know next to nothing about the extent of Iraqi casualties) and extensive control of the news media. As in the earlier cases of Grenada and Panama, official management of news reporting during the Gulf War allowed the winning side to shape the international community's knowledge and assessment of the conflict.

As in Panama, the political objectives that guided the allied military operations in the Gulf were poorly articulated. The military cam-

[1] The last time the United Nations approved this sort of military intervention was in Korea in 1950.

paign against Saddam Hussein succeeded so overwhelmingly that—at least at first blush—the allied victory appeared total. Within several months, however, as President Bush's domestic support plummeted to unprecedented depths, the U.S. government began to reap the consequences of its vague presentation of war aims and of the benefits that the American public could hope to receive from victory.

Other theaters of conflict, especially Yugoslavia and Somalia, have spawned a new rationale for intervention, this time based on humanitarianism. This new "right of humanitarian intervention" has multiplied opportunities for orchestrating United Nations–sponsored interventions throughout the world, thereby strengthening and expanding the international community's ability to wield influence in domestic conflicts. This new atmosphere has clearly affected the political calculations of most Latin American leaders. The incontestable triumph of the values of the winning side in the cold war, the demonstrated ability of that winner to resolve other conflicts in far-flung corners of the world, and indeed the very idea of a unipolar world dominated by a sole superpower have led most Latin American governments to conclude that they have little to gain by following their own paths when the new hegemon's path is so clearly marked.

These new political facts of life have brought changes in the formal hemispheric security structure that have touched every aspect of the inter-American system. The OAS has successfully rebuilt itself, thanks in part to the U.S. decision in 1989 finally to pay up its arrears. Although this development did not immediately produce the expected benefits, it signaled a first step toward the organization's possible usefulness in the middle and long terms, as shown by its successful revitalization. Canada at last joined the OAS, abandoning the standoffish stance it had maintained throughout the cold war, and the newly elected secretary general—João Baena Soares—was expected to bring new dynamism to the organization in accordance with its new circumstances.

Democracy has been the leitmotif of these transformations. Meeting in Santiago, Chile, in June 1991, the Twenty-first General Assembly of the OAS adopted resolution 1080, which stated:

> [I]n the event of actions that produce an abrupt or irregular interruption in democratic political procedures or in the legitimate exercise of power by a democratically elected government in any member states of the Organization . . . a meeting of foreign ministers or an extraordinary session of the General Assembly shall be held within a period of ten days . . . in order to assess the facts collectively and take the appropriate decisions, in accordance with the charter and international law.

The Permanent Council of the OAS was also entrusted with formulating proposals to preserve and strengthen democratic government. We should point out that the resolution originally called for the automatic expulsion from the OAS of any member state that experienced a violent breach of constitutional order.

At the Twenty-second General Assembly of the OAS, held in Nassau, Bahamas, in May 1992, the delegates approved resolution 1182, urging the secretary general:

> to convene as soon as possible a session of the Permanent Council in order to decide whether or not to convoke a series of extraordinary meetings of the General Assembly, to be held prior to December 31, 1992, which will consider the incorporation into the OAS Charter of new provisions regarding the possibility of suspending from OAS membership the governments of any member states that come to power by means described in resolution 1080 (the Declaration of Santiago), and also regarding the need to confront the region's critical level of poverty, which constitutes one of the most dire threats to democracy.

In accordance with the mandate of the Twenty-second General Assembly, an extraordinary general assembly was convened in Washington, D.C., in December 1992 to reform the OAS Charter. Delegates to that meeting approved by majority vote Article VIII of the charter, referring to the suspension of member states from the OAS. The article states:

> Any member of the Organization whose democratically constituted government is overthrown by force can be suspended from exercising the right of participation in sessions of the General Assembly, the Consultative Meeting, the Councils of the Organization, and the Specialized Conferences, as well as the commissions, working groups, and other existing bodies.

The Assembly approved another resolution (AG/RES 1(XVI-E/92)) calling for "inclusion in the Charter of arrangements for more effective and operative provision of technical cooperation, in order to promote efforts to eliminate extreme poverty." These reforms were adopted at an extraordinary session held in Managua, Nicaragua, in June 1993 under the auspices of the Twenty-third General Assembly. The Managua session also called for an extraordinary General Assembly on Inter-American Cooperation for Development (AGECID), which was convened in Mexico in 1994. The subject of democracy dominated the ongoing hemispheric debate, the first phase of which concluded with reform of the OAS Charter. Nevertheless, the operational aspects of a new security system based upon the new political outlook began to appear in other areas of the hemispheric system as well.

Regarding the Rio Pact there is rather little to say, except that its structure and operation responded explicitly to cold war concerns, which has degraded the ability of this body to face the challenges of the new era. The Rio Pact involved itself in actions directed exclusively toward hemispheric defense, which has rendered it unfit to act in matters of security more broadly considered. In fact, no Rio Pact member has tendered any proposal to energize this organization or make it more relevant to the hemisphere's new security priorities.

Such was not at all the case, however, with the Inter-American Defense Board. Beginning in 1991, a number of proposals were offered to change the nature of the board, which, as previously noted, is a consultative body established during World War II, prior to the founding of the OAS and the Rio Pact. It was charged with formulating plans for hemispheric defense, although not with carrying them out.

In 1991 the United States spearheaded the establishment of the Association for Democracy and Development for Central America (ADD). In the name of promoting democracy, this association was intended to channel all manner of international assistance—political, economic, and social—to Central America under U.S. supervision. Members of this association included the United States and Canada, the European Community countries, Japan, and the so-called Group of Three (Colombia, Venezuela, and Mexico). At its plenary meeting held in Ottawa, Canada, in February 1992, the ADD resolved that the Inter-American Defense Board should help in developing plans for the removal of land mines from the Central American countries. The association forwarded this decision to the OAS secretary general, who in turn communicated it to the IADB. Operational plans for the demining were prepared in time for the Twenty-second OAS General Assembly, held in Nassau in May 1992. It was even proposed at this meeting that the IADB itself carry out the job, the implication being that the board would at last receive de facto operational authority.

The Inter-American Defense College (IADC) has continued to discharge its vital function of instructing Latin Americans in U.S. strategic doctrine, and specifically in American conceptions of hemispheric security. The college's budget has recently been increased, which has allowed a larger number of students to take advantage of its programs. Another interesting development is the higher percentage of civilian students; in 1993, civilians outnumbered military personnel in IADC courses. Since its inception, the college—like the Inter-American Defense Board—has been statutorily headed by an American.

Regarding human rights we can also discern a tendency to strengthen supervisory mechanisms that allow greater involvement of external actors in the internal jurisdiction of Latin American states. In recent years the Inter-American Human Rights Commission (IAHRC) has been increasingly active in monitoring human rights conditions within member states. Civil liberties and other political rights have become an increasingly important part of the human rights agenda. Accompanying this mounting concern with political rights has been the growing involvement of external actors in overseeing national elections in member countries and verifying the outcomes. This has occurred in Haiti (March 1991), Surinam (May 1991 and 1992), El Salvador (1991), Paraguay (June 1991 and December 1991), Peru (November 1992), and Venezuela (December 1992). In each case the OAS secretary general issued a report assessing the election's integrity.

This evolving set of regional priorities has been accompanied by a series of political crises that have tested the ability of the inter-American system to defend its newly redefined security interests. The first of these crises struck in Peru on April 5, 1992, when President Alberto Fujimori suspended congress and the judiciary, citing corruption and ungovernability to justify his action. As ordained in OAS resolution 1080, an ad hoc meeting of foreign ministers was immediately convened in Washington, D.C. The ministers imposed sanctions on the Peruvian government which, despite its having been legitimately elected, had breached institutional order by suspending the legally constituted powers. Shortly thereafter the Peruvian government invited an OAS mission to visit the country and assess the human rights situation there. Interestingly, Fujimori simultaneously withdrew Peru from membership in the Rio Group, all members of which must have a democratic government. This requirement had caused Panama's expulsion from the Rio Group in February 1988.

In May 1992 Fujimori personally appeared at the second ad hoc meeting of foreign ministers, held in Nassau, Bahamas, under the auspices of the Twenty-second OAS General Assembly to discuss the Peruvian situation. He promised to hold elections for a new congress in November 1992 and requested technical assistance from the OAS in carrying them out. The elections subsequently took place with the support and under the supervision of the OAS, and Fujimori's party obtained a majority.

A similar situation arose in Guatemala in May 1993, when President Jorge Serrano Elías suspended the congress and the court system. An ad hoc meeting of foreign ministers was immediately convened in accordance with resolution 1080, and the OAS secretary general himself visited Guatemala to meet with the main political participants in the crisis. President Serrano rapidly lost the backing of most social sectors, including the armed forces, and three days after the *autogolpe* he and Vice President Gustavo Espino Salguero were officially disqualified by the Constitutional Court. The following Sunday, the congress elected Ramiro de León Carpio as constitutional president of Guatemala to complete Serrano's term of office, due to expire in February 1996.

In both of these cases the OAS, acting as spokesman for the hemispheric community, decisively shaped the course of events. In the Peruvian case, the OAS brought direct pressure for the restoration of democratic order. In the case of Guatemala, the secretary general's presence was likewise decisive in shaping events. The restoration of constitutional government in Guatemala was the main topic of discussion at the Twenty-third OAS General Assembly, held in Managua just a week after Serrano's *autogolpe* and only two days after de León Carpio assumed the Guatemalan presidency. In each case, pressure from the international community contributed importantly to the restoration of constitutional order.

There were two other cases during these same months in which chief executives were removed from office before the expiration of their constitutional mandates: Brazil in December 1992, and Venezuela in April 1993. In each case, the national congress disqualified the president from continuing to exercise his executive powers because of alleged irregularities in the handling of public funds. Constitutional procedures were followed in each case, and the processes were begun and concluded without any intervention from the hemispheric community. In each case, the armed forces—which wield decisive power in each country—refrained from taking advantage of the political instability to seize greater power for themselves, probably because they feared the overwhelmingly negative response that such action would have elicited at the hemispheric and global levels.

Haiti represents a very different case, perhaps the most difficult case of democracy building that the hemispheric system has faced since the cold war ended. In November 1990 Jean-Bertrand Aristide was democratically elected as president of Haiti. A few months later, in September 1991, General Raoul Cédras, supreme commander of the armed forces, seized power in a military coup and forced President Aristide into involuntary exile.

This new breach of constitutional order in the hemisphere not only drew the immediate attention of the inter-American system and helped to strengthen the force of OAS resolution 1080. It also transcended the bounds of the hemispheric system. In late 1992, the OAS resolved to pass the entire matter on to the United Nations Security Council, which imposed an economic embargo on the beleaguered island. The United Nations and the Organization of American States named a joint representative who entered into discussions with the

Haitian disputants. The two Haitian sides eventually forged an agreement—the Governors' Island accord of July 1993—which, among other things, called for the return of President Aristide by October 30. The most striking difference between the Haitian case and those of Peru and Guatemala was the direct role of the armed forces in disrupting constitutional order, a situation for which the inter-American system had no solution. Ultimately the combined pressures of United Nations mediation and a U.S. threat to use military force induced the Haitian armed forces to reach a negotiated settlement with Aristide, under which the deposed president resumed his office. This development suggests that the United States continues to seek international legitimation for its preferred courses of action while also preserving the unilateral option.

Finally, we ought to mention Cuba's role in the evolution of this new security strategy. This country lost its strategic importance with the end of the cold war and no longer constitutes a threat to the United States. Most Latin American and Caribbean countries have established closer relations with Cuba in recent years, despite a total absence of encouragement or support from the United States. Nevertheless, by 1994 no state had moved for Cuba's readmission into the OAS or any other inter-American body. The first Ibero-American Summit in 1991 gave Cuba a vital opportunity for political dialogue with its neighbors. Fidel Castro personally attended this meeting and met with his fellow Latin American heads of state and government, just as he did at subsequent summits in Madrid, Spain (1992) and in Salvador de Bahia, Brazil (1993).

Clearly the United States and other Latin American countries now view Cuba as the only exception in an almost wholly democratic hemisphere. These same observers declare that Cuba will inevitably have to liberalize its political system, since the termination of Soviet support has made the current regime unviable. The end of the cold war has been interpreted—at least in the Western Hemisphere—as signifying total collapse of the socialist model, dooming the Cuban path, at least in theory.

It remains an interesting fact that even those OAS member states that would willingly support a U.S. intervention in Cuba have failed to advocate this action within OAS councils. Perhaps the likely problems and uncertainties of a Cuban intervention have deterred these countries thus far from offering such a proposal. Nevertheless, we should not dismiss the prospect that, sooner or later, Cuba will become the central concern of the OAS, whether due to a perception that gradual liberalization has made its readmission appropriate, or to a felt need to take action to accelerate, provoke, or support the process of change within Cuba. The rise of Cuba as the central subject of debate within the Rio Group during the early 1990s is symptomatic of likely future priorities for the OAS as a whole.

Mexico in an Evolving Inter-American System

Mexico has responded to the new security situation with more reserve and caution than has any other Latin American country. As often happened in the past, Mexico's cautious stance left it isolated when the OAS Extraordinary Assembly, held in Washington in December 1992, called for a vote on reforms to the organization's charter which were intended to strengthen democracy. Nevertheless, the Mexican government has been one of the region's most active diplomatic players in efforts to promote democracy, and many of the positions it has taken have shaped subsequent developments in the region.

Mexico maintained its opposition to the U.S. military invasion of Panama, condemning it as a violation of principles embodied in the OAS and UN Charters. Even so, the government issued a statement on the domestic situation in Panama that did not justify the invasion but nevertheless recognized some rationale for it. Merely by commenting on internal Panamanian affairs, the Mexican government sparked a vigorous public debate about whether or not it had departed from the traditional noninterventionist principles of Mexican foreign policy.

At the Twenty-first OAS General Assembly, held in Santiago, Chile, in 1991, Mexican opposition was decisive in killing a draft resolution that proposed the automatic expulsion from the OAS of any member country in which the democratic system was overthrown as a result of a coup d'état. Mexico's opposition in this instance, as in others, arose from its long-standing fear that institutionalized mechanisms for assisting democratic consolidation might be used for other objectives, particularly to promote the strategic interests of specific national actors within the system. Another reason for Mexico's reluctance to support automatic pro-democratic mechanisms within the OAS was the ambiguous nature of the concept of democracy itself and of what constitutes democratic breakdown. One cannot speak of a single democratic model that applies equally to the political systems of Haiti, the United States, and Venezuela.

Following the breakdown of constitutional government in Peru in April 1992, the Mexican government argued that expulsion of the Fujimori government from the OAS would do little to promote the restoration of democracy there. At the Twenty-second OAS General Assembly in June 1992 Mexico reiterated its opposition to proposals for the automatic expulsion of member states, denounced proposals to turn the Inter-American Defense Board into a de facto operational military agency, and opposed the adoption of a new security agenda that implied last-resort military action against a raft of threats ranging from drug trafficking to human rights violations, environmental degradation, and even free-market economic reform policies. Indeed, Mexico successfully moved for the creation of a special commission to revise the very concept of hemispheric security; this commission was to issue its final report in 1994.

The Mexican government has also rejected the idea of expanding the definition of human rights to include political topics such as elections. It argues that such matters fall within each state's internal jurisdiction, and that consequently no state can be forced to accept external supervision of electoral activities.

The Mexican government's position regarding democracy has emphasized the need to foster cooperative action among Latin American countries to fight economic and social ills, which constitute the main threats to the survival and consolidation of democratic government. Its proposal to this effect was approved at the December 1992 extraordinary assembly of the OAS, and the Twenty-third General Assembly in Managua incorporated it into the OAS Charter.

The proposal as adopted reflects Mexico's position by forthrightly asserting the objective of strengthening democracy, but it differs regarding the appropriate means to achieve that objective. In the case of Haiti, Mexico supported from the very start the international community's efforts to restore democracy there, but it drew the line at military intervention, just as President Aristide himself had repeatedly done.

Regarding Guatemala's constitutional breakdown in 1993—an especially delicate case in light of that country's close physical proximity to Mexico—the Mexican government backed the efforts of the OAS, and especially of its secretary general, to resolve the crisis. It was also the first country to offer support in situ to the new president immediately after the restoration of constitutional authority.

Regarding the delicate peace process in El Salvador, Mexico has maintained its support for the activities of the UN secretary general and has even contributed police personnel to serve as observers under the auspices of the UN Operation for El Salvador (ONUSAL). This decision, which was unprecedented in Mexican foreign policy, was intended to ensure Mexico's continued participation in the secretary general's "Group of Friends" as it sought to guarantee the final implementation of the peace accords signed in Chapultepec, Mexico, in 1992.

Mexico also participated actively with Spain, Colombia, and Venezuela in the "Group of Friends" that supported the Guatemalan peace process. Mexico was especially active between February and

May 1993, a period of intense negotiation between the Guatemalan government and guerrilla representatives in Mexico City. These talks were finally broken off in the wake of President Serrano's seizure of emergency powers.

Although Mexico helped to establish the Association for Democracy and Development in Central America, it distanced itself from any actions that it took to imply foreign intervention to support democratic consolidation. Within the association, Mexico has focused its efforts on programs of economic and social development. In this and other instances, the Mexican government has refused to participate in cooperative efforts that might restrict the actions of recipient governments.

Mexico has been heavily engaged diplomatically in each of the above-mentioned cases. It has been the first to hail the restoration of democratic order in those countries that have fallen victim to coups d'état. Mexico has also worked hardest to prevent an excess of good intentions from producing negative results, especially the legitimation or even institutionalization of automatic intervention by the hemispheric community in domestic affairs of member countries. Although such interventions might have the declared objective of strengthening democracy, they can easily be diverted to advance special interests of powerful countries in the system, as has happened in the past.

Mexico has special historical reasons for holding this view. One of these is the antecedent use of military means to solve political conflicts within the region. Beyond defending the principles of nonintervention and self-determination of peoples which underlay Mexico's position on the question, Latin America's historical experience shows that such military actions eventually produce outcomes that are less democratic and more politically unstable. Although foreign interventions might be inspired by good intentions, they cannot fail to advance the national interests of those countries that advocate and conduct them, with all the risks that this situation implies. Finally, the recent experiences of the United Nations in its humanitarian interventions in Somalia and Yugoslavia have underscored the enormous legal and practical problems involved in managing the scope and conduct of such operations.

The Cuban case offers the best proof that the diplomatic exclusion and isolation of an undemocratic regime does not necessarily promote the internal political changes that are anticipated by those who apply the sanctions and enforce the isolation. The recent cases of Peru and Guatemala have shown that continued diplomatic engagement with such countries can foster eventual democratic restoration by preserving flexibility and communication. In each of these cases the OAS wielded positive influence at the moment of political crisis without having to expel the country in question or resort to military intervention. In the case of Peru, the OAS even provided technical support for the November 22, 1992, elections, which chose a new congress and marked a return to constitutional order.

Although Mexico shares the hemispheric community's concern for strengthening democracy in the region, it differs from some countries on how the hemispheric community should achieve this goal. Specifically, it rejects any use of military means to defeat threats to hemispheric security. That is, Mexico opposes a militaristic understanding of hemispheric security, as well as any effort to legitimize or institutionalize external military intervention as a means to resolve essentially domestic conflicts.

In the several years that have passed since the end of the cold war, most conflicts arising within member countries of the inter-American system have been resolved, in some cases under the auspices of the hemispheric community, without resort to interventionist measures. Panama in 1989 and Haiti in 1994 are the sole exceptions. Nevertheless, the tendency of some within the OAS to promote interventionist actions has not yet been stamped out. In much of Latin America and the Caribbean—and especially in the Southern Cone countries, where the armed forces have a long tradition of usurping political power—the threat of external intervention constitutes a deterrent to soldiers who might take advantage of political crises in order to seize power. For the United States, the attractiveness of military arrangements is consistent with that nation's long-standing tendency to give top priority to solutions of a political or strategic character, especially with regard to Latin America.

The end of the cold war has made necessary a fundamental change in our understanding of what constitutes a threat to democracy and hemispheric security. External threats have receded, and the main internal and external challenges to regional stability—ranging from drug trafficking to extreme poverty—call for a new response based on ever greater cooperation and hemispheric solidarity. These new challenges cannot be met successfully by creating security agencies for interventionist purposes. Far from solving the structural problems that give rise to such threats, such interventions would serve only to replace one group of hard-line political incumbents with another more moderate group. They would not, however, solve the root problems that threatened the region's democracies in the first place.

Mexico is well positioned to defend its interests in a sovereign and autonomous way. Its foreign policy is coherent and consistent, built upon firm principles that have proven their worth over time. For fifty years Mexico has enjoyed political and social stability, and the armed forces have shown no inclination to subvert democratic institutions and seize political power from the civilian authorities. Mexico has also benefited from the economic modernization program begun in the early 1980s and strengthened in 1994 with the entry into force of NAFTA. Finally, it enjoys the benefit of a highly experienced political class and a professional foreign service.

Mexico's foreign policy toward Central America—a high diplomatic priority in recent years—has been effective in promoting political stability and economic and social development as a way to preserve and strengthen democracy there. Mexico has achieved these good results without having to compromise its own autonomy by acting jointly with other countries.

One frequently hears it said that by signing NAFTA, Mexico "lowered its guard" against assaults on its sovereignty by the United States, its most important commercial partner. One can also argue, however, that Mexico has in fact strengthened itself vis-à-vis the United States by joining it in a common free trade arrangement. In 1983 Mexico faced one of the worst financial crises in its modern history, dominated by a huge foreign debt owed mainly to U.S. creditors. Most observers wagered that the transfer of power that year from José López Portillo to Miguel de la Madrid would bring an end to Mexico's diplomatic activism in Central America, since the government would need the U.S. government's good will in order to restructure successfully its financial relations with the outside world. Nevertheless, as a member of the Contadora Group, established in January 1983, Mexico adopted policy positions toward Central America—intended to foster peace and regional stability—that differed sharply from those of the United States. Mexico's divergent policies toward Central America did not hinder its own return to financial health, as shown by its three successful public debt restructurings and two private debt restructurings accomplished between 1982 and 1988.

Some observers have suggested that NAFTA has distanced Mexico from the other Latin American and Caribbean countries, with whom it shares strong ties of history and culture. The reaction of these countries to NAFTA's difficulties in the U.S. Congress, however, belied these suggestions, showing instead that NAFTA brought Mexico closer to its regional neighbors rather than distancing it from them. Virtually every country in the region urged the treaty's approval. This has helped to improve Mexico's relations with its neighbors, since most now harbor desires of joining the treaty as well.

All of the above considerations lead one to conclude that Mexico retains considerable flexibility in responding to proposals for redirecting the inter-American system. It can either yield to majority opinion or try to move the process in a new direction, always reserving the option, as it has in the past, of rejecting those political and security initiatives that it believes contradict Mexico's national interests and that might bring pressures in other areas for changing the country's national project.

The Events of 1994

The political and economic events of 1994 produced very important changes in how Mexicans view their national reality. The indigenous and peasant problem—specifically, the January 1994 armed uprising in Chiapas in defense of local Indian and peasant interests—is nothing new. Nor are the complexities of the country's electoral system unknown to most Mexicans. The only event of early 1994 with which Mexicans were totally unfamiliar was a high-level political assassination, the first to take place since the murder of President-elect Alvaro Obregón in 1928. These destabilizing events took place during a particularly important and sensitive election year. On August 21, 1994, Mexico elected a new congress and president, who took office on December 1, 1994. The events of 1994 created significant concern and uncertainty, which both boosted voter turnout and complicated the conduct of the election itself.

This new situation produced some changes in perceptions of subjects touching upon foreign policy. Between 1989 and 1993, the Mexican government followed a coherent and consistent policy toward the complex evolution of the hemispheric system in matters of democracy and security. Fernando Solana, who served as Mexico's foreign minister from December 1989 until December 1993, when he became minister of public education, was the main implementer of Mexican foreign policy in the Western Hemisphere context. As foreign minister, Solana consistently opposed all proposals that implied either the creation of new agencies with supranational authority to intervene in the domestic political or security affairs of OAS members, or the provision of such authority to existing agencies. Mexico's opposition helped to blunt all such interventionist initiatives, which otherwise might well have been adopted. Mexico participated vigorously in the inter-American system, never withdrawing from the debate despite disagreements and difficulties in forging consensus. The current absence of any hemisphere-level military agency with operational authority is due in large measure to this consistent and firm policy of the Salinas government, which Foreign Minister Solana played a vital role in implementing.

With respect to democracy, one of the most hotly debated subjects within Mexico was the possible participation of international organizations—especially the Inter-American Human Rights Commission—as observers of the August 1994 elections. The Mexican government welcomed technical assistance from international organizations in carrying out the elections, as has been provided to Nicaragua, Peru, Venezuela, Haiti, and El Salvador. In fact, a large number of Mexican journalists and members of various civic associations stepped forward to observe the elections. The government welcomed this participation but continued to draw the line at granting these associations or individuals any authority to judge the election results, asserting that this function belonged solely to the Mexican electoral authorities.

Nevertheless, an important consequence of the political events of 1994 was increased support on the part of some political sectors and groups for the presence of international electoral observers to ensure the honesty of the August 1994 elections. The PRI's initial 1994 presidential candidate, Luis Donaldo Colosio, publicly declared his support for international observation of the election. He asserted that this presence would serve the interests of the opposition parties by pressuring the electoral authorities to comply fully with the electoral law, and it would benefit the ruling party by increasing the domestic and international credibility of a PRI victory.

As a result of pressure from various political groups, the Federal Electoral Institute (IFE) decided to permit participation of international electoral observers, and it delineated both the authority that such observers, or "visitors," would enjoy and the limits to which they would be subject. By inviting international electoral observers, Mexico did not necessarily suffer any loss of sovereignty, since Mexicans themselves decided to welcome the presence of such observers at various stages of the election. In principle, this situation did not contradict Mexico's traditional defense of its national sovereignty, since the presence of international observers resulted not from any external imposition but from a consensus among the country's main political actors. This decision neither served as an opening wedge for unwanted interference by international organizations in Mexico's internal affairs, nor did it imply any change in the country's firm opposition to the creation of any hemisphere-level political or military organization with supranational authority.

In matters concerning the Western Hemisphere, Mexican foreign policy has maintained its solid defense of national sovereignty, despite the winds unleashed against it by the end of the cold war. Mexican foreign policy between 1989 and 1994 has remained strong enough to face the challenge of internal political evolution, while it has continued to influence decisively the evolution of the hemispheric system. Mexico has sought in this way to defend its legitimate interests in preserving sovereignty and nonintervention in its internal affairs.

Bilateral Tensions and Cooperation

4

Mexico and U.S. Grand Strategy: The Geo-strategic Linchpin to Security and Prosperity

Michael J. Dziedzic

During the cold war, the United States enjoyed an enormous geopolitical advantage: whereas the Soviet Union was encircled by adversaries, the United States was blessed with benign neighbors and secure land borders. Along our southern frontier, stability was largely a by-product of Mexico's single-party, pseudo-democratic political order. Coincidentally, just when Mexico's erstwhile corporatist regime was beginning to show serious signs of decay, the Soviet empire itself succumbed to prolonged dry rot, sloughing off its vassal states along with its neo-imperial pretensions. Superpower rivalry ceased to be a driving force in global affairs, and the United States assumed a position of unchallenged prominence. Mexico, owing to its stability and its peaceful ways, was a passive yet essential contributor to the ultimate success of our containment policy, the U.S. grand strategy of the cold war.

Ironically, in the post–cold war order we inhabit today, geopolitical dominance no longer carries with it the same cachet as in earlier eras. The global polity no longer seems to operate by the same rules, although new arrangements are still evolving. Like the Roman god Janus, the international system currently displays two contradictory faces. The more sanguine outlook sees promise in the demise of great power rivalry. This has allowed economic affairs, once considered "low politics," to emerge as a dominant factor in inter-state relations. The positive-sum logic of comparative advantage and market integration are presently in ascendancy over the zero-sum dictums of the domino theory and competing alliances. According to this school of thought, a peaceful new order might evolve under the influence of expanding free trade and democratic governance. The opposing view is fundamentally pessimistic, anticipating instead a "new world disorder" and a horde of disruptive non-state actors (international criminal enterprises, terrorists, refugee migrations, global pollutants, and so on) operating transnationally without regard for state sovereignty. It is premature to say which of these contrasting images will ultimately gain ascendancy. Both may continue to coexist for some time, Janus-like, until their dialectical tension is resolved, or perhaps until the zero-sum logic of the geopoliticians eventually reasserts itself.

The burden of this chapter is to establish the geo-strategic relevance of Mexico for the United States. Just as the global order has evolved, so also has the nature of Mexico's strategic significance. During the cold war, and indeed during World Wars I and II as well, Mexico was prized as a *geopolitical* fulcrum. On the southern flank of the United States, it was coveted as a source of leverage to pry us away from other vital pursuits. As the post–cold war system has begun to take shape, Mexico's *geo-economic* importance has become much more salient. The North American Free Trade Agreement (NAFTA) is a manifestation of this. Mexico's successful incorporation into the domain of vibrant, free market economies (or its failure to incorporate) will be a major determinant of the viability of our contemporary enlargement strategy. Concurrently, Mexico has also become a choke point for an array of *geo-social* or transnational afflictions that respect no national boundaries. Thus it will play a pivotal role in the emerging struggle to ward off the direct consequences of what pessimists refer to as the new world disorder. If Mexico were to succumb to such forces, the United States could scarcely expect to avoid the full and direct consequences of any "coming anarchy" (Kaplan 1994). Thus Mexico has been, and will continue to be, pivotal to the success of U.S. grand strategy.

Clearly there are both historic opportunities and serious risks at play in the U.S.–Mexican strategic relationship. To capture the full extent of Mexico's geo-strategic relevance, therefore, the analysis that follows draws a contrast between potential best-case and worst-case scenarios. This methodology is used to evaluate each aspect of Mexico's geo-strategic importance for the United States (that is, the geopolitical, the geo-economic, and the geo-social).

Mexico: The Geopolitical Fulcrum

Geopolitical theorists consider geographic factors to have great, even decisive, bearing on how powerful a state may become. Friedrich Ratzel, for example, argued that states must seek additional living space (*lebensraum*) or they will perish; Alfred Thayer Mahan considered control of sea-lanes to be essential; and Sir Halford Mackinder calculated that whoever controlled the Eurasian "heartland" would dominate the world (Glassner and de Blij 1990). In Mexico's case, geopolitical significance is a function of its location on the southern flank of a superpower. The significance of this juxtaposition for the United States has been most pronounced when: (1) the United States has been enmeshed in a *struggle for power internationally*; or (2) Mexico has been riven by *domestic unrest internally*.

Geopolitics and Great Power Rivalry

During the twentieth century, great power rivals of the United States sought to exploit Mexico's strategic location on two particularly noteworthy occasions. One involved the infamous Zimmermann telegram of 1917, a German démarche calculated to divert U.S. war-making potential away from the European battlefield. The German foreign minister, Arthur Zimmermann, hoped to entice Mexico to declare war on the United States on the eve of his nation's initiation of unrestricted submarine warfare, an action that was certain to provoke outrage in the United States. In return, Germany pledged to help Mexico "regain by conquest her lost territory in Texas, Arizona, and New Mexico" (cited in Tuchman 1957: 7). Since the United States and Mexico had already skated close to the brink of war on a couple of occasions during the upheavals of the Mexican Revolution (1910–1917), this ploy was far from an idle matter. If it had been successful, the capacity of the United States to play a role in determining the outcome of the war in Europe would have been vitiated. The plot had the opposite effect, however, when British intelligence intercepted the telegram and adroitly brought it to the attention of U.S. authorities.[1]

During the cold war, U.S. policy makers perceived similar Machiavellian designs behind Soviet and Cuban meddling in Central American insurgencies. Applying the logic of the domino theory to those developments, President Ronald Reagan admonished the country in a March 1986 speech that acquiescing to the Sandinista takeover in Nicaragua would mean "consolidation of a privileged sanctuary just two days driving time from Harlingen, Texas. . . . They

[1] I deal with this issue in greater detail in Dziedzic 1989a: 4–6.

have in mind being a launching pad for revolution up and down, first of all, Latin America" (Reagan 1986). Assessments by U.S. strategists throughout this era concluded that Mexico was the ultimate strategic objective of Soviet maneuvers in the region. As recently as the 1990 Annual Report to Congress by the Defense Department, this geopolitical logic was cited as the fundamental rationale for our policy in the region. As noted in that report, "If we fail to support our friends and allies now, as they confront the growing security threat in Central America, we can expect to face a more serious threat much closer to our own borders in the future" (Carlucci 1989: 27).

If Mexico had been destabilized, of if an adversarial relationship had developed between the United States and Mexico, the strategic "correlation of forces" would have tilted markedly in favor of the Soviets. Our southern flank could no longer have been treated as an "economy of force" zone. The United States would have been compelled to squander precious resources on securing the border. Though this was not to be, Mexico's geopolitical utility cannot be gainsaid. A strategic assessment from the late cold war period captures the essence of the matter, stating, "The absence of significant security threats close to home has helped the United States to play a global military role in the years since 1945" (Ikle et al. 1988: 11).

Geopolitics and Internal Stability in Mexico

The contemporary absence of a struggle for global hegemony diminishes but does not eliminate the geopolitical impact of Mexico. Turbulence on our very threshold would still have profound consequences for our capacity to cope with the broader international environment and to shape it in a way that is more consistent with our interests. Even in the absence of a great power rival to foment or exploit instability along our southern border, our strategy of engagement and enlargement would be severely hamstrung. National security policy is not exclusively dedicated to managing threats, however. The global order also presents opportunities for promoting national interests and values. A well-ordered, resurgent, and self-confident Mexico could become a vital partner in the formation of a hemispheric community of pluralistic, prosperous, and peaceful states.

One does not need to search assiduously through the annals of our diplomatic history to find a time when the United States was still largely disengaged from the global balance of power yet deeply entangled in Mexico. The Mexican Revolution produced two serious armed interventions by the United States: the 1914 occupation of Veracruz, and the 1916–17 expedition by General "Blackjack" Pershing in pursuit of Pancho Villa. Though Villa proved too wily a quarry for Pershing to snare, that year-long expedition, in particular, came perilously close to precipitating open warfare.[2] Two aspects of this latter episode illustrate the strategic significance of Mexico for the United States. First, roughly half the active forces in the United States Army were ultimately committed to securing the border. Including the soldiers under Pershing's command and national guardsmen called to active duty to protect the border from Villa's continuing depredations, some 100,000 troops were assigned to the mission.[3] Second, our attention was diverted by this squabble until a mere two months before entry into the conflict in Europe.

It would seem axiomatic, therefore, and as immutable as geography, that Mexico is of vital geopolitical importance to the United States, even in an epoch when great power rivalry is quiescent. The logic is not complex: it would simply be impossible to remain serenely aloof from widespread domestic disorder there. If we reason by analogy, the Mexican Revolution produced a dramatic "spillover effect" in the form of Pancho Villa's brazen raid on Columbus, New Mexico. Should Mexico once again become ungovernable under the weight of its contemporary political and economic crises, spillover onto vital interests of the United States would be unavoidable. The border is too long and porous, too many Americans have interests in Mexico, and too many Mexicans would be interested in seeking sanctuary in the United States.[4] Under such circumstances, the clamor to "seal the border" could be irrepressible.

As a practical matter, an immediate response would be demanded, and the only institution with the requisite surge capability would be the armed forces. The number of troops that might become involved would depend heavily on the actual scenario and on the concept of operations adopted. In addition, extensive terrain analysis would be required. In the absence of such planning, it is only possible to project a crude estimate. Nevertheless, two army divisions, or more, could easily be required. Apart from the fiscal implications of such a commitment, if instability along the border were to last for several months or more it would make a shambles of our present

---

[2] According to Weigley, "war seemed almost inevitable" after a clash between Pershing's forces and Mexican government troops at Carrizal in April 1916 (1967: 348). See also Katz 1981: 309–11.

[3] According to Matloff (1969: 372), the United States Army numbered only 210,000 men, if one includes the 75,000 National Guard troops federalized for duty on the Mexican border.

[4] Tangible U.S. interests include 500,000 U.S. citizens who reside in Mexico and $30.6 billion in direct investment in fixed assets (two-thirds of all foreign direct investment in Mexico). In addition, investment in equity from all foreign sources has fluctuated from a high of $60.9 billion in January 1994 down to $19 billion in February 1995, as a result of the peso crisis (U.S. Embassy 1995: 66, 91).

military strategy. Current national strategy stipulates that the United States must maintain a military capability:

> sufficient to help defeat aggression in two nearly simultaneous major regional conflicts. . . . Obviously we seek to avoid a situation in which an aggressor in one region might be tempted to take advantage when US forces are heavily committed elsewhere. More basically, maintaining a "two war" force helps ensure that the United States will have sufficient military capabilities to deter or defeat aggression by a coalition of hostile powers or by a large, more capable adversary than we foresee today (White House Office 1995: 7).

There is already considerable skepticism that our present force posture would be adequate to conduct two "nearly simultaneous" major regional conflicts. If several of the army's ten remaining divisions were no longer available to meet contingencies abroad, this would create an acute and unsustainable force-strategy mismatch.

In a geopolitical sense, therefore, political order in Mexico is a core interest of the United States. The burdens of securing our southwestern border could have a debilitating, even crippling, impact on our capacity for global engagement. Admittedly, positing a potential need to secure the border is an extreme and, perhaps, unlikely worst-case scenario. The inescapable reality, however, is that political stability in Mexico is essential to the success of our strategic aspirations.

Geopolitical Benefits of Politico-Economic Transition in Mexico

Although Mexico is currently undergoing an unsettling and potentially turbulent process of political and economic transformation, the ultimate outcome could conceivably be a genuinely pluralistic polity and a robust economy. The strategic stakes for the United States in fostering this highly desirable outcome are extensive. In the realm of regional security affairs, collaboration at both the *bilateral* and *multilateral* levels could be expanded and invigorated. There is considerable room for improvement in both at present.

The Bilateral Security Relationship—The U.S.–Mexican military relationship remains essentially frozen in its late cold war configuration, in spite of profound changes in global affairs. It is currently unthinkable, for example, that U.S. and Mexican ground forces would engage in combined exercises in Mexico. This stands in sharp contrast to the transformation in U.S.–Russian relations, which has already led to combined peacekeeping exercises on both Russian and U.S. soil.

Although extensive interaction does take place between law enforcement agencies engaged in counter-drug activities, the Joint Mexican-U.S. Defense Commission remains moribund. At present, the bilateral security relationship is largely informal, episodic, lacking in institutionalization, susceptible to politicization, burdened by lingering suspicions, and encumbered by obsolete stereotypes. This is especially true of the military dimension of the relationship, but dealings with the Foreign Ministry are not fundamentally different. When it comes to many national security matters, we are neighbors, but our neighborhood is only embryonic.

Despite the impoverished condition of U.S.–Mexican security relations today, a solid foundation now exists upon which to construct the architecture for future cooperation. Barriers that once precluded closer ties have vanished along with the cold war. One obstacle had been a divergence in threat perceptions. Mexico never viewed communist subversion in the region with the alarm that U.S. policy makers did. Now, in contrast, there is a convergence around the notion that the illicit drug trade is a genuine, if unorthodox, threat to the security of both nations.

Another impediment had been Mexico's deeply rooted concern about the conduct of the United States itself. Within the Mexican armed forces, this went beyond anxiety about overweening influence by the "Colossus of the North" in their economic and cultural affairs. NAFTA constitutes a watershed, therefore, because it is a symbolic recognition that the United States is no longer considered a plausible security threat.[5]

As a result, an implicit security community has come into being. Not only is it unthinkable that force would be used to resolve bilateral disputes, but virtually any threat to the security of one nation would constitute a threat to the other as well. By eschewing the notion that it must guard against the United States militarily, Mexico has opened the door to meaningful collaboration against common security threats. Before stepping over the threshold, however, military leaders will, at a minimum, require time to build confidence in the evolving relationship.[6] The gap once separating these two "distant neighbors" is shrinking, and it will continue to do so—if the fruits of *economic*

---

[5]While this is now apparently the official viewpoint, it is still fairly common for serious people to express concern that the northern half of Mexico will once again be hived off and incorporated into the United States. There is even the suspicion by some that NAFTA is a ruse by the United States to expand its influence in Mexico.

[6]The notion that NAFTA represents the abandonment of the perception that the United States was a potential enemy was articulated to me by a senior member of the Mexican general staff in May 1995. Even more emphatic was this officer's insistence that the pace of further change must not be rushed.

integration become manifest and as confidence in Mexico's embryonic process of *democratization* strengthens.

As a result of NAFTA, the salience of "North America" as a geopolitical entity and as a unifying factor in national security affairs may be significantly enhanced.[7] For a document that does not explicitly mention security matters, this trade accord is, nevertheless, freighted with implications for regional security cooperation. As the economies of Canada, Mexico, and the United States inexorably merge under its influence, NAFTA could serve as a catalyst for closer coordination on a panoply of common concerns, including national security. The agenda for the annual summit meeting of G-7 countries, for example, regularly embraces pressing security concerns, in addition to coordination of macroeconomic policies.

Perhaps the most immediate and compelling reason for the three NAFTA partners to establish a mechanism to coordinate their actions in the field of national security will be to manage the inevitably disruptive consequences of economic and political change in Mexico. As the relationship matures, a more conventional pattern of military-to-military interaction could emerge, perhaps involving expanded personnel exchanges, common training, combined exercises, and coordinated planning. The accent would likely be on such mutual security concerns as disaster relief, counterterrorism, control of arms smuggling, support for law enforcement efforts against international criminal organizations, and regulation of any other potentially threatening transnational phenomenon. Indeed, the web of regular governmental interaction and interpersonal relations among policy makers has become much more extensive as a result of the process of NAFTA treaty negotiation and implementation. Presumably this will spill over into other issue areas if Mexico's market-oriented economic program begins to demonstrate broad and sustainable results.

Whether an effective regime of security cooperation ultimately emerges in North America also hinges on the extent to which all three countries come to share a common democratic ethos. Essential ingredients include respect for human rights, toleration of dissent, and military obeisance to civil authority regardless of the political party in power. There must also be a willingness to hold individuals accountable for violating the public trust. When any regime falls seriously

[7] "North America" may appear on the map, but for those who live here its usage has been imprecise, and for policy makers the concept has been largely irrelevant. For most Mexicans, a "North American" is a resident of the country immediately to their north. For those in the United States and Canada, it is a term reserved for themselves. For policy makers in the U.S. State Department, it doesn't exist; Mexican affairs are handled along with other American Republics, while Canada belongs to the European Bureau.

short in these areas, military cooperation can become indistinguishable from conspiracy to repress political freedom.

On balance, although important limitations remain, the environment for constructing a cooperative security regime in North America is more promising today, especially with NAFTA. As will be discussed at length below, the United States will remain vulnerable to the cancerous effects of geo-social forces unless effective mechanisms of cooperation are forged with other sovereign states. There are no more vital partners in this campaign than our contiguous neighbors. The ultimate significance of the U.S.–Mexican security relationship could be to create a community of interests in which both neighbors regard each other as essential contributors to mutual security in our own geopolitical neighborhood.

Hemispheric Security Cooperation—While governments in the Americas (with the exception of Cuba) generally endorse free market economic programs and democratic governance, advancement in multilateral security affairs has not kept pace. The recent clash between Peru and Ecuador demonstrates that warfare has yet to be abandoned as a means of resolving inter-state disputes. Within the OAS, there is a growing awareness not only that the post–cold war era has opened a window of opportunity for crafting a new hemispheric security regime, but also that there is a price for neglecting to do so. As stated in "A New Vision of the OAS":

> In recent years, fundamental changes have occurred in the regional and international context that promote greater cooperation and significant strengthening of collective action for peace. . . . Unfortunately, this trend has been broken by the recent military confrontations between Ecuador and Peru (Gaviria 1995: 23).

For the past several years, the OAS has been grappling with this matter, primarily through the mechanism of a temporary working group on hemispheric security. A central issue is whether the Inter-American Defense Board (IADB) ought to be formally linked to the OAS. At present, there is no working relationship other than the funding that is provided by the OAS for the operation of the Board. OAS Secretary General Caesar Gaviria has taken the position that, "It is essential that the inter-American defense system and our organization integrate basically, and that the system's activities complement and interact with the various components of the OAS" (Gaviria 1995: 24). To date, however, consensus about the desirability of forging a viable regional security organization has been elusive.

Initiatives to invigorate the IADB have consistently met with resistance, the most intransigent of which stems from Mexico. The Mexicans oppose rejuvenation of the IADB because of fears it could be transformed into a coercive mechanism that could be used to undermine state sovereignty. Mexico also insists upon a very rigid and traditional definition of the casus belli that might trigger collective security provisions under the Rio Treaty. From the Mexican perspective, drug trafficking, internal subversion, arms smuggling, disaster relief, or promotion of democracy are not *continental* security issues. Since that treaty is concerned with defense against an extra-hemispheric threat, its relevance in the contemporary world is nil. It has become one of Mexico's more predictable foreign policy objectives to keep both the Rio Treaty and the IADB in that harmless condition.

Mexico was also decidedly unenthusiastic about the U.S.–proposed hemispheric Defense Ministerial meeting in Williamsburg in July 1995. Initially, Mexico was inclined to skip the session entirely. After considerable courting from the United States, they ultimately decided to send their ambassador to the United States, while most other nations had their defense minister or another senior minister in attendance (Aldinger 1995). Thus collective action to deal with contemporary transnational security concerns is greatly retarded by Mexico's aversion to multilateral military initiatives.

Mexico is, once again, the linchpin for a policy outcome that is highly desirable for the United States. In this instance, support is not likely to be forthcoming soon. If and when Mexico overcomes its paranoia about multilateralism, however, the long-term dividends could be extraordinary.

Perhaps the paradigm case for such regional advancement is Western Europe. Since World War II, prosperity in that historically war-torn region has been a function not only of economic integration and democratization but also of collaborative security ties among the states of that subregion. While NATO might be faulted for incoherence in out-of-area operations such as Bosnia, there is no doubt that it has been essential to preserving the peace in Europe since World War II. This pertains not only to containment of Soviet expansionism but also to the absence of warfare within Western Europe itself.

Thus it is not utopian to aspire to the same outcome as the nations of the Americas progress down an analogous path. Even flinty realists like Henry Kissinger advocate pursuit of such an objective. He makes the following comparison:

> The two regions where moral consensus can undergird cooperative relationships are the Western Hemisphere and the North Atlantic area. In both, the key countries have, to all practical purposes, foresworn the use of force in their relations with each other. In each, institutions already exist capable of serving as building blocks of a cooperative world order (Kissinger 1995a).

This is certainly one of the loftier goals sought by the present U.S. grand strategy of engagement and enlargement. As Vice President Gore (1995: 8) asked rhetorically in his keynote address to the assembly of defense ministers at Williamsburg, "Can we develop a framework for hemispheric security that will assure the integrity of our borders, reduce the potential for conflict, increase cooperation and develop means for the fair and speedy resolution of problems?" For the moment, one of the more significant factors militating against such a cooperative security regime in the Americas is Mexico's aversion to multilateralism.

On balance, Mexico's geopolitical salience has declined somewhat in the post–cold war epoch because, at the global level, there is presently no contender for power who could benefit from destabilizing our southern flank. Nevertheless, Mexico remains vital to the success of U.S. grand strategy. In a negative sense, serious instability would likely vitiate our military strategy, which is predicated upon maintaining a force posture adequate to engage in two "nearly simultaneous" major regional conflicts.

Just as consequential, however, are the positive contributions that a stable, prosperous, and self-confident Mexico could make. In geopolitical terms, U.S. security would be profoundly reinforced if Mexico were to become a partner in managing transnational threats that permeate our common border and in constructing a peaceful community of nations in our hemisphere. Thus Mexico's future circumstances will exert a powerful influence over U.S. ability to seize the abundant opportunities present in the post–cold war environment. This is also true of its geo-economic function as a bridge to the rest of the Americas.

Mexico: Geo-economic Bridge of the Americas

Geopolitics is associated with "high politics." These are matters of great moment; the very survival of the state may be at stake. The dominant preoccupation is the relative power of the state, and the logic is decidedly zero-sum. Geo-economics, in contrast, has traditionally been considered "low politics." One of the distinguishing features of the post–cold war order, however, is the absence of any U.S. rival capable of threatening our way of life. With survival assured, at least for the moment, prosperity has become a dominant consideration. Thus, geo-economics appears to be gaining ascendancy over more traditional geopolitical matters. In international politics today, as in recent U.S. presidential politics, "It's the economy, stupid."

Geography has become a prominent macroeconomic consideration as a result of the current trend toward subregional, regional, and global economic integration. As this process unfolds, it will be vital for the United States that these trading regimes remain both *open and fair*.

With regard to open trade, if regional trading blocs were to become exclusionary, a future world order could arise in which trade in Europe is conducted under German hegemony and economic interaction in Asia is centered on Japan or China. Apart from negative economic consequences, closed regional trading blocs could degenerate into competition for global dominance, producing a much riskier international environment for the United States.

Concerning fair trade, the issue of market access is pivotal. For U.S. grand strategy to succeed, states engaging in unfair trading practices ought not to profit at our expense. Especially in Asia, the gap between principles of free trade and actual practice has become worrisome. At least a portion of the annual U.S.$65 billion trade gap with Japan, for example, is allegedly due to invisible, nontariff barriers.[8] Until recently, China's flagrant pirating of U.S. intellectual property also usurped a share of our potential market, another dimension of the fair trade issue. As Kissinger has observed, "The majority of Asian countries are undergoing a transition that produces tension between the internationalism required by global economics and the nationalism many leaders believe helps internal political cohesion" (Kissinger 1995b).

The challenge in Mexico is quite different. In this case, they have embraced the logic of the marketplace with the zeal of the newly converted. There is no escaping the demonstration effect that the results of this experiment will have on policy makers elsewhere. As our NAFTA partner, Mexico has dedicated itself to shrinking its public sector and competing for markets abroad. With the sixteenth largest economy in the world, its future economic performance will be a bellwether for our enlargement strategy.[9] It is geographically and culturally positioned to serve as the bridge between English- and Spanish-speaking America. If Mexico demonstrates that the neoliberal economic formula works, this will provide a powerful fillip in the direction of a global economic community that is both open and fair. The opposite is also true.

---

[8] U.S. concerns over such practices recently evoked threats to impose a 100 percent duty on Japanese luxury cars.

[9] As of 1992 (World Bank 1994: 18–19).

The Geo-economic Significance of Bilateral Trade

If we consider the magnitude of two-way trade, a nation's proclivity to "buy American," and prospects for expanding our export market there, Mexico may be our most valuable trading partner. In 1994, the total value of U.S.–Mexican trade amounted to U.S.$100.3 billion, a bilateral volume surpassed only by Japan and Canada (U.S. Department of State 1995a: 4). Whereas the United States ran a $66 billion deficit with Japan in 1994, the tally sheet was $1.3 billion in our favor with Mexico (*New York Times* 1995: World Bank 1994: 4). Nor are there invisible domestic sales arrangements hindering access to the Mexican consumer. Fully 69 percent of Mexico's imports came from the United States in 1994 (U.S. Department of State 1995a: 4).

The potential for market expansion is suggested by the growth that occurred during the first year after NAFTA went into effect. In 1994, U.S. exports to Mexico increased by $18.8 billion, a 23 percent increase over the previous year (U.S. Department of State 1995a: 4). Depending on the nature of the jobs created (manufacturing or service sector), every billion dollars of additional imports generates from 16,500 to 23,300 new jobs. This equates to some 310,000 to 438,000 jobs for U.S. workers as a result of the growth in exports to Mexico (Davis 1995: 20). The enormous pent-up demand for consumer goods in Mexico has scarcely been satiated. With almost 90 million consumers, most of whom would prefer to buy U.S. products, the principal factor influencing expansion of our market there will be the rate of growth in their consumer spending. U.S. geo-economic interests are thus closely linked with vibrant and sustained growth in the Mexican economy, a positive-sum relationship that is a hallmark of trade that is both free and fair.

Mexico is a vital trading partner for reasons other than its consumers. Indeed, ten to fifteen years ago, most Americans associated Mexico with its hydrocarbon potential, not its market potential. In recent years, plentiful global supplies of oil have seemingly reduced the significance of this strategic commodity; however, the United States has inexorably increased its reliance on foreign sources to satisfy its energy needs.

Prior to the Arab oil embargo of 1973, the United States imported 35 percent of its crude oil (Stabler and Tanner 1977). Today that figure has risen to 52 percent.[10] The volatile Persian Gulf region still accounts for 22 percent of our imports. Offsetting this, since 1990 Mexico has increased the proportion of crude oil it exports to the United States from 50 percent to over 70 percent. Currently it accounts for 11 percent of our imports (British Petroleum 1994: 16; U.S. Department

[10] In 1993, the United States consumed 16.41 million barrels of oil per day. Of this quantity, 8.527 million barrels were imported (British Petroleum 1994: 8, 16).

of State 1995a: 94–95). With proven deposits of 50.9 billion barrels, it possesses the seventh largest pool of crude oil in the world and the second greatest reserves outside the Persian Gulf region (British Petroleum 1994: 2).

The geo-strategic significance of secure oil supplies is evident to anyone who experienced the "oil shocks" of 1973 and 1979. As the Department of Energy blandly notes in its *International Energy Outlook* for 1994:

> Historically, supply disruptions have been associated with more negative impacts than just an increase in petroleum prices. Typically, major supply disruptions have also been associated with increases in consumer prices, increased unemployment, and a decline in gross domestic product (U.S. Department of Energy 1994: 23).

Thus Mexico is a vital geo-economic partner for the United States, shielding us from future disruptions in oil supplies from the Middle East. Indeed, during the Gulf War, Mexico was the first country to respond to U.S. appeals for increased production to offset the reduction in supply caused by that conflict.

The Geo-economic Significance for Multilateral Trade

In the aftermath of its brush with bankruptcy in 1982, Mexico abandoned its exhausted, protectionist economic policies in favor of a free market, export-oriented model. In so doing, it was in the vanguard of Latin American countries making this move; its promising results helped to precipitate a conversion that has swept the globe. Unfortunately, in following our example, Mexico not only did as we say, they also did as we do; they spent too much, saved too little, and borrowed to cover the deficit.[11] Pressure on the peso mounted, culminating in a very hard landing in early 1995. This event was not just an isolated affair between Mexico and its creditors; indeed, the international financial system nearly went into panic.

The ripple effect of the peso crisis was global in scope. International financiers were inclined to bolt like sheep out of all emerging economies. This affected not only Latin America but Central Europe and the entire Third World as well. Had the United States not acted resolutely to arrest the hemorrhage of capital out of Mexico and the developing world more generally, leaders in many of these countries might have been compelled to question the wisdom of continuing to

---

[11] Concerns about the country's stability and rising U.S. interest rates also contributed to pressure on the peso in 1994.

embrace our economic model. Global economic activity could easily have suffered a major blow. Following close behind would have been our own prosperity, prestige as a world leader, and prospects for enlarging the realm of capitalist economic systems.

The relative success or failure of Mexico's integration into NAFTA could have a major bearing on the pace and even the extent to which the remainder of the Americas proceed down the free trade path. There is little enthusiasm today in the U.S. body politic for additional trade accords, and those who opposed NAFTA find justification for their stance in Mexico's current economic difficulties. The countries of Central and South America, along with the Caribbean, are actively pursuing their own subregional trade regimes (for example, the Central American Integration System, SICA; the Southern Cone Common Market, Mercosur; and the Caribbean Common Market, Caricom). The December 1994 Summit of the Americas established 2005 as the date for creation of a free trade area embracing the entire hemisphere. Whether the various subregional groupings ultimately amalgamate into a vigorous free trade community for the Americas, however, could be affected considerably by the extent to which Mexico prospers—or falters—under NAFTA.

If our own geographic region fails to integrate economically while Europe and Asia proceed to do so, the United States would be at a clear geo-economic disadvantage. As a hedge against a "worst case" division of the globe into regional trading blocs, the United States can scarcely afford to neglect its neighbors. On the other hand, the United States would be deprived of a geo-economic advantage if its own traditional market in the Western Hemisphere was to be excluded from a global pattern of economic liberalization. Historically we have had a major share of the market in the Americas and, assuming free trade, would continue to benefit from proximity and lower transportation costs. Finally, like Mexico, most of Latin America has accepted the neoliberal economic paradigm. It is central to the strategy of enlargement that these efforts flourish; a dynamic regional free trade regime bridging North and South America would provide a major stimulus in that direction. For geographic, cultural, and chronological reasons, Mexico is, or certainly ought to become, that bridge.

Mexico: Geo-social Barrier or Conduit?

While economic prosperity may be a national priority at the moment, great civilizations have as often collapsed from within as succumbed to the depredations of an external foe. In the future, our greatest vulnerability may be our social order; the most acute external dangers may arise not from any nation-state but rather from a host of transnational threats to our social institutions and domestic well-being. Among the more likely pathogens are international criminal enterprises, terrorist organizations, environmental pollutants, and mass migrations of desperate refugees fleeing civil unrest or the collapse of the state.

Since these non-state entities have no regard for international boundaries, the only way to cope with them effectively is with the cooperation of other states. To combat this "coming anarchy," the most vital allies are one's neighbors. Given our acute concerns about illegal immigrants and illicit drugs, there is no more crucial ally in this developing geo-social struggle than Mexico. As the social tapestry of the United States and Mexico becomes more extensively interwoven, any fraying around the edges of one sociopolitical order will inevitably cause an unraveling in the other. NAFTA is but one of the dynamics contributing to our growing interdependence. The presence of 13.5 million citizens of Mexican American origin is another powerful sinew binding our two nations together.

In geo-social terms, the United States is buffered somewhat from various transnational threats because it is bounded by oceans on two sides. On one of the land borders, moreover, the social order is stable and state institutions are responsive. The essence of our grand strategy, therefore, must be to ensure that Mexico also develops as a full collaborator against, rather than becoming a conduit for, the flow of invidious transnational agents across our southern border.

One of the more crucial considerations for the near term will be the capacity of Mexico's political institutions to respond to these invasive threats. At present their political system is in the midst of a profound transition. Like two tectonic plates, the ossified and autocratic regime dominated by the Institutional Revolutionary Party (PRI) is buckling against the democratic aspirations of the Mexican people. From illiterate Indians of Chiapas to affluent housewives in Mexico City, subterranean pressures are building within the Mexican polity. The PRI-controlled ancien régime is crumbling; we just don't know how far up the political Richter scale future tremors will register. While sufficient political space remains for Mexico to construct a peaceful, democratic outcome, grand strategy cannot be predicated on mere wishful thinking. The United States does not have a permanent and inalienable right to stable and cordial neighbors. Rather, this is a circumstance our national strategy should strive, perhaps above all else, to preserve.

The geo-social consequences of an incapacitated state or extensive civil strife in Mexico would be strategically devastating for the United States. Just two of the more unsettling outcomes would likely be: (1) a flood of *illegal immigrants* streaming northward, and (2) a law enforcement void for the *drug underworld* to exploit.

Under normal circumstances today, neither the flow of illegal immigrants nor the shipment of illicit drugs has been effectively curtailed. Nor are they liable to be, at an acceptable price, unless Mexico is willing and able to render effective collaboration. Jessica Mathews describes just one of the inherent limitations:

> At one of the busiest Mexican border crossings, customs officers are told to spend no more than one minute examining each northbound tractor-trailer in order to prevent huge traffic jams. And while the volume of air freight is exploding, new rules make the government liable for damage caused to perishable goods—flowers, food, animals—by inspection delays. What more natural than to use these same shipments, especially to the busiest airports, to smuggle drugs and other contraband (Mathews 1995).

If political stability were to be seriously degraded in Mexico, the task of controlling our nearly 2,000–mile frontier would be immensely, perhaps impossibly, compounded.

The Geo-social Consequences of an Immigration Crisis

At present, the U.S. body politic is in a surly, xenophobic mood. The torch held aloft by the Statue of Liberty is obscured by a "Proposition 187" placard. We no longer invite ashore the huddled masses; rather, we wish to send them packing. The number of economic migrants leaving Mexico today, however, would be dwarfed by those abandoning the country in the midst of political turmoil.

The magnitude of any northward migration would, of course, be dependent upon circumstances. During the civil war in El Salvador, roughly 1 million refugees (about 20 percent of the citizenry) fled. The preferred destination was the United States. Given that Mexico has a population eighteen times that of El Salvador, and that some 10 to 15 million Mexicans live within a few miles of the U.S. border, it is plausible that a million or more Mexicans might seek safe haven in the United States under conditions of serious internal unrest.

Even if the resources were forthcoming and the political will existed to take draconian measures along the border, we still would not be able to insulate ourselves from serious disorder in Mexico. One virtually immutable constraint is our own Constitution.

The Constitutional Constraints—Once an illegal immigrant has set foot on U.S. soil, certain constitutional protections attain. Deportation, therefore, becomes a legal proceeding encumbered by numerous limitations:

> Deportation proceedings afford the alien a number of constitutional rights: a right against self-incrimination, protection against unreasonable searches and seizures, guarantees against ex post facto laws, bills of attainder, and cruel and unusual punishment, a right to bail, *a right to procedural due process, a right to counsel,* a right to notice of charges and hearing, as well as a right to cross-examine [emphasis added].[12]

As a result, deportation is not necessarily swift or certain. The infamous case of the *Golden Venture* is illustrative. This ship, laden with illegal Chinese immigrants, was detained in New York harbor before it could disgorge its human cargo in June 1993. Two years later, deportation proceedings for 175 of the 276 asylum seekers still had not been completed.[13] If fewer than 200 illegal immigrants can retard the deportation process for two years, the consequence of perhaps a million or more additional Mexican immigrants flooding our court system would be nothing short of gridlock.

To forestall deportation, all that is required is a request for a hearing. If the majority of illegal immigrants opt to do this, the federal government would be left with but two choices: to establish detention centers to house this mass of humanity while their lengthy legal proceedings unfold, or to admit them into the country on a provisional basis until their hearings can be held.

In the present context, when one of our most pressing domestic priorities is to balance the federal budget, coping with an immigration emergency would be fiscally ruinous. At a minimum of $40 per day for each detainee, housing a million asylum seekers would cost $14.6 billion a year. The 175 Chinese detainees from the *Golden Venture* cost the U.S. government $6 million over two years, not to mention the considerable legal expenses of contesting their appeals for asylum.[14] The political cost of the latter option would perhaps be unacceptable as well. It certainly would not serve as a deterrent to further waves of migrants. The only other possibility is immediate deportation, but this can be prevented if an asylum hearing is requested. Nor does deportation cause the problem to go away, since this would frequently be followed by a subsequent crossing attempt.

The Domestic Political Constraints—A second major consideration would be the 13.5 million Mexican Americans already living legally in

---

[12] Killian and Beck 1987: 310. I am grateful to Tom Walters of the U.S. Border Patrol for bringing these constitutional limitations to my attention.

[13] Thirty had been granted political asylum as of April 1995, forty-five had been released on bond or admitted to the United States for humanitarian reasons, and sixteen had exhausted their appeals and had been involuntarily deported (Dunn 1995).

[14] At that rate, housing and feeding a million detainees for a year would require $18 billion.

this country (U.S. Department of Commerce 1992: 3). Most retain strong emotional ties to the *"patria"* and would be vitally concerned about the plight of family members in Mexico. Many would no doubt mobilize to protest any "militarization" of the border. A significant number could also be expected to provide sanctuary for relatives seeking to evade immigration authorities. Confrontations could erupt between citizens sympathetic to the plight of Mexican "refugees" and those enraged by massive violations of national sovereignty. The situation could be especially inflammatory along the southwestern border. Federal, state, and local law enforcement authorities could easily be overtaxed merely by the secondary effects of such an immigration crisis. Activation of the National Guard and Reserves would seem almost inevitable, and, depending on the extent of border coverage desired, active duty troops could also be required. In this manner, political strife in Mexico would almost certainly have profound reverberations in the United States.

A diversion of federal funds, on the order of $15 billion simply to run detention centers, could be a budget buster. This figure exceeds the entire Foreign Operations budget for fiscal year 1995 ($13.7 billion), which funds U.S. foreign assistance (economic support fund, developmental and military assistance, and multilateral aid) and export promotion programs (Nowels 1995: 1–3). Even more potentially disruptive would be confrontations between volatile social groups on opposite sides of this issue. A stable Mexico, therefore, is essential both to our domestic deficit-reduction strategy and for social tranquility. At present, the two countries consult regularly and collaborate effectively on this issue. Recently, for example, Mexico agreed to "strengthen and expand a law enforcement effort directed at curtailing criminal trafficking in immigrants" (*International Enforcement Law Reporter* 1995). It is very much in our interest, therefore, that Mexico's institutions of law and order function effectively, and also that their domestic capacity to employ their people begins to keep pace with their burgeoning labor force.

The Geo-social Consequences of an Unchecked Drug Cancer

In the campaign to stanch the flow of illegal drugs into the United States, perhaps only Colombia is as important as Mexico. It is Mexico's misfortune to be situated between the globe's most lucrative market for narcotics and the source of the world's best-selling illicit drug: cocaine. For reasons of geography, therefore, Mexico has become a conduit for more than half the cocaine abused in the United States. Given its proximity, Mexico is also a major supplier of other narcotic substances that are produced domestically: 20 percent of the heroin seized in the United States and 60 to 80 percent of imported marijuana originate in Mexico. As stated in the annual *International Narcotics Control Strategy Report*, "It [Mexico] is therefore critical to U.S. drug control efforts" (U.S. Department of State 1995b: 140).

The highly corrosive effects of the drug trade upon Mexico's institutions of law and order have prompted the government to treat this scourge as a threat to the nation's security. To interdict the flow of cocaine across its territory, Mexico has established the Northern Border Response Force. This unit, equipped with helicopters and other air assets, was responsible for over 80 percent of the 22 tons of cocaine seized last year. In addition, Mexico's armed forces have typically assigned 25,000 troops (about a quarter of the army), to the eradication mission. In 1994, over 50 percent of the opium crop and 45 percent of marijuana cultivation were eradicated through such efforts, according to U.S. Department of State assessments (1995b: 147).

The capacity of the Mexican government to constrict its coca corridor suffered notably in 1994, owing largely to disruptions in Chiapas. Cocaine seizures were reduced by half from the previous year, and eradication of marijuana and opium fields was also down by almost 10 percent (U.S. Department of State 1995b: 147). This illustrates the vital stake the United States has in bolstering the performance of Mexico's institutions of law and order and how internal disturbances can have a debilitating effect on their capabilities.

Certainly we benefit from Mexico's exertions against the drug trade and the resulting reduction in the volume of drugs entering the United States. Even more vital in the long run, however, is the integrity of their governmental institutions in the face of this hydra-headed threat. That integrity can be dangerously eroded in many ways. Traffickers may suborn key members of the police, armed forces, and judiciary; drug barons may establish virtual fiefdoms in strategic areas of the country; the tenacity of subversive movements can be exacerbated by a nexus with drug smugglers; democratic processes may be contaminated by the nouveaux riches of the drug industry; and the reins of government could even fall into the grip of the drug underworld. Loss of control over the apparatus of the state is obviously the most extreme concern.

This has already happened on several occasions to Mexico's neighbors. Most notable are the 1980 drug coup perpetrated by General Luis García Meza in Bolivia and Panama's degeneration into a virtual franchise of the Medellín cartel in the late 1980s under General Manuel Noriega.[15] More recently, even Colombia's democratically elected president, Ernesto Samper, has been seriously tainted: his campaign treasurer has been arrested for allegedly accepting cam-

---

[15] I discuss these situations at some length in Dziedzic 1989b.

paign contributions totaling $6 million from the Cali drug cartel, and his former campaign manager, who had assumed the defense minister's post, also had to resign amidst the furor (*Washington Post* 1995).

The gravity of the threat to Mexico's political regime has been manifested in a series of shocking, high-profile assassinations that have suspicious indications of possible drug linkages. Perhaps the most ominous is the September 1994 assassination of Secretary General José Francisco Ruiz Massieu of the ruling PRI party. Allegations that both the Tamaulipas cartel and the brother of former president Carlos Salinas de Gortari were involved have been especially persistent. There are even indications President Salinas himself may have been a party to this plot. These are serious warning signs that control of the state itself is imperiled.

The United States has an acute interest in bolstering the Mexican state against the savagery of the drug underworld. Should Mexico become colonized by the barons of the drug business, it would likely serve as much more than a corridor for cocaine trafficking. The door would probably be thrown open to many other transnational criminal enterprises involved in illegal arms sales, auto theft and prostitution rings, money laundering, and smuggling of aliens from around the world. Perhaps most ominous, now that the magnitude of our national vulnerability has been so graphically demonstrated in Oklahoma City, would be the crippling effect this could have on our capacity to prevent atrocities by international terrorists. While Mexico might not be converted into a safe haven for terrorists, little effective intergovernmental cooperation could be expected. Administration of justice would probably break down totally, and an adversarial relationship would likely develop with the United States, as occurred during the Noriega period in Panama. NAFTA would likely be scrapped and replaced by a draconian border control regime. Mexico's process of democratization would become mere farce. Thus fundamental U.S. interests would be sacrificed, and our society would be exposed directly to the destructive toxins of terrorism, international mafiosi, and unchecked waves of migrants. It is evident that the United States has an enormous stake in ensuring that Mexico functions as an effective barrier against, rather than as a conduit for, such transnational menaces.

Mexico at the Crossroads: Crucible for U.S. Strategy

From a geopolitical perspective, our capacity to remain fully engaged on the global stage would suffer grievously if serious unrest were to erupt on our southern border. At a minimum, our present military strategy would be emasculated. Just as vital, however, are the positive contributions that a close geopolitical partnership between the United States and Mexico could make. Not only would the task of confronting our mutual security concerns along the border be immensely facilitated, but prospects for fashioning a cooperative security regime throughout the Western Hemisphere would be greatly advanced.

Our future geo-economic prospects also hinge on prosperity in Mexico. We have major bilateral interests in the growth of Mexico's purchasing power (which translates almost directly into markets for the United States) and in assured access to oil, as a buffer against Middle East instability. Multilaterally, a flourishing economy in Mexico will serve as a solid bridge for incorporating the balance of Latin America into a free, fair, and open trading community.

In the long run, Mexico's geo-social relevance may be the most consequential, as we strive together to overcome the destructive potential of such transnational forces as international crime, mass migration, disease, and ecological collapse.

During the cold war, our grand strategy was galvanized around containment of Soviet expansionism. Mexico's remarkably stable political order afforded the United States a decisive advantage over the encirclement confronting the Soviet Union. Today the essence of our national strategy is to enlarge the realm in which free peoples and free markets flourish. Once again, Mexico will be a linchpin for the realization of these strategic aims. It is presently in the midst of a perilous and unsettling transition from corporatism and protectionism to more open political and economic processes. We would be foolhardy to take the outcome for granted simply because of Mexico's exceptional record of stability during most of this century. As one of Mexico's leading political thinkers, Jorge Castañeda (1995: 76), has observed, "The United States should count its blessings: it has dodged instability on its borders since the Mexican Revolution, now nearly a century ago. The warnings from Mexico are loud and clear; this time it might be a good idea to heed them."

It would be a rather pyrrhic victory for the United States if our strategy of enlargement were to succeed elsewhere while engendering a chronic governability crisis on our own border. Perhaps only Russia and China are as strategically vital to us; however, neither holds as much promise for genuine political and economic pluralism in the near future. Thus Mexico holds not only enormous strategic risk if neglected but also surpassing potential if its fragile process of political and economic liberalization bears fruit. This surely will be one of the defining tests of U.S. leadership and strategy of the post–cold war era.

References

Aldinger, Charles. 1995. "Americas' Defense Officials Powwow," *Washington Times*, July 24.

British Petroleum. 1994. *BP Statistical Review of World Energy: June 1994*. London.

Carlucci, Frank C. 1989. *Report of the Secretary of Defense Frank C. Carlucci to the Congress on the FY1990/FY1991 Biennial Budget and FY 1990–94 Defense Programs*. Washington, D.C.: U.S. Government Printing Office.

Castañeda, Jorge G. 1995. "Ferocious Differences," *Atlantic Monthly* 276 (1): 68–76.

Davis, Lester A. 1995. *U.S. Jobs Supported by Goods and Service Exports: Including Special Focus on Exports by High Technology Industries*. Washington, D.C.: U.S. Department of Commerce.

Dunn, Ashley. 1995. "Golden Venture Passengers Are Opting for China over U.S. Jails," *New York Times*, April 28.

Dziedzic, Michael J. 1989a. *Mexico: Converging Challenges*. London: International Institute for Strategic Studies.

———. 1989b. "The Transnational Drug Trade and Regional Security," *Survival*, November/December, pp. 533–48.

Gaviria, Caesar. 1995. "A New Vision of the OAS: Working Paper of the General Secretariat." Washington, D.C.: Organization of American States, April.

Glassner, Martin Ira, and Harm J. de Blij. 1990. "The Geopolitical View." In *Theories of International Relations*, edited by James A. Hursch. Washington, D.C.: National Defense University Press.

Gore, Al. 1995. "Keynote Address." *Defense Ministerial of the Americas*. Washington, D.C.: U.S. Department of Defense.

Ikle, Fred, et al. 1988. *Discriminate Deterrence: Report of the Commission on Integrated Long-Term Strategy*. Washington, D.C.: U.S. Government Printing Office.

International Enforcement Law Reporter. 1995. Vol. 11, no. 3 (March): item VII-A.

Kaplan, Robert. 1994. "The Coming Anarchy," *Atlantic Monthly* 273 (2): 44–76.

Katz, Friedrich. 1981. *The Secret War in Mexico: Europe, the United States, and the Mexican Revolution*. Chicago: University of Chicago Press.

Killian, Johnny H., and Leland E. Beck, eds. 1987. *The Constitution of the United States of America: Analysis and Interpretation*. Washington, D.C.: U.S. Government Printing Office.

Kissinger, Henry. 1995a. "For U.S. Leadership, a Moment Missed," *Washington Post*, May 12.

———. 1995b. "Heading for a Collision in Asia," *Washington Post*, July 26.

Mathews, Jessica. 1995. "We Live in a Dangerous Neighborhood," *Washington Post*, April 24.

Matloff, Maurice. 1969. *American Military History*. Washington, D.C.: U.S. Government Printing Office.

New York Times. 1995. "Dollar Falls against Yen, but Gains Slightly in Mark," May 2.

Nowels, Larry. 1995. *Appropriations for FY1996: Foreign Operations*. Washington, D.C.: Congressional Research Service.

Reagan, Ronald. 1986. Remarks by the President at a White House meeting, March 3. *Public Papers of the Presidents of the United States*. Washington, D.C.: National Archives, Public Papers 300.

Stabler, Charles, and James Tanner. 1977. "There's Plenty of Oil on Hand Right Now, but Outlook Is Bleak," *Wall Street Journal*, October 31.

Tuchman, Barbara W. 1957. *The Zimmermann Telegram*. London: Lowe and Brydone.

U.S. Department of Commerce. 1992. *1990 Census of Population: General Population Characteristics*. Washington, D.C.

U.S. Department of Energy. 1994. *International Energy Outlook: 1994*. Washington, D.C.

U.S. Department of State. 1995a. *Mexico: Economic and Financial Report–Spring 1995*. Washington, D.C.

———. 1995b. *International Narcotics Control Strategy Report: March 1995*. Washington, D.C.: Bureau of International Narcotics Matters, U.S. Department of State.

U.S. Embassy–Mexico. 1995. *Mexico: Economic and Financial Report: Spring 1995*.

Washington Post. 1995. "Campaign Official Tied to Drug Money," July 27.

Weigley, Russell F. 1967. *History of the United States Army*. London: Batsford.

White House Office. 1995. *A National Security Strategy of Engagement and Enlargement*. Washington, D.C.: The White House.

World Bank. 1994. *The World Bank Atlas 1994*. Washington, D.C.: The International Bank for Reconstruction and Development.

5

Mexico's National Security Policies and Institutions in the Post–Cold War Era

Manuel Villa Aguilera

The Nature of a Mexican Security Doctrine

In recent decades Mexico's national security agenda has been subordinated to other more pressing concerns. In the domestic sphere, national security has been overshadowed by electoral reform and the expansion of political participation, especially since the 1960s. In foreign affairs it has been subordinated to a much larger and wide-ranging set of doctrines arising from the cold war ideological context. Mexico's actions in defense of national security have thus tended to be limited either to conflicts that were too extreme to be ignored, or to low-intensity conflicts that were quelled with relative ease.[1]

Throughout the cold war, Mexico maintained a low profile in everything that related to national security actions or mechanisms. It

---

[1] Latin America's experience during the cold war can be divided into three separate periods: (1) the immediate postwar period, lasting from 1946 to 1958 and characterized by repression of leftist parties and popular fronts that had gained strength during World War II, (2) the period of open anticommunism, begun with the abortive Guatemalan revolution of 1954 and consolidated with the successful Cuban revolution of 1959, and (3) the militarization of the conflict during the 1970s and 1980s.

This periodization is useful in helping to explain both the Mexican government's policy toward the United States during these years and its concern to maintain its international autonomy, democratic convictions, and linkages with social groups. A vast scholarly literature exists for this period, expressing a variety of viewpoints and arguments. My own views on the subject can be found in Villa 1986. See also Parkinson 1974. A different perspective can be found in Aguayo 1990.

took this stance in foreign policy for political-strategic reasons, and in the internal sphere it pursued domestic security as a means to achieve the larger goal of national stability.

The end of the cold war and the exhaustion of the state-centered model of development had various domestic and international consequences. These included the creation of new commercial blocs, economic liberalization, social mobilization, political reform, and heightened electoral competition. This confluence of developments has brought about a new state of affairs that calls for a reexamination of the concept of Mexican national security as well as its specific policy implications and operational mechanisms.

I disagree with the contention of the editors of this volume[2] that Mexico has avoided public discussion of national security issues largely because it fears that the articulation of a national security doctrine might cause Mexico's national interests to be identified with those of the United States. This contention is far more significant than the casual reader might at first realize, as much for what it says as for what it leaves unsaid. Although it serves as a useful initial approach to the question, it is even more useful as a point of departure for illuminating what yet remains hidden.

I doubt very much that the editors have identified the real reason why Mexico has failed to formulate an explicit national security doctrine. That failure has resulted instead from other causes related to what I regard as the main problem in Mexican–U.S. relations: difficulty in establishing communication based upon a sensitive understanding by each country of the other's perspectives, interests, and modes of expression. I suggest, in other words, that the difficulty lies in finding areas of agreement while accepting disagreement on other questions as genuine, healthy, legitimate, and deserving of toleration. These differences should be seen as expressions of distinct national traditions worthy of being preserved, cultivated, and strengthened.

Communication problems can lead Americans to conclude mistakenly that Mexico ought to adopt the national priorities of the United States. Clearly the reverse also happens, as Mexicans frequently express superficial opinions or judgments about the United States.

[2] I refer here to the text provided by Sally Shelton Colby, John Bailey, and Sergio Aguayo, which helped to frame the first discussion among the contributors to this volume, and specifically to the passage stating: "Mexico has avoided public discussion of its own national security, largely out of concern that articulation of a national security doctrine would lead to the United States' identifying its security interests with those of Mexico. Such a development would traditionally have been considered by Mexican elites to be too risky as it would have raised the specter of intervention, conflict, and too close a relationship with the United States."

Americans, however, are far more guilty of this particular fault than are Mexicans.

Some have suggested that Mexico in fact formulated a national security policy but kept it hidden in order to keep it from being identified with U.S. security policy and thereby undermining the legitimacy and importance of Mexico's own national traditions and interests. According to this view, since the United States considered it appropriate to have a clear and assertive national security policy, Mexico found it necessary to do the same, although it chose not to acknowledge the fact.

Another possible explanation, however, can be too easily and quickly dismissed. This argument holds that Mexico's distinctive political system, based on a unique national power structure, made it unnecessary for the country to possess its own national security doctrine. As a result, the preservation of national stability came to depend upon institutional means and principles other than the standard policies and strategies for promoting national security. I believe that this explanation comes closer to the truth.[3]

Mexico's National Project and Geography

As is well known, the doctrine and instruments of national security are products of the cold war, although their origins are traceable to the formation of the sovereign state. Sovereignty is a capacity for national self-preservation, expressed and realized through the state.

[3] The concept of national security includes three basic components. The first of these is *doctrine,* consisting of a principled national posture resting on fundamental national values. The second aspect of national security is *policy,* consisting of the set of specific purposes and actions that can be subordinated to an explicit doctrine of national security or to national principles of a different nature. Brazil's military dictatorship during the 1970s provides a good example of the combination of doctrine and policy. The various Central American dictatorships that modernized (that is, Americanized) their armed forces during the last two decades of the cold war provide cases of national security policy prevailing over doctrine.

Operational agencies constitute the third component of national security. In extreme circumstances these agencies can function without a corresponding security doctrine or policy. Such is the case, for instance, with security agencies that act pragmatically in the absence of clear and general principles, perversely substituting their own political rationales and actions for doctrine and policy. Haiti is an example of this extreme case of an authoritarian police regime. Mexico lies at the other extreme, exemplifying a government based upon national principles, internal policy guidelines, and a subordinated security apparatus devoted to solving specific national security problems.

In my view, national security analysis should distinguish carefully among these three components. The frequent failure to draw these distinctions leads to confusion and dangerous value judgments.

National security doctrine is simply the expression of the means by which the state defends and enhances its independence.

Throughout the cold war era the doctrine of national security gave justification, purpose, and legitimacy to the policy of national self-preservation internally, to resist popular socialist mobilization or communist infiltration, and externally, to defeat Soviet-bloc aggression or establish a regional balance of power. Brazil provided the most typical Latin American case of such a national security doctrine.

Mexico's political system throughout the cold war, unlike those of most other Latin American and Third World countries, faced no significant political challenge from the Left. Such political challenges as existed in Mexico were marginal, coming from relatively insignificant political parties rather than from the population at large, except in certain isolated areas. Moreover, Mexico's neighbors posed no threat that called for a rigorous national security doctrine.

For these reasons, I suggest that Mexico did not need a broad and hard-line national security doctrine. Its political system already enjoyed the advantages of a homegrown national project, institutionalized authority, and popular legitimacy. Countries lacking these advantages were precisely those that adopted the national security doctrine during the years when popular mobilization and socialism seemed to pose the clearest threat to national security. The absence of such internal challenges explains why Mexico viewed the formulation of a national security agenda and doctrine as an implicit capitulation to U.S. national interests and perspectives. By adopting such a doctrine, in other words, Mexico would have tacitly acknowledged that it faced an internal threat of popular mobilization when clearly no such threat existed.

The Mexican Revolution gave birth to a political system that has drawn support—at varying levels over time—from both the principle and practice of popular participation and social mobilization. This social involvement is precisely what most Latin American countries failed to generate during the cold war era. Moreover, the Mexican government has maintained a high—albeit unofficial—level of communication with most elements of the Left. The relative secrecy of this communication has resulted more from the need of leftist leaders to protect themselves from accusations of collaboration than from any desire by government or PRI officials to conceal it. Disaster has ensued whenever the government has neglected this communication, as happened in 1968 when violent repression of student demonstrators severely shook the political system.

The Mexican Left has derived its strength more from its impact on public opinion than from effective mobilization, except when it forged alliances with sectors close to the government. As a result, throughout the cold war years the Mexican Left was more a cause for concern in the United States than in Mexico itself. Moreover, Mexico has never had a strong Right disposed to act as the agent of U.S. interests. Although some residual groups from the revolutionary era aspired to this role, they had paled to insignificance by the early 1940s.

Brazil occupied the other extreme from Mexico as the prototypical country whose entire national project in the 1960s and 1970s rested on the doctrine of national security. Other South American countries that took this route during these same years were Argentina and Chile. In Mexico, however, the national project that emerged from the principles of the revolution reduced questions of national security to their operational dimensions. Electoral reform—a recurring theme in Mexico since 1963—subsequently shifted the government's dealings with the radical Left from open confrontation to electoral contestation.

As this summary indicates, cold war imperatives caused national security in Mexico to become subordinated to other concerns. Mexico's political system had sufficient absorptive capacity to manage the domestic challenges that arose during those years. An illustration might be helpful here. The start of the cold war unleashed a relentless persecution—almost a frontal war—throughout Latin America against labor unions and subsequently against communist parties. This U.S.–inspired crusade brought heavy pressure to bear against Peronism in Argentina, the "New State" of Getulio Vargas in Brazil, and the Popular Front in Chile. In Mexico, this cold war campaign led to proscription of the Communist Party but not to repression of the labor movement.

Far more than labor unions in other Latin American countries, the Mexican labor movement was under the ruling party's effective control. Unlike other weak labor organizations, however, Mexican labor's relative lack of independence allowed it at least to survive as a coherent political actor, even though it lost ground in economic terms. At the same time, it successfully stayed within the boundaries set for it by the framework of cold war politics.

This example illustrates a dual capacity of Mexico's political system that allowed it to limit significantly the operational scope of the instruments of national security. The system successfully assimilated pressures from both the United States and domestic society to find points of equilibrium that could guarantee the system's stability on both institutional and negotiated grounds.

Today the growing relationship between Mexico and the United States will encourage the inclusion of ever more subjects in the bilateral agenda, as well as the formulation of new initiatives for protecting the national interest. The connections between national security and foreign policy will become increasingly evident in both countries. Mexico will face the challenge of formulating its own active national security policy, in order to avoid having to acquiesce in U.S. actions that contradict its interests.

At present, a new line of risks has arisen that will find its place on the national security agenda. This agenda raises a new problem since it neither addresses internal security nor distinguishes it from defense against external threats. In other words, external developments have encouraged the formation of a new security agenda common to both Mexico and the United States. Although this shared agenda might confer some benefits, it is also highly dangerous since the perspectives and interests of both countries are bound to clash. Although a collaborative approach is clearly appropriate in certain areas such as economic security, its usefulness is less clear in the political realm. Although Mexico must find firm, aggressive, and imaginative ways to define its future national security priorities, full acceptance of the security agenda of its most important neighbor could become something like "sleeping with the enemy."

This observation leads us to ask once again why Mexico needs the doctrine, policy, and instruments of national security. Paradoxically, only after the cold war ended did Mexico begin to face stiff pressure to develop a national security policy and a broader, more complex, and more detailed security agenda. If we accept the above-referenced framework statement for this volume, we must conclude that throughout the cold war era Mexico has required a definite national security agenda, despite the consequent risk of coinciding with U.S. interests and allowing them to predominate over Mexico's own interests.

This observation not only helps to explain why Mexico has failed to develop a national security doctrine. It also highlights two basic differences between Mexico and the other Latin American countries. First, Mexico has possessed a distinctive national project and an institutional order with enough social support to minimize internal threats. Second, Mexico's geopolitical situation has not presented any significant external threats.

The Imperative of Clear Communication

In light of the above observations, one might wonder why Mexico now needs a security policy and apparatus that is more complex, active, and well defined than before. Have internal threats increased, or has the end of the cold war caused Mexico's interests to be subsumed by those of the United States, as some observers fear? Are others correct to think that Mexico must increase its vigilance against foreign intervention intended to promote political change, which has thus far lagged behind economic reform? These concerns have now joined the other specific components of Mexico's security agenda, such as border issues, drug trafficking, and trade.

The following proposition might help to elucidate the problem. National sovereignty—the basic concept that concerns us here—is a capability that can be exercised only by the state and the instruments of government. Viewed in this context, national security policy consists of the various instruments and measures of self-defense available to the state for exercising to the fullest extent the peculiar and exclusive capability known as national sovereignty.

Such instruments and measures for self-preservation are considerably less universal and interchangeable than is often supposed. Moreover, some nations—the United States, for instance—might have an interest in homogenizing these instruments, although nothing of the sort has yet occurred. A preliminary problem thus arises from the different codes used by each national security instrument to translate signs and symbols arising from specific situations. Another problem arises from different ways of perceiving these signs and symbols, which could prompt one to regard them as risks or threats.

Problems thus arise from the tendency of officials from each government to project very similar attitudes toward these defense measures, which are directed toward protecting clear and recognized points of vulnerability, especially with regard to migration at one extreme and drug trafficking at the other. Agreement among these officials is viewed with suspicion by certain sectors of public opinion in each country. These problems are well defined and specific, and they are being addressed by specialized governmental agencies. Despite their complexity and even dangerousness, these security problems are increasingly viewed from a perspective that tends to homogenize them, although disagreements occasionally emerge over how to deal with them.

The largest and most fundamental questions, however, are linked to problems that are much harder to define or enumerate on a list of specific risks. These problems have to do mainly with maintaining communication and interaction in extremely diversified and competitive contexts that span both the internal and external spheres. The process of enumerating specific risks has opened spaces for confluence that are so complex and diverse that they come to demand a national security policy in order to ensure that negotiation and interchange do not produce conflict but instead promote communication and agreement.

Increasing National and Bilateral Complexity

The far-reaching changes that Mexico underwent between 1989 and 1993, as well as those that occurred over a longer time as the Mexico–

United States relationship deepened, have generated new questions that now enjoy priority status.

In domestic affairs, the governmental and political reforms begun in 1988 are the consequence of three fundamental changes. The first involves the proliferation and diversification of social and political actors, which has forced the government and state to adjust to a new situation of pluralism that exerts pressure for stable democratization. Government officials have accommodated these pressures on the assumption that Mexico's political institutions are able to withstand political liberalization. The second fundamental change has to do with the multiplication of social demands and with society's increased ability to express those demands directly rather than through intermediaries such as political parties. In other words, the government will have to develop a new social policy that can respond rapidly to the demands arising from pluralism. Finally, the country faces the proliferation and dynamism of new economic actors, both domestic and foreign. In many cases the external and domestic actors will be associated with each other, further complicating the situation.

The state must therefore be ready to heed this diverse collection of political, economic, and even social processes that interconnect with their counterparts in the United States. In other words, the Mexican government's public policies often include elements relating directly to the United States.

The bilateral relationship is becoming more and more an everyday matter. It does not consist, for the most part, of issues that are susceptible to negotiation solely by representatives of specific government agencies, without citizen input. It consists, rather, of problems that flow and unfold day by day, putting both the agencies and their representatives constantly at risk of being overtaken by events. Aspects of daily life, including local culture, thus frequently obstruct decision making and action.

In effect, the boundary between the domestic and external spheres shifts constantly, producing an area of overlap that steadily gains greater permanence and continuity. In my opinion this zone will be an ongoing source of problems, demands, and signals that together will produce situations that both governments should interpret in such a way as to avoid falling into misconceptions. This situation underscores the dangers of miscommunication and a lack of clarity in symbols and signals.

The real problem facing a national security strategy could thus be that it generates a series of circumstances that either hinder the management of situations and the provision of adequate attention to issues or simply impede the clear and precise definition of each government's interests and positions regarding specific problems it must confront. It is therefore necessary to eliminate misleading signals which can produce disorientation, tension, or conflict. Bad communication and mistaken perceptions—both of problems and interests—can undermine the ability of governments to respond and act decisively, which is today a very serious problem.

If such confusion exists and generates controversy, paralysis, or increased tension, it will become harder to resolve conflicts among citizens or interests, as well as conflicts between either of these and the government. Likewise, it will be harder to resolve disputes between the governments of Mexico and the United States. It thus seems to me that the specific items on the security agenda are overshadowed by the basic need for clear communication based on permanent and accurate translation, so as to guarantee in every case that symbols, signals, and information are free of confusing elements that might hinder common action.

These considerations are not meant to imply that the public agency responsible for national security should deal directly with all problems. On the contrary, its intelligence functions will focus on the ability to foresee and facilitate communication so that the relevant personnel, national agencies, and corresponding officials might always have access to free-flowing communications. Such an atmosphere of open communication will help at the very least to reduce tension as much as possible while allowing the specific agencies or forces—both social and economic—to act in an environment free of obstacles to efficient and realistic action.

The most important problem between Mexico and the United States is the existence of shared and converging interests, with influences and effects that are undesirable but cannot be avoided. Despite these similarities, the national projects of these countries remain starkly dissimilar. Consequently, there is both much that brings these countries together and much that separates them. The intensity of the interchange and fluid communication between them has strategic implications.

The New Security Agenda

The downfall of communism in Central and Eastern Europe has not merely required the West to modify its security arrangements. It has also forced a reexamination of the very concept of security. The need to reformulate this concept has occasioned a new debate in which some have continued to address the subject in the traditional terms of political and strategic interests, while others have used a broader definition encompassing problems related to ecology, population, and the economy.[4]

The global security environment of the 1990s is undoubtedly more complicated than in the past. During the 1980s, numerous countries acquired an impressive arsenal of long-range weapons with high capacity for precision and destructive power. In coming years various internal conflicts arising from historical or contemporary animosities will generate instability, including the possibility of nuclear-armed civil war. The situation in Central and Eastern Europe remains uncertain. The Western powers, moreover, have become concerned about the Third World, which now appears to be the main source of latent security threats arising from such phenomena as nationalism and religious fundamentalism.

For the United States as for all industrialized countries, the need to redefine national security strategy tends to foster considerable uncertainty in a world tending ever more toward multipolarity than unipolarity. The U.S. government is particularly concerned to establish a new equilibrium among conflicting objectives. The debate over security strategy has raised options ranging from isolationism and unilateralism, on the one hand, to engagement and leadership, on the other.

Various researchers have tried to redefine the concept of security in broader terms to include global economy, population, and environmental issues. They believe that despite the end of the cold war, Western societies continue to perceive external threats to their ways of life and thus to their security. These new threats are not military, and they cannot be pinpointed. They seem to arise from fear and uncertainty generated by such things as unemployment, rampant social change, pollution, and new diseases such as AIDS. The concept of security thus crosses national boundaries to comprehend economic, environmental, and social issues. Viewed from this perspective, security and defense are no longer synonymous, since security refers to political ends while defense refers to military means. In other words, the new security agenda addresses social as well as state interests.

A Redefinition of Latin American Security

The basic assumptions underlying the concept of security as applied to the inter-American system have changed in important ways. As an area traditionally subject to U.S. hegemony, Latin America became entangled in the cold war from the very start. That involvement dic-

[4] Key contributions to this debate include Bagley and Tokatlian 1991; Deutch 1992; Eberle 1991; Eberstadt 1991; Gosnell 1991; Insulza 1991; Pfaltzgraff 1991; Smith 1991.

tated the region's post–World War II alliances and restricted its autonomy. The inter-American military system helped to weaken civil institutions in the Latin American countries by subjecting their military policies to U.S. national security doctrine.

The premise of anticommunism that undergirded the inter-American military system has now lost its relevance. Although the United States might conceivably abandon its unilateral stance toward the region in coming years, it will still tend to impose its own tactics in order to achieve its objectives.

The United States currently views the problem of drug abuse as a top national priority. This concern seems justified, given the harmful impact of drug abuse on public health and economic productivity, as well as the enormous financial costs of fighting the drug trade. Since a large share of the drugs entering the United States comes from Latin America, the U.S. government has come to view drug trafficking as a national security issue. Consequently it has pressured the governments of drug-producing Latin American countries to suppress drug cultivation, processing, and trafficking. Those efforts have been highly ineffective in fighting the drug trade, exposing instead the U.S. government's misunderstanding of the true nature of the drug problem in Latin America.

Initially, governments in Latin America did not respond to these pressures since they correctly regarded the drug trade as a problem pertaining to the United States. As drug traffickers became organized, however, they acquired so much power and influence that they began to pose a clear threat to several of these same governments. Concurrently, the economic and technical "help" provided by the United States for the war against drugs increased in step with its pressures on Latin American governments.

The drug-trafficking problem is linked to that of poverty. Millions of poor and desperate people throughout Latin America are searching for ways to improve their living conditions. Various movements, among them liberation theology, are arising with growing strength, inspiring popular rebellions against the oppressive socioeconomic status quo. Poverty and social instability offer fertile soil for the growth of drug trafficking, since criminal drug enterprises exploit the poverty of the rural population. The United States therefore has an interest in working hard to overcome the poverty and ignorance that predominate throughout Latin America.

Conclusion: Accepting Mexico's Distinctiveness

In light of the above discussion, Mexico faces the huge challenge of determining how to continue to promote national modernization without causing the United States to feel threatened, either because it reads the signs poorly or simply due to a natural reluctance to accept the consequences of change in Mexico. The latter concern might be provoked, for instance, by any of the following: a change in the Mexican government's relationship with the labor movement, a reform of the party system itself or of its relationship with civil society, or a root-and-branch reform of government institutions (especially those having to do with public security and the administration of justice). These political changes are urgently needed, since political reform in Mexico has tended to lag behind changes in the economy and civil society.

The first step in developing productive relations with Mexico consists of understanding its heterogeneity and diversity—and in not confusing the meaning of, or understanding superficially, the first level of signs. For example, the United States must explain honestly and rigorously exactly what threat it faces from Mexico's notably autonomous political system, which the United States prefers to characterize as "authoritarian." In other words, to what extent is the United States willing to recognize the legitimacy of Mexico's distinctive institutional model, which is self-supporting, pursues its own objectives, and seeks to strengthen democracy within the context of the country's own historical logic and dynamics? Will it, on the other hand, insist that Mexico dismantle its institutions and adopt a model that reflects U.S. values?

This propensity of the United States to impose its own values and institutional models on Mexico should be understood in light of an unavoidable fact: the convergence of U.S. and Mexican interests at the grassroots level, which tends to hinder both democratization and modernization in Mexico. This association of interests finds expression in efforts by the United States to promote democratization as it defines the concept. Such efforts typically raise issues that hold relevance for a national security agency carrying out genuine and important political intelligence work.

Such a national security agency should take care to design and manage its signals correctly and transmit them clearly, so that the security agencies of both countries might avoid prejudgments and misunderstandings when they come into contact. Such clearness of signals can also clarify each country's perception of the problem and its assessment of possible solutions.

The negotiations over the North American Free Trade Agreement have taught a basic lesson regarding Mexican–U.S. relations—negotiation is possible only in the absence of mixed signals. Mexico and the United States have common interests in favor of certain projects and in opposition to others. It is inappropriate to carry support for or opposition to a project to the point of affiliating with one of the contending parties or of being played off by one party against the other.

References

Aguayo, Sergio. 1990. *Perspectivas de la seguridad nacional mexicana: cuadernos del diplomado*. México, D.F.: Centro de Investigaciones en Seguridad Nacional.

Bagley, Bruce, and Juan Gabriel Tokatlian. 1991. "Droga y dogma: la diplomacia de la droga en Estados Unidos y América Latina en la década de los ochenta," *Pensamiento Iberoamericano* 19 (January–June): 235–55.

Deutch, John M. 1992. "The New Nuclear Threat," *Foreign Affairs* 71 (4): 145–58.

Eberle, James. 1991. "Security: New Ideas, Old Ambiguities," *World Today* 47 (2): 30–32.

Eberstadt, Nicholas. 1991. "Population Change and National Security," *Foreign Affairs* 70 (3): 115–31.

Gosnell, Wayne P. 1991. "A Time to Build: U.S. Policy for Latin America and the Caribbean," *Military Review* 71 (6): 42–50.

Insulza, José Miguel. 1991. "Estados Unidos y América Latina en los noventa," *Pensamiento Iberoamericano* 19 (January–June): 217–33.

Parkinson, F. 1974. *Latin America, the Cold War and the World Powers, 1945–1973: A Study in Diplomatic History*. Beverly Hills, Calif.: Sage.

Pfaltzgraff, Robert L., Jr. 1991. "The Emerging Global Security Environment," *Annals of the American Academy of Political and Social Sciences* 517: 10–24.

Smith, W.Y. 1992. "U.S. Security after the Cold War," *Washington Quarterly* 15 (4): 23–38.

Villa, Manuel. 1986. "La crisis del intervencionismo estatal en América Latina: Argentina, Brasil, Perú, y México, 1960–1975." Doctoral thesis, El Colegio de México.

6

Challenges of Unfinished Modernization: Stability, Democracy, and National Security in Mexico

Guadalupe González González

The Incongruities of Mexican Modernity

Mexico is passing through a period of profound change that began before the end of the cold war was even foreseen, much less accomplished. The origins of the current stage of transition go back to the 1970s, when the protectionist economic development model that made possible the "Mexican miracle" of the 1950s and 1960s entered into crisis and when the legitimacy of the authoritarian, corporatist, and presidentialist postrevolutionary political regime began to erode. Even though evidence of the regime's growing political instability preceded the symptoms of economic stagnation, the government appears to have given much higher priority to the latter problem. From the 1970s onward it has followed a strategy of slow and gradual political liberalization; yet ever since the 1982 financial crisis that followed Mexico's brief oil boom, the government has pursued rapid and thoroughgoing economic reforms intended to dismantle the old development model.

Between 1989 and 1994 Mexico underwent deep-going changes that marked the "end of a historical epoch" ushered in by the Mexican Revolution in the early years of the twentieth century (see Garza Elizondo 1994) and the dawn of a new era that began with the end of the cold war but has yet to be defined. Three domestic developments during the 1990s support the view that Mexico's contemporary history has entered a new epoch. The first of these is the exhaustion of the corporatist political system of the hegemonic party, undermined by the growing electoral strength of opposition parties, the eroding cohesion among the ruling elite, and growing differences among political actors regarding the pace, type, and extent of political reform. The second is the adoption of a new development model based on openness to foreign trade and investment, economic deregulation, and privatization through constitutional reforms and new international agreements. The third development relates to Mexicans' growing awareness that the dichotomous "Salinastroika" model of rapid economic reform and slow political modernization can produce modernization in Mexico only at the expense of the country's political stability and social peace.[1] Aguilar Camín observes that Mexico's political system has begun to break down because both the economic modernization paradigm promoted by top government officials and the political modernization proposals advanced by civil society "depict a modernity meticulously opposed to the institutional framework that Mexico constructed during the postrevolutionary epoch that began in the 1920s" (1992a: 39).

Just as Mexico's postrevolutionary epoch is coming to an end, the international system is undergoing epochal change as a result of economic globalization, the end of the cold war, the emergence of new regional associations, and growing internationalization of domestic political processes. The deep and turbulent transformation of the international system forces us to rethink the national security problems faced by countries of the so-called Third World (see Azar and Moon 1988a)—that is, countries that lack power resources and occupy a subordinate place in the international order.[2]

The academic literature on national security, which focuses on the analysis of problems facing the great powers, has underestimated the importance of domestic factors in shaping threats, power resources, and strategies for state survival (Azar and Moon 1988b: 12). Analysts have not paid adequate attention to the impact of such factors as domestic political structure and governmental fragility, economic un-

[1] In an interview in 1991, President Carlos Salinas offered the basic justification for his national modernization program, subsequently popularized by the national and international press as "Salinastroika." The president indicated that Mexico should reject the "Gorbachev route" of simultaneous economic and political reform, and instead accelerate economic reform while postponing political reform. This strategy was intended to guarantee change without endangering stability. "When you are introducing such a strong economic reform," Salinas stated, "you must make sure that you build the political consensus around it. If you are at the same time introducing additional drastic political reform, you may end up with no reform at all. And we want to have reform, not a disintegrated country" (Salinas de Gortari 1991: 8).

[2] Escudé (1993) argues that in peripheral states with weak political structures and relatively little international power, the logic of the construction of the national interest tends to be subordinated to functions of internal legitimation of undemocratic regimes.

derdevelopment, and deep-seated ethnic, political, and social tensions upon the national security policies of peripheral countries.

This chapter will examine various aspects of Mexico's national reality, having as its main explanatory axis the linkages between certain internal problems and national security at the levels of theory, discourse, and political practice. It will analyze some of the most important changes that have occurred in Mexico's political life and their possible implications for national security. Many of these changes are symbolic and related to political culture; others have to do with the country's economic and social realities. Most, however, result from the unstable equilibrium between state and society.

The review presented below of the multifaceted changes currently under way in Mexico leads us to suggest that the most important challenges facing the country at the dawn of the twenty-first century are political and social in nature. Mexico in the 1990s is fragmented by marked regional, cultural, ethnic, and economic estrangements.[3] The country faces dire problems of social and political integration that could become threats to internal stability and peace.

The chapter makes three main arguments. The first holds that Mexico is potentially more unstable now than at any other time since the consolidation and institutionalization of the Mexican Revolution during the 1940s. What does this mean in terms of national security? A superficial examination might lead one to conclude that domestic instability in itself threatens national security. We might learn more, however, by evaluating the potential for instability in terms of the nature of the tensions that produce it, as well as its possible extent with reference to the basic components of security: territorial integrity, social peace, self-government, and rule of law. The problem is not so much a higher level of political instability and uncertainty as it is the exhaustion of undemocratic models for stability and the emergence of violent forms of social and political change.

The second argument maintains that the principal challenge in safeguarding Mexico's national security and stability is the need to accelerate and complete the transition from the current semi-authoritarian political system to a fully democratic one.[4] The strategic goal is to transform the very foundations of domestic stability and domestic peace—that is, to replace the fragile equilibrium of

---

[3] See Soledad Loaeza's "Comentario" in Pérez Gay 1992.

[4] The characterization of Mexico's postrevolutionary political system as authoritarian is based on the model developed by Juan Linz. The general features of authoritarianism include a high level of concentration and centralization of political power (presidentialism); the prevalence of clientelistic means of policy formulation (corporatism); limited political pluralism (dominant-party system); low level of social mobilization (weak civil society); weak rule of law (lack of correspondence between the formal structure and actual operation of the institutional political structure); and, finally, the existence of a broad consensus within the governing elite. See Linz 1964.

"authoritarian stability" with a temporary "democratic instability." The outbreak of armed violence in Chiapas during the run-up to Mexico's 1994 presidential election placed in stark relief the limits of the current regime's ability to contain and channel the growing demands of a fragmented and pluralistic society through the traditional means of bossism, corporatism, electoral fraud, and concentration of political power in the president. Chiapas was another in a growing series of conflicts and social movements that confirmed the pressing need for Mexico's political modernization.

The third argument suggests that the construction of a democratic and modern state that can guarantee domestic stability and peace involves more than establishing a transparent electoral environment and a competitive party system. It also requires the completion of political reform in two areas that are endemic sources of instability, institutional corruption, and political violence: the inoperability of the system of administration of justice, on the one hand, and the systemic weakness of federalism, on the other. The acute problems and weaknesses that currently beset Mexico's justice system not only undermine individual rights (legal freedom and security) but also cast doubt on the vigor of the rule of law, public security, and thus social peace.[5] Regarding federalism, the centralized control of political decision making and public resources has created problems for lower levels of government and fostered increased political tensions between the center and the regions. As Aguilar Camín (1992b: 578) indicates, regional identification has become a source of mobilization and radical political behavior which can be controlled only by developing the capabilities of local and regional levels of government.

The Domestic Dimension in National Security

In approaching a basic definition of "security,"[6] our point of departure is Azar and Moon's contention that the meaning of national security is closely linked to threats to a combination of basic national values (1988b: 1–14). This preliminary approach to the problem is clearly inadequate, however, since the perceived security threats and the national values under protection lack any fixed or permanent definition; they differ by country, thematic area, and time period. The term "national security" lacks univocal meaning and is instead subject to the political and operational interpretations of governments and societies in different historical contexts (Mangold 1990: 4).

---

[5] For an analysis of the condition of Mexico's administration of justice system, see González Compeán and Begné 1994; Procuraduría 1993; de la Barreda 1988.

[6] For a discussion of the concept of national security and its application in Mexico, see Aguayo 1993; Meyer 1993.

At this point we should propose an initial distinction between the abstract notion of national security, on the one hand, and its operational definition in various national, thematic, and historical contexts, on the other (see Herrera-Lasso 1988). As a guide for concrete state action, the operational definition of national security is largely contextual and lacks fixed meaning. Mangold asserts that security "inevitably means different things at different times and in different places, depending on what people have to protect, and the nature of the threat" (1990: 4).[7] As Chabat notes, the contingent nature of the concept means that "what one particular state views as a national security threat, another state might not regard as a problem at all" (1994: 99–100).[8]

Even though any general definition of the security concept has limited usefulness, a basic conceptual framework must serve as our point of departure in formulating an operational definition that captures the precise content of the national values considered "vital" in the case of Mexico. In minimal terms, national security involves defense of the national territory, including its airspace and national waters; protection of the population's physical integrity and property rights; and preservation of national sovereignty, understood as the state's supreme and exclusive authority to discharge the tasks of government, the administration of justice, and the application of law according to the internal constitutional order and without subjection to external dictates. A country's national security, as traditionally understood, involves the basic components of the modern state: territorial unity, political sovereignty, state monopoly of the legitimate use of force (through control of the military and police), and exclusive jurisdiction over the administration of justice.

The security problem has been commonly understood in terms of physically protecting the state from external threats, especially from violent military threats. Accordingly, any country's central security concern is to resist external aggression in any form (war, border conflict, espionage, and so on). From this perspective, military force becomes the basic means for confronting the permanent insecurity that results from the absence of any central international authority. As we

---

[7] Elguea proposes this same distinction in the following words: "Negative security implies the capacity to eliminate or reduce a negative relation in which threats are posed against the life of a population, borders, stability, et cetera. Positive security, by contrast, implies the capacity to preserve or maintain a positive relation, that is, certainty that the basic needs of the population or country for natural resources, means of communication, and the like will continue to be satisfied" (1990: 228).

[8] In treating the concept of national security, Chabat distinguishes among three levels of analysis that underscore its contingent nature. These three levels are nongovernmental definition, official discourse, and "really existing national security," that is, the actual content of security resulting from political practice.

will see below, this definition of security does not help us resolve certain fundamental problems.

The conventional understanding of security outlined above is partial and limited. In the first place, defining security in terms of defending the interests of the nation-state against external or internal threats emphasizes the *negative* aspects of the phenomenon while neglecting the *positive* aspects having to do with the state's provision of protection and well-being to its citizens (Elguea 1993: 228).

Second, the conventional understanding tends to define national interests in terms of defending intangible goods ("national values") such as national character, identity, culture, and prestige in a way that allows those who control the state apparatus to abuse their power. For these reasons, the conventional definition shows a strong statist bias; it regards the state as the juridical personification of the nation.[9] The linkage between nation and state is especially complicated in cases of multinational societies or countries that have not yet concluded the nation-building process.

Third, Buzan indicates that both the traditional understanding of national security and its corresponding thematic agenda clearly reflect the perspective of the Western great powers (1988).[10] Ethnocentrism permeates the classical notion of national security, limiting its usefulness in analyzing the problem under conditions of state fragility, economic weakness, social fragmentation, and national disintegration, all of which characterize many peripheral countries. Elguea identifies the conceptual problem in observing that the conventional notion of security based on protecting territory and sovereignty from external threats ignores the internal dimensions of the problem.[11]

Peripheral countries face varied and complicated threats that go beyond external military aggression or the disequilibria of the geopolitical context. The root causes of violence, instability, insecurity, and war in most Third World countries have little to do with the defense of territory or sovereignty. They derive instead from internal conditions of social conflict, endemic poverty, population growth, ethnic diversity, and the weakness of state and political institutions.

---

[9] The traditional conception does not distinguish clearly between national security understood as security of the social community of towns, nations, and groups sharing a given territory, on the one hand, and security of the state as a governing system, on the other. The latter understanding assumes an automatic identification or organic linkage between nation and state. For an analysis of problems in applying the assumptions of the conventional perspective to the study of Third World countries, see Azar and Moon 1988c: 279. For a discussion of this problem as applied to the Mexican case, see Herrera-Lasso and González 1993.

[10] Buzan's analytical propositions regarding the problem of international security in the post–cold war era can be found in Buzan 1990.

[11] Elguea offers a different perspective which links national security to the problems of precarious development. See Elguea 1993.

Azar and Moon assert that, contrary to the situation in developed countries, "security challenges in many parts of the Third World are of endogenous rather than exogenous origin" (1988b: 12).

In order to understand the context of the formation of national security policy in peripheral countries, we must pay greater attention to its internal dimension, and especially to such domestic political characteristics of the state as coalitions and institutions. Viewed from an integral perspective (Buzan 1988: 16), the state's capacity to preserve national security is as much a function of its internal strength (its level of sociopolitical cohesion and consensus) as of state power in the more traditional sense of the term (quantity of resources in comparison with other states). Conditions for stability and peace are especially precarious when extreme incongruities exist between the two dimensions of state capacity (strength and power)[12] or when state structures have not been consolidated internally.

State weakness, in the internal sense of fragile sociopolitical cohesion, is manifested in high levels of political violence, intense ideological polarization, precarious and fragmented legitimacy, militarization, repression by police and the military, and recurrent changes in the structure of political institutions and constitutional order. Are these problems really national security concerns? In countries with weak state structures, political power lacks widespread legitimacy. Thus national security lacks a widely accepted meaning since society enjoys no consensus or agreement on values, ideology, institutions, or national political project. In this situation the very meaning of security is subject to dispute, and in extreme cases government authority faces multiple threats from guerrilla movements, separatist outbursts, political factionalism, and coups d'état.

What are the national security implications of violence and domestic instability under conditions of political fragmentation and weak state legitimacy? This question poses a serious dilemma. If we agree that legitimate national security concerns encompass conflicts arising from the absence of orderly mechanisms for transferring power, the inability of judicial mechanisms to resolve internal disputes legally, the incapacity of government institutions to channel social demands, and so on, then we risk giving the state and government apparatus an extremely powerful instrument for legitimizing the use of force against its own political opponents. In this case, state institutions become a primary source of violence, directly threatening the security of social sectors regarded as "enemies" of domestic order.

If we exclude domestic conflicts from the national security agenda, however, other equally serious problems will arise. First, one cannot

[12] A paradigmatic case of such an incongruity is that of the former Soviet Union during the second half of the 1980s in its dual condition of world power (the external dimension) and weak state (the internal dimension).

completely separate the functions of governmental security structures (protection of citizens' physical integrity, individual guarantees, property rights, and minimal levels of well-being and public services) from national society as a whole, since government inefficacy can lead contending social, ethnic, or religious groups to resort increasingly to indiscriminate violence (Buzan 1990: 103). Second, in today's world the state apparatus continues to bear principal responsibility for guaranteeing the security of its corresponding national society (Mangold 1990: 20). No juridically recognized supranational or subnational entity can substitute for the state in providing justice, public security, and legal enforcement, and thus in ensuring impartial or neutral resolution of intrasocietal conflicts.

In light of this dilemma, we must find ways of establishing internal order so that the state's security functions are limited by the general interest through the creation of effective means to oversee state institutions as they carry out these functions. One reason to establish a system of checks and balances in national security matters is to avoid a polarization of forces that might eventually lead to internal conflict, either between government and society or among various social groups.

In order to add an internal dimension to national security analysis, one must do more than simply point out that instability and conflict have domestic causes. One must also explain in specific terms how domestic conflicts affect conditions of national security, understood as protection of the vital interests of an entire sociopolitical entity (the totality of individuals and social groups who live together within a state) and not simply of the state apparatus that governs it.

The specialized literature identifies three paths—disintegration or secession, intervention, and ungovernability—by which domestic ruptures and tensions can become national security problems. In the first case, opposition movements mount secessionist efforts, hazarding the state's disintegration, to the detriment of the interests of other inhabitants of the same territory. In the second case, internal polarization and fragmentation provoke the direct intervention of external actors or the internationalization of the conflict. Lacking political, military, or juridical resources, or the authority to impose their own solution, domestic actors begin to lose control of the situation. In the third case, violence, political fragmentation, and social instability become chronic and endemic (sometimes to the point of latent civil war), gravely degrading the state's ability to ensure minimal conditions of governability,[13] administration of justice, and protection of citizens' physical integrity and individual rights.

---

[13] The term "governability" is used here in an essentially instrumental sense to refer to the capacity of government structures to design and execute effective public policies responsive to the unsatisfied demands of broad social sectors. The capacity to

Here we are applying Elguea's argument that "a broadening of the meaning of the concept of security for Latin American countries should include as another important component, in addition to defense of national territory and sovereignty, the maintenance of the capacity for economic growth and social progress" (1993: 70). We should clarify that in identifying the internal economic, social, and political causes of instability and conflict, we are not elevating them to the level of national security concerns. Elguea offers some criteria to help in understanding the linkages between national security and the problems of chronic underdevelopment. He asserts that "only those national interest priorities that represent a threat to survival of the nation and cause recourse to armed force and violence constitute true national security interests" (1993: 70). Shaky economic, political, and social development can induce internal actors to resort to armed force and disrupt the peace. In this way, the absence of justice, democracy, freedom, and social well-being can undermine domestic peace, provoking war or at least more widespread recourse to force. Social conflict and political instability endanger security when they lead to the use of force and organized violence, and when they become polarized to the point of provoking the militarization of society. Thus "any war [internal or external] is—by definition—a problem of national security for the country in which it is fought" (1993: 66).

No security threat arises, however, when conflicts sparked by social change or the inadequacies of political institutions follow political, legal, and peaceful channels. From this perspective, the fundamental criterion for identifying social conflicts as security problems is the potential for both state and non-state actors to resort to organized violence and systematic armed force in managing internal conflicts.

If the goal of national security policy is to generate conditions that discourage organized violence, then the state's security apparatus should limit itself mainly to the efficient discharge of its functions of deterring, delimiting, and defusing such violence. The problem of limiting the use of this apparatus (including the armed forces, public security forces, and intelligence agencies) to the goals of deterring, delimiting, and defusing organized violence (but not conflict in general) can be viewed from various perspectives.

The problem's first facet is preventive in nature and refers to the establishment of institutional mechanisms that permit the development of nonviolent means of defending social interests under conditions of injustice and social polarization. This implies that, in normal circumstances, the state's security apparatus should contribute to the peaceful management of social, political, and economic change. To

---

govern effectively refers as much to the ruling elite's skill in forging basic political agreements that build social support for its public policy proposals as to the infrastructural power of the state apparatus. See Mann 1986.

the extent that the state uses its security apparatus not to maintain that normality but instead to impose social equilibrium through force, its very actions will foster conditions of conflict, with organized violence as its ultimate expression. In that case, national security policy will have acted against its own objectives.

A second facet of the problem involves the delimitation of conditions that under extreme circumstances legitimize the state's and other actors' recourse to violence. The basic idea is that the use of force constitutes not an instrument of first instance but rather a last resort once all means of peaceful resolution have been exhausted.[14] The state weakens its own ability to protect national security when the use of violence becomes the leading edge of its policy. Security agencies should not treat violence as their main policy instrument simply because they enjoy a monopoly over its legitimate use: their inclination should be to avoid it, not to initiate it. The quelling of conflict, not its control through the use of violence, is the objective of national security policy.

The quelling of violence, the third facet of the problem of limiting the use of force, requires the state's security apparatus to enjoy sufficient intelligence, logistical, and offensive capacity to neutralize, isolate, and limit armed conflict once it appears. In accordance with this conception of security, the need to contain organized violence at the societal level cannot justify such official acts of violence as repression, torture, or violations of individual rights. Even under conditions of civil war, legal criteria must restrict to the utmost the state's use of physical force. The legal framework that governs national security activities under conditions of internal war should seek to reduce as much as possible the injuries and other costs resulting from the use of force.

The foregoing discussion implies that once the use of violence becomes inevitable, the state's security apparatus should apply military and police force only in a way that is discriminate (directed exclusively against belligerent forces), proportional (the destructive consequences should not exceed the anticipated benefits in terms of reestablishing peace), and limited (the political objective is to quell violence, not to annihilate those who use it). Only by establishing systems of checks and balances and effective oversight of the state's national security agencies can one ensure that force and violence will be employed in a limited and controlled way.

---

[14] For an analysis of just war theories, see Elguea 1994.

The Domestic Face of National Security in Mexico

How useful is this conceptualization of national security in analyzing the Mexican case? The national security doctrine of the Mexican government rests on an integral and broad vision of the phenomenon, one closer to the unconventional notions of Buzan, Azar and Moon, and Elguea than to the restricted conventional definitions stressing external threats and military power. In 1980 Defense Minister Félix Galván López delivered one of the Mexican government's first public statements on national security, defining it as "the maintenance of social, economic, and political equilibrium, guaranteed by the armed forces" (quoted in Ronfeldt 1984: 20). According to the official doctrine explicitly set forth during the 1980s,[15] national security is "the permanent condition of peace, freedom, and social justice that federal government power produces within an institutional and legal framework by means of political, social, economic, and military actions" (Secretaría 1989). The conception described above reflects the prevalence of a nonmilitarist discourse stressing the subordination of the armed forces to the constitutional order, the importance of political and juridical mechanisms for overseeing and controlling the military apparatus as it quells internal conflicts, and the need to guarantee conditions of economic development and social well-being that reduce instability and ungovernability.

In addition to the conceptual linkage between development and security in the Mexican case, we should also consider the ideological linkage between official pronouncements on defense and security matters and the nature of the political regime. Mexico's national security doctrine has been defined in terms of defending the economic and social values of the national, nationalistic, and popular project forged during the Mexican Revolution. Pellicer (1983) asserts that until the end of the 1960s the economic dimension of national security was prominent in the government's security considerations, especially its interest in preserving sovereignty over natural resources, securing state dominance in "strategic" economic sectors (such as petroleum, communications, and electricity), and controlling the activities of foreign capital in Mexico. Ronfeldt refers to the close linkage between the nature of the postrevolutionary political system and the

---

[15] Until 1980 Mexican governments had no explicit national security doctrine. Official discourse was based on the defense of national sovereignty, political independence from superpower-dominated blocs, promotion of disarmament, control of national resources, and rejection of external interference in national politics. Regarding internal tasks, the practice of national security consisted in using the armed forces as a last-resort political stabilizing factor to combat the radicalization of social opposition movements (such as the student movement of 1968 and the guerrilla movements of the 1970s). See Benítez Manaut 1994.

traditional understanding of national security when he asserts that, in stressing the social and economic dimensions of security, the traditional Mexican vision reinforced and legitimized the nationalist goals of strengthening the state's role in the economy and in social development (1984: 21).

Mexican political discussion of security has tended over time to stress its social and economic aspects at the domestic level, while in the foreign sphere it has emphasized the defense of national sovereignty and political independence from the United States. This dual content formed what has been called Mexico's "nationalist and populist" version of national security. In this way revolutionary nationalism—the political doctrine shaping the national project born of the Mexican Revolution—became the primary and almost sole ideological feature of the Mexican armed forces.

Apart from the ideological and doctrinal aspects of national security, in the area of official security practice the armed forces and police organizations have carried out the important function of political stabilization—as the "option of last resort" (Benítez Manaut 1994: 187)—in moments of political crisis, broad social mobilization, extreme tension between the government and sectors of civil society, or increased violence associated with illegal activities. Direct military involvement in resolving internal crises and quelling political violence has generally taken the form of temporary and small-scale repression, accompanied at times by "civic" activities such as the construction of roads, hospitals, housing, and communications networks. In extreme cases the army has participated in resolving worker and peasant conflicts, stabilizing tensions in rural zones, repressing social movements such as the 1968 student uprising, launching counterinsurgency campaigns, and controlling drug trafficking.

Ever since the 1940s, when power was peacefully transferred from Mexico's last military president (General Manuel Avila Camacho) to the civilian elite, the army has participated neither visibly nor directly in national politics, although it has remained an institutional member of the postrevolutionary political regime. Its role, therefore, has not become "residual," as Ronfeldt asserts; instead, it has remained an important guarantor of political stability.[16]

This pattern of institutional civil-military relations has allowed the maintenance of a demilitarized political system whose stability and internal strength have been sustained principally by the effective functioning, until recently, of its institutions for political control, me-

---

[16] The argument that the armed forces help to stabilize the Mexican political system is fully elaborated by Benítez Manaut (1994). He argues that the Mexican army plays a calming and stabilizing role in the national political climate, since it has abjured any deliberative or decision-making political role and does not press for a constant increase in military spending.

diation, and cohesion (that is, the hegemonic party, corporatism, and presidentialism), with use of repression as a last resort (see Serrano 1995). Nevertheless, it bears asking to what extent the current exhaustion of the political system's traditional mediatory mechanisms, uncertainty regarding the ruling party's political future, ruptures within the political elite, and rising prospects for conflict and organized violence (political, common, and guerrilla) all affect the political role of the army as an institutional pillar of the state and stabilizing factor for the regime, test the army's professional capacity, and expand its size and influence.

Since the early 1980s, the security challenges facing the armed forces have increased in number, intensity, and diversity as political tensions within Mexico have worsened and simultaneous outbursts of violence have become more common. The army has intensified its nationwide struggle against illegal drug and arms trafficking in response to the increasing use of Mexican territory as a transit point for cocaine shipments to the United States. Simultaneously, corruption and incompetence within the police forces responsible for preserving security and public order have led the civil authorities to look increasingly to the army for support in monitoring elections and social mobilizations in Mexico's zones in conflict.[17]

Although the army's increased involvement in maintaining public order has not yet led to openly repressive actions, it has nonetheless provoked sharp domestic criticism that has undermined the prestige of military commanders (see Aguilar Zinser 1990, 1994). These attacks have been as much political as professional. As various studies have shown, the army's ability to conduct concurrent military actions in multiple areas of conflict has been hampered by insufficient physical resources, intelligence gathering, and technical capacity. The Zapatista uprising in Chiapas and the presence of armed groups elsewhere (such as in the state of Guerrero) have forced the army to expand and diversify its operations in especially sensitive and conflict-ridden areas of Mexico. The army suffered intense criticism for human rights abuses allegedly committed during its twelve days of combat with the Zapatistas in January 1994; this criticism revealed certain differences between military commanders and civilian authorities. In the same way, the Chiapas insurrection and the outbreak of organized rural violence in Guerrero have led necessarily to a vastly increased military presence in those states, which could lead to greater militariza-

[17] The increased participation of the Mexican armed forces in maintaining public order as a direct response to the incompetence and corruption of the nation's police forces has been fully and systematically studied by Serrano (1995: 448).

tion of those areas while discouraging political settlements of their conflicts.[18]

On the other hand, there is evidence of discontent among elements within the army that distrusted the Salinas administration's modernizing reforms (which they viewed as contrary to the nationalistic values in which they were socialized) and demanded greater decision-making participation for themselves in areas for which public opinion holds the armed forces responsible. Nevertheless, despite the military's expanded role in fighting the international drug trade and domestic guerrillas and in restoring public order in the wake of local-level postelectoral conflicts, we have no solid evidence of a clear tendency toward greater militarization of the political system, or toward increased politicization and autonomy of the armed forces, which have remained subordinate to constitutional order and civil authority.

These developments do not indicate a substantial erosion of military subordination or loyalty to the civilian authorities. Nor do they indicate a political or ideological breach between the armed forces and the government that might presage direct military intervention in politics, even temporarily. Nevertheless, the gradual erosion of the army's prestige and the relative decline of civil-military cohesion highlight the need for institutional changes that will expand opportunities for open and efficient participation by the armed forces in the formulation of national security policy. Additionally, if the armed forces are to respond effectively to Mexico's increased domestic turmoil, their apparatus and strategies must be modernized, especially through the development of a flexible rapid-response capability. As the armed forces become more exposed to domestic and foreign public opinion, the government will have to develop mechanisms that facilitate more open, smooth, and transparent interaction between the armed forces and society at large (Meyer 1994).

Some analysts expect the 1990s to mark the end of the "exceptionalism of Mexican stability" as compared with the rest of Latin America. They view the guerrilla insurgency in Chiapas and the existence of armed groups in other rural zones as evidence that Ronfeldt's assertion (1984: 11) that "time after time [the] political system [in Mexico] has demonstrated a profound capacity to absorb internal conflicts and crises without becoming unstable" no longer applies. Until January 1994 one could hardly doubt the ability of the Mexican political system to guarantee internal systemic stability, but thereafter it became harder to sustain that case.

---

[18] In considering the possible implications of the increased military presence in Mexico's most conflictive zones, we must remember that in the 1950s Mexico began a gradual process of demilitarization that made it in 1994 one of the world's least militarized countries. According to Benítez Manaut (1994), Mexico's military expenditures during the 1980s represented only 0.6 percent of GDP.

In fact, the very mechanisms that formerly assured Mexico's internal stability (single-party system, absence of strong opposition parties, centralization of political power in the hands of the executive, corporatist control of society, manipulation of elections, local bossism) have now become the main sources of national tension and discord. As a result, future political stability (understood as the ability to channel conflicts politically) will depend increasingly on the state's capacity to lead a thorough and rapid political reform, completing the process of slow liberalization begun during the 1970s and permitting the strengthening of democratic institutions, especially a competitive party system.

Some interpretations of the Chiapas uprising suggest erroneously that Mexico faces a Hobson's choice: either an escalation of armed violence leading eventually to nationwide civil war, or an imposition of authoritarian stability through military repression of the insurgency. Instead, Mexico now confronts the strategic need to modernize its political structures as a necessary condition for restoring internal peace. The threat of instability resides precisely in the indeterminate character of Mexican political modernity—that is, in the historic moment when the breakdown of the corporatist apparatus intersects with the inadequacy of Mexico's democratic institutionality.

Several factors prompt us to conclude that, indeed, Mexico is potentially more unstable at the threshold of the twenty-first century than at any other time since the "Mexican miracle" began to falter at the end of the 1960s. The current period of instability can be distinguished from turbulent moments in the recent past—the student movement of 1968, the outbreak of urban and rural guerrilla violence in the 1970s, the economic and financial crises preceding the presidential elections of 1976 and 1982, and the "electoral crisis" of 1988—by three features of what theoreticians of democratic transitions call "foundational moments."[19]

First, tension and conflict appear simultaneously at the national level and in various and heterogeneous regional settings. The simultaneous and dispersed nature of these outbursts (drug trafficking, guerrilla insurgency, violent postelectoral mobilization) endangers internal peace. Further, it tests not only the flexibility of political institutions in defusing conflicts and constructing sociopolitical pacts that

[19] "Foundational moments" in the transitional process refer to abnormal moments in which the breakdown of an authoritarian regime can have various outcomes, including the installation of political democracy, the restoration of authoritarianism under a new guise, or the emergence of a revolutionary regime. The rules of the game that govern these political transitions are typically vague and fluid; they are subject to vigorous dispute among actors seeking not only to defend their particular interests but to define the procedures that govern competition among all political actors. These moments are characterized by a high degree of uncertainty. See O'Donnell, Schmitter, and Whitehead 1986.

ensure conditions of governability and peaceful transfer of power; it also tests the capacity of the security and army apparatus, under conditions of simultaneous challenges on various fronts, to prevent localized incidences of violence from joining together and escalating to the national level.

Second, the mobilization of important sectors of civil society coincides with an exacerbation of divisions within the political elite—over the presidential succession; Zedillo's breaching of the compact of mutual protection between incoming and outgoing presidents[20]; the pace, modalities, and extent of political liberalization; and, in local-level postelectoral conflicts, the center's imposition of candidates and its political concessions to opposition parties.

The third feature of these transitions is the impossibility of channeling conflicts politically without enacting fundamental political reforms. These include, but are not limited to, separating the ruling party from the government apparatus, holding clean and transparent elections, recognizing opposition victories, and accepting the possibility of alternation in power.

The current stage of transition in Mexico, in the second year of the Zedillo administration, is characterized by extreme internal political uncertainty and economic instability. Prior to the peso crisis of December 1994, factors that favored the concerted management of Mexico's political transition were the relatively strong institutionalization of economic reform and the success of the adjustment policy in controlling inflation and strengthening public finances. The fact that Mexico avoided bankruptcy in the 1980s and early 1990s and received substantial new investment as a result of the North American Free Trade Agreement (NAFTA) gave the Salinas government some maneuvering room to satisfy unanswered social demands and to lead a pacted political transition within minimal conditions of economic certainty.

The economic model had significant weaknesses, however. It gave inadequate attention to social needs; it eroded the political system's capacity to forge agreements among diverse social and economic sectors; it exposed Mexico to the vagaries of the world economy; and, finally, it was overly dependent on highly speculative and mobile international private capital flows. Even though the government's

[20] President Zedillo's decision to initiate judicial proceedings against Raúl Salinas, older brother of former president Salinas and the presumed intellectual author of the assassination of PRI party leader José Francisco Ruiz Massieu, broke abruptly with one of the most important of Mexican authoritarianism's unwritten rules: that ex-presidents and their families will have full political protection against allegations of irregularities, illegal enrichment, or abuse of power during their administrations. While this unwritten guarantee assured a high degree of discipline and cohesion within the governing group during periods of transition between administrations, it also functioned as a strong and systemic incentive for corruption.

economic strategy between 1988 and 1994 restored the macroeconomic stability lost in the 1970s, it failed to maintain satisfactory levels of sustained growth (given current rates of population increase), and its social consequences were quite unequal, with the least protected and most backward social sectors bearing most of its costs.

Mexico's main macroeconomic indicators showed considerable improvement by mid-1996. Financial markets had steadied, interest and inflation rates had fallen, the exchange rate had stabilized at between 7.40 and 7.60 pesos per dollar, and the agricultural and industrial sectors registered positive growth rates during the second trimester of 1996. Despite this improvement, which resulted from the consistent application of adjustment policies and the financial support program negotiated with the U.S. Treasury Department and the International Monetary Fund, Mexico's economic stagnation had produced a sharp decline in living conditions[21] and given rise to several outbursts of popular unrest and an alarming increase in crime and public insecurity. Moreover, indicators of macroeconomic stabilization clashed with pessimistic microeconomic forecasts that poor living conditions for salaried workers and heavy financial pressures upon small and mid-sized businesses would continue in the medium term.

Especially notable were the fragility of the financial and banking system and high levels of private indebtedness among businesses and individuals. According to the annual report of the Bank of Mexico, families and businesses went from a net creditor position vis-à-vis the financial system in 1990 (equivalent to 15.6 percent of GDP) to a net debtor position of 11.2 percent in December 1994. By 1995 Mexico faced a situation of internal insolvency that gravely threatened the banking system and much of the middle class, despite the government's support efforts. In view of these conditions, one cannot speak of a recovery of growth based upon solid and stable foundations.

What have been the implications of Mexico's current economic crisis for the democratization process? A tentative response to this question requires us to stress two key aspects of the crisis that beset Mexico during 1995 and 1996. First, the financial instability provoked by the loss of confidence among important economic actors resulted not only from strictly economic considerations but also from eminently political factors (such as the resurgence of political violence, increased conflict within the Institutional Revolutionary Party [PRI], and institutional corruption).

Second, the magnitude of the crisis far exceeded its economic costs, and its main impact was felt in the spheres of society and public security. The huge social costs occasioned by Mexico's prolonged re-

[21] Real salary levels fell by 12 percent in 1995 alone, and it was hoped that the total decline for 1996 would not exceed 20 percent (Lustig 1996).

cession and failure to restore growth suggest that the economic crisis has had a contradictory impact on the democratization process. On the one hand, the crisis revealed the weakness of the domestic foundations of national security, given the absence of stable conditions of social progress and the considerable external vulnerability of the economic modernization program, and it has greatly reduced the Zedillo government's ability to contain social discontent and counter the opponents of economic liberalization. On the other hand, the crisis has helped to accelerate the dismantling of the political and institutional framework of authoritarianism.

Although recession and financial disorder have not yet provoked either a social uprising or an organized opposition movement among the popular sectors most affected by the crisis,[22] in the medium run the government can maintain social peace only by ensuring that improved macroeconomic indicators translate into improved living standards.[23] In the short run, however, ongoing social discontent and violence, especially in rural areas, could have a significant impact on economic policy, especially in the areas of social spending and agricultural modernization. If the government fails by 1998 to produce a sustained economic recovery that results in new job creation, domestic pressures will build for a sustained increase in social spending and eventually for populist measures to relieve economic suffering, with negative consequences for the health of public finances.

Mexico faces two main economic challenges during the current stage of political transition. The first, which President Zedillo defined in his initial State of the Nation address as the keystone of his economic policy, is the restoration of sustained growth on solid and stable foundations (Zedillo 1995). The government's current strategy consists in designing policies that promote domestic savings, raise productivity, and stimulate job creation without relaxing stringent monetary, fiscal, and exchange rate policies and thereby sparking a

[22] Lustig (1996) notes that despite the disorder produced by the financial crisis, traditional peasant and worker associations have not formed a national movement to protest the government's adjustment program and that new social movements (such as the "Barzón" debtors' association) have been neutralized in part by the government's efforts to resolve the problem of nonperforming bank loans (through its programs to restructure credit in investment enterprises, support endangered banking institutions, strengthen bank capital by purchasing nonperforming loans, and support agrarian debtors).

[23] Reducing the rate of inflation has been the most signal success of the macroeconomic stabilization strategy followed by the governments of de la Madrid and Salinas de Gortari. The annual inflation rate fell from 159.2 percent in 1987 to just 8 percent in 1993. The second most important success was the elimination of the chronic public-sector deficit and reduction of the public debt from 74.7 percent of GDP in 1988 to 32 percent in 1993. See Sarmiento 1994.

new financial crisis. These conflicting imperatives imply that the expected positive results will appear only over the long term.

The second challenge, which Zedillo's economic agenda does not acknowledge, is to modify the economic liberalization and deregulation programs so as to ensure more equitable distribution of the fruits of macroeconomic stability without undermining the confidence of private economic actors and fostering renewed instability and financial crisis. For this reason, as Sarmiento (1994: 19) has observed, what at the beginning of the 1980s was an economic challenge has become in the 1990s an eminently political and social one.

The following discussion will analyze some incongruities and contradictions in the current political transition in Mexico that have a potential or real impact on domestic stability and peace, and that will shape the future direction of official national security policy. We refer in particular to three aspects of the problem: (1) erosion of the ideological foundations of the cohesion and legitimacy of the Mexican political system (the crisis of revolutionary nationalism); (2) the inadequate and precarious nature of the democratic institutional framework (parties, elections, legislature, judicial system, federalism) and the debilitation of the corporatist institutional framework, which has become a source of instability and political violence; and (3) the systemic sources of instability (institutional corruption, chronic poverty, and a weak apparatus for administering justice) that account for the upsurge of organized violence in Mexico, especially among drug traffickers and guerrillas.

Most of these phenomena directly threaten the security of the postrevolutionary political regime, with important collateral consequences for public security in various parts of the country. However, they also provide evidence of the weakness of the internal foundations (political legitimacy, economic development, and social progress) of national security in a country that suffers strong social and regional imbalances and has not yet established the political-institutional democratic rules needed to resolve with minimal use of violence and coercion the conflicts fostered by its own social diversity.

The Dependence of National Security on Legality

The financial crisis sparked in December 1994 by the peso devaluation and subsequent massive capital flight marked a reappearance of the economic instability that typically characterizes the change of presidential administrations in Mexico. In this case, however, the crisis occurred not at the end of the outgoing president's term but at the start of the new *sexenio*. Between 1994 and 1996 Mexico's political transition entered a new stage marked by a novel factor—the new president's political weakness and his consequent need to forge alliances outside the PRI and to use democratic means to recover the legitimacy of which the economic crisis had deprived his government—that would hasten the steady erosion of both the ruling party's corporative institutionality and the ideological foundations of the postrevolutionary political system (the crisis of so-called revolutionary nationalism). In sharp contrast with his predecessor, Ernesto Zedillo took office armed with electoral legitimacy. But he was also politically weak, a late-chosen substitute candidate with little support within the ideologically and politically fractured PRI. Zedillo inherited a government weakened by institutional corruption and identified with an increasingly vulnerable economic policy. The confluence of three factors—change of government, economic crisis, and political instability—pushed Mexico toward a difficult political transition just as the government was losing its ability to control key economic variables and the timing and substance of political change.

Presidential weakness has had a twofold impact upon Mexico's democratic transition. It has undercut arbitrary and unchecked presidential power. But it has also increased the sources of ungovernability; a weakened central leadership cannot subdue local-level bosses and reactionary elements within the PRI that oppose political liberalization. Despite Zedillo's political weakness, his government has shown great consistency in managing economic policy. Zedillo has also shown a determination to implement reforms that will ensure clean elections in 1997, to revamp the administration of justice system, and to reach a negotiated settlement in Chiapas. Arbitrary presidential power, which is the axis of the clientelistic system of political power, is increasingly hard to maintain within a context of economic liberalization: unchecked power clashes with the growing need to ensure the uniform and predictable application of laws that govern economic activity in order to sustain acceptable levels of investment. Unlike Salinas, who sought to separate economic modernization from political reform, the Zedillo government has given top priority to strengthening the rule of law. In the president's view, no strategy for economic growth can give the results that Mexico needs unless the rule of law and public security are also guaranteed.

Mexico's difficult political situation during the first two years of the Zedillo presidency suggests that the postrevolutionary regime that for six decades ensured political stability despite huge socioeconomic inequalities has, after a prolonged period of debilitation that began in 1968, entered a terminal phase. Short-run factors linked to the change of government, the armed rebellion in Chiapas, and the assassination of the PRI's presidential nominee in 1994 have combined with structural factors to force a redefinition of the Mexican political system. Absent solid institutional alternatives to the system of authoritarian control, Mexico's current incomplete democratization requires that the country implement a drastic and rapid opening of the political system—without provoking a crisis of governability, instability, and violence.

The stability of Mexico's postrevolutionary regime rests on six foundational conditions: economic growth; institutionalization of the armed forces; high levels of ideological consensus and cohesion within the political elite; an influential network of corporative organizations within a state party system; the mediating role of a strong president; and a high capacity for reformism. Most of these conditions are currently weak. The reproduction of consensus among political elites has diminished as their access channels to power have been closed—by the downsizing of the state apparatus through privatization and reduced public spending, by the more efficient administration demanded under the new economic model (which obstructs the participation of traditional political groups in the distribution of power), by intensified competition between the technical-bureaucratic and political-clientelistic sectors of the ruling elite, and by the escalating costs of discretionary presidential power in terms of administrative efficiency.

The corporative system of clientelistic relations that formerly ensured the control of social demands and mediation among sectors, regions, and the state has been eroding and fragmenting. Presidentialism, another pillar of regime stability, also faces a stiff challenge which will probably extend into the next presidential administration. The outbreak of war in Chiapas, the murder of the PRI's presidential candidate, and the economic crisis of early 1995 have gravely injured the institution of the presidency. The Zedillo administration marks the end of presidentialism and the beginning of a restricted presidential regime in which negotiation and co-government will become the norm as opposition parties achieve greater representation at all levels of government (Molinar Horcasitas 1994).

The Chiapas conflict and the 1995 economic crisis forced the Zedillo government to abandon all hopes of following its predecessor's practice of postponing political reform until economic reform had restored investor confidence and economic growth. The Salinas government's decision to declare a unilateral cease-fire in Chiapas, to open negotiations with the insurgents, and to name as interior minister Jorge Carpizo, a lawyer and academic without strong ties to the PRI or the political elite, marked a change of strategy. In view of the likely high costs of a strategy of military repression and political retrenchment, the Zedillo government has chosen to pursue a new and definitive electoral reform and to contain the armed violence in Chiapas through political dialogue.

Even though the situation remains precarious, we should not conclude from the foregoing analysis that current indications of political uncertainty and instability will lead inevitably to civil war, endemic ungovernability, or a coup d'état. Despite the fragility of negotiations in Chiapas and the agreements on electoral reform, a peaceful and pacted transition in Mexico is attainable. The various forms that this transition could take are not limited to the electoral sphere. We must remember that the current signs of instability stem from diverse causes, with both positive and negative implications for a peaceful transition from semi-authoritarianism to democracy. Some of these signs are the natural consequences of the regime's democratization. Others indicate an institutional decomposition both of certain state agencies and of the structures of political organization, representation, and participation.

References

Aguayo Quezada, Sergio. 1993. "The Uses, Abuses, and Challenges of Mexican National Security: 1946–1990." In *Mexico: In Search of Security*, edited by Bruce M. Bagley and Sergio Aguayo Quezada. New Brunswick, N.J.: Transaction.

Aguilar Camín, Héctor. 1992a. "El cambio mundial y la democracia en México." In *Coloquio de Invierno. "México y los cambios de nuestro tiempo."* Vol. 3. México, D.F.: Fondo de Cultura Económica/UNAM/CONACYT.

———. 1992b. "La nación y el territorio: comentario general." In *El nacionalismo en México*, edited by Cecilia Noriega Elio. Zamora, Mex.: El Colegio de Michoacán.

Aguilar Zinser, Adolfo. 1990. "Civil-Military Relations in Mexico." In *The Military and Democracy: The Future of Civil-Military Relations in Latin America*, edited by Louis Goodman, Johanna Mendelson, and Juan Rial. Lexington, Mass.: Lexington.

———. 1994. "Acerca del ejército mexicano: actuación bajo premisas de lealtad y confianza," *Ideas de Excélsior*, April 12.

Azar, Edward E., and Chung-in Moon, eds. 1988a. *National Security in the Third World: The Management of Internal and External Threats*. Aldershot, England: Center for International Development and Conflict Management.

———. 1988b. "Rethinking Third World National Security." In *National Security in the Third World*, edited by E.E. Azar and C. Moon. Aldershot, England: Center for International Development and Conflict Management.

———. 1988c. "Towards an Alternative Conceptualization." In *National Security in the Third World*, edited by E.E. Azar and C. Moon. Aldershot, England: Center for International Development and Conflict Management.

Benítez Manaut, Raúl. 1994. "Las fuerzas armadas mexicanas a fin de siglo: su relación con el Estado, el sistema político, y la sociedad," *Sociología* 9 (25): 187–216.

Buzan, Barry. 1988. "People, States, and Fear: The National Security Problem in the Third World." In *National Security in the Third World*, edited by E.E. Azar and C. Moon. Aldershot, England: Center for International Development and Conflict Management.

———. 1990. *People, States, and Fear: An Agenda for International Security Studies in the Post–Cold War Era*. Boulder, Colo.: Lynne Rienner.

Chabat, Jorge. 1994. "Seguridad nacional y narcotráfico: vínculos reales e imaginarios," *Política y Gobierno* 1 (1): 99–100.

de la Barreda, Luis. 1988. "El poder judicial y la democracia en México." In *México: el reclamo democrático*, edited by Rolando Cordera, Raúl Trejo Delarbre, and Juan Enrique Vega. México, D.F.: Siglo Veintiuno.

Elguea, Javier A. 1990. "Crisis y seguridad nacional." In *México en el umbral del milenio*. México, D.F.: Centro de Estudios Sociológicos, El Colegio de México.

———. 1993. "International Security and National Development." In *Mexico: In Search of Security*, edited by Bruce M. Bagley and Sergio Aguayo Quezada. New Brunswick, N.J.: Transaction.

———. 1994. "El sangriento camino hacia la utopía: la violencia y el desarrollo en América Latina," *Perfil de la Jornada*, February 19.

Escudé, Carlos. 1993. "International Relations Theory: A Peripheral Perspective." Working Paper No. 1. Buenos Aires: Universidad Torcuato Di Tella.

Garza Elizondo, Humberto. 1994. "El avance en materia exterior resulta aún insuficiente," *Ideas de Excélsior*, January 7.

González Compeán, Miguel, and Alberto Begné. 1994. "La administración de justicia en México: apuntes preliminares." Mimeo.

Herrera-Lasso, Luis. 1988. "Democracia y seguridad nacional." In *México: el reclamo democrático*, edited by Rolando Cordera, Raúl Trejo Delarbre, and Juan Enrique Vega. México, D.F.: Siglo Veintiuno.

Herrera-Lasso, Luis, and Guadalupe González. 1993. "Reflections on the Use of the Concept of National Security in Mexico." In *Mexico: In Search of Security*, edited by Bruce M. Bagley and Sergio Aguayo Quezada. New Brunswick, N.J.: Transaction.

Linz, Juan. 1964. "An Authoritarian Regime: Spain." Mimeo.

Lustig, Nora. 1996. "Mexico: The Slippery Road to Stability," *Brookings Review*, Spring, pp. 4–9.

Mangold, Peter. 1990. *National Security and International Relations*. New York: Routledge.

Mann, Michael. 1986. "The Autonomous Power of the State: Its Origins, Mechanisms, and Results." In *States in History*, edited by John A. Hall. Oxford: Basil Blackwell.

Meyer, Lorenzo. 1993. "Prologue." In *Mexico: In Search of Security*, edited by Bruce M. Bagley and Sergio Aguayo Quezada. New Brunswick, N.J.: Transaction.

———. 1994. "Necesario, mayor interacción entre el ejército y la sociedad," *Ideas de Excélsior*, April 12.

Molinar Horcasitas, Juan. 1994. "Fin del presidencialismo," *Reforma*, June 27.

O'Donnell, Guillermo, Philippe C. Schmitter, and Laurence Whitehead. 1986. *Transitions from Authoritarian Rule*. Part 4, *Tentative Conclusions and Uncertain Democracies*. Baltimore, Md.: Johns Hopkins University Press.

Pellicer, Olga. 1983. "National Security in Mexico: Traditional Notions and New Preoccupations." In *U.S.–Mexican Relations: Economic and Social Aspects,* edited by Clark Reynolds and Carlos Tello. Stanford, Calif.: Stanford University Press.

Pérez Gay, José María. 1992. "Nación y Estado en Alemania y México," *Foro Internacional* 32 (4): 449–54.

Procuraduría General de la República. 1993. *La procuración de justicia en México: problemas, retos, y perspectivas.* México, D.F.: PGR.

Ronfeldt, David. 1984. "The Modern Mexican Military: An Overview." In *The Modern Mexican Military: A Reassessment,* edited by D. Ronfeldt. Monograph Series, no. 15. La Jolla: Center for U.S.–Mexican Studies, University of California, San Diego.

Salinas de Gortari, Carlos. 1991. "North American Free Trade: Mexico's Route to Upward Mobility," *New Perspectives Quarterly* 8 (1): 4–9.

Sarmiento, Sergio. 1994. "El gran experimento: la economía bajo Salinas," *Este País* 34 (January): 18–19.

Secretaría de Programación y Presupuesto. 1989. *Plan Nacional de Desarrollo 1989–1994.* México, D.F.: SPP.

Serrano, Mónica. 1995. "The Armed Branch of the State: Civil-Military Relations in Mexico," *Journal of Latin American Studies* 27 (2): 423–48.

Zedillo, Ernesto. 1995. "Mensaje al Congreso de la Unión," *Comercio Exterior* 45 (September): 703–11.

Civil and Military Responses

7

Controlling Drugs: Strategic Operations and U.S. and Mexican National Interests

Jorge E. Tello Peón

In 1990 President Carlos Salinas de Gortari unveiled his administration's National Antidrug Program, thereby elevating the antidrug struggle to priority status as an official concern. The Salinas administration conducted an intensive program of drug control and prevention unprecedented in Mexican history. On July 13, 1993, the president underscored the importance of the drug problem for Mexico by calling upon the Central and South American countries to cooperate in forging multinational initiatives to fight the drug trade effectively while safeguarding the sovereignty of each Latin American country.

The Clinton administration shares the Mexican government's determination to defeat the drug barons. Mexicans have taken careful note of Clinton's publicly stated resolve to reduce U.S. drug consumption through programs to prevent drug abuse and to prosecute domestic drug suppliers.

This chapter will offer a summary review of relevant aspects of Mexico's struggle against the drug scourge. It will also outline the cooperative efforts of the United States and Mexico to fight this problem.

The Current Situation

Drug consumption in the developed countries has risen precipitously in recent years. At the global level, a significant increase in demand for and addiction to narcotics and psychotropic drugs has encouraged a huge expansion of drug-trafficking activity. As a result, drugs have poured across national borders and infiltrated all corners of society, encouraging false expectations among their users and bringing in their train various destructive social repercussions. Caught unawares, many societies and governments did not move quickly to confront the drug threat and effectively evaluate the success of their antidrug efforts. As a consequence, many societies suffered serious harm.

Mexico has served the international drug-trafficking network as a bridge between the main areas of coca cultivation and the principal cocaine market, the United States. The transshipment of cocaine through Mexico has not led to increased cocaine consumption in that nation, however, which suggests that cocaine demand has certain cultural correlates that are alien to the Mexican people.

The production and trafficking of illicit drugs have increased steadily to the point that they now touch most parts of the world. Within Mexico, the area sown in marijuana and poppies has continued to grow, despite the expansion of programs to eradicate these crops and develop alternative ones.

As drug production and distribution have expanded in quantity and range, traffickers have redoubled their efforts to expand the international market for their product. They seek to incorporate into this market countries that previously served only as areas of cultivation or as transit points. This propagation of drug consumption has changed the forms and routes of drug trafficking, as traffickers try to evade the controls and obstacles set up by national drug enforcement authorities.

Assessing the Problem at the Hemispheric Level

The production, consumption, and trafficking of drugs has expanded throughout the Western Hemisphere, just as it has at the global level. Although addiction to the so-called hard drugs used to be found almost entirely in industrialized countries, it has now appeared in developing societies as well. Although drug trafficking and consumption are hardly new to the Western Hemisphere, the types of drugs consumed—and consequently the types of addicts seeking treatment—have become increasingly diverse.

Specialization in drug production and trafficking has helped to generate higher yields and wider profit margins for drug producers and distributors. The international bosses who control the drug trade have broadened their contacts with lesser drug-trafficking organizations in an effort to expand and diversify the supply of illicit drugs.

Economic problems have increased the vulnerability of most Latin American countries to the snares of the drug trade, since most of these countries lack the necessary human and other resources for detecting and controlling drugs. The production and consumption of narcotics and psychotropic substances have consequently expanded throughout the hemisphere, defeating the increasingly effective preventive measures taken by national antidrug agencies.

The steady expansion of the drug trade in the Western Hemisphere has been accompanied by increased illegal traffic in weapons and explosives. Organizations that conduct these illicit dealings have forged clandestine links among themselves, thereby increasing their ability to escape detection by law enforcement authorities. The drug trade has also infiltrated the financial systems of certain countries through the laundering of drug profits. This aspect of the drug phenomenon is particularly destructive since it destabilizes national economies and sometimes distorts production in certain economic sectors.

The international community's concern about the drug threat has prompted a recent increase in antidrug cooperation among nations, especially through information exchanges. Concerned governments have also begun to reassess existing multilateral strategies for fighting the drug trade in order to improve their effectiveness and likelihood of success.

Mexico's Efforts to Control the Drug Trade

Between December 1988 and June 1993, the Salinas administration scored some major successes in the fight against drugs. Authorities seized 197,297 kilograms of cocaine, 1,141 of opium paste, 662 of heroin, and 2,277 of marijuana. During this same period, authorities eradicated 51,644 hectares of marijuana and 45,661 hectares of poppies. The quantity of illegal drugs confiscated by the Mexican government exceeded the combined amount seized by the U.S. and Canadian governments during the same period. Mexico went further than any other Latin American country during 1992 and 1993 in reducing the total land area sown in illegal drug crops by means of aggressive programs of eradication and alternative crop development.

During the first half of 1993, the Federal Public Ministry[1] arrested 3,870 people on drug-related charges. Among the most important of these drug traffickers were Joaquín "Chapo" Guzmán Loera and his key associates.

---

[1] Editors' note: The Federal Public Ministry is the division of the Mexican Attorney General's office that is charged with investigating federal crimes, bringing indictments, and conducting prosecutions.

Integrality: The Principle Guiding Drug Control in Mexico

Mexico has an integral understanding of the multidimensionality of the drug trade and a broad view of its manifestations and consequences. The Mexican government has tried to address the various aspects of this multidimensional phenomenon in an integral, plural, and dynamic way.

For instance, the government has encouraged the development of global measures for clearly differentiating the various aspects of the drug process. These include production, consumption, treatment of addiction, public health measures, prosecution and disruption of drug-trafficking organizations, eradication of illicit crops, and the prosecution of related crimes such as money laundering, illegal trade in weapons and precursor chemicals, terrorism, and corruption.

Mexico views the drug phenomenon as an extremely serious social problem arising from various interrelated causes, both internal and external, one whose solution must be sought at the global level rather than within national borders. The drug problem tends to arise when a culture of excessive consumerism excites expectations that a society cannot satisfy for all of its members. The inability to fully satisfy these expectations produces in some members of the society a state of anxiety and emotional instability, which they may try to escape through drug use. Although this phenomenon can be seen in many areas of the world, it is particularly evident in the industrialized societies. In addition to exaggerated consumerism, drug abuse is driven by other causes, including poverty, unemployment, social marginalization, economic uncertainty, lack of education, and the destructive social consequences of the actions of drug traffickers themselves.

Because the factors that underlie the drug problem are global in scope and implications, Mexico correctly perceives that drug control policies must not rest exclusively on prosecution or repression. One of the most serious obstacles to success in the fight against drugs at the global level is the fact that many societies do not share this perception.

Mexico's National Program for Drug Control

Programs to treat drug addiction and fight drug trafficking stand out among the Mexican government's initiatives to safeguard public health and defend national interests. These objectives have animated the government's antidrug efforts. In order to control the drug trade, the appropriate authorities must accurately identify the main problems that trafficking has generated in Mexico and evaluate the steps taken thus far to address those problems.

Policies, strategies, and proposals for fighting the drug industry must be rooted in the concept of integrality—that is, within a global perspective on a problem with many interrelated facets. Treating a single facet in isolation will not help resolve the larger problem.

In January 1992 the Mexican government presented its National Program for Drug Control, Evaluation, and Implementation, which set forth the policy, strategy, and action agenda that would guide the government's drug control activities. The National Program aimed to systematize the government's antidrug efforts by formulating integral, solid, and dynamic policies to promote law enforcement, public health, and education. It also sought to design complementary policies, prioritize tasks, coordinate resource utilization, and strengthen mechanisms for cooperation and collaboration at all levels of government.

The National Program also called for the development of dynamic and efficient strategies that involve participation by all levels of government and the population at large. By means of these strategies, the government hoped to build support for the creation of a common front, involving both civil society and government agencies, against the drug trade and drug abuse.

All Mexican government agencies involved in the struggle against drugs collaborated effectively in carrying out the National Program during 1992. The Planning Center for Drug Control (CENDRO), a decentralized office[2] under the authority of the attorney general, has strengthened coordination among the various agencies responsible for preventing drug abuse and controlling the drug trade within Mexico. It has assisted in developing measures against narcotics and psychotropic substances at the federal, state, and municipal levels by providing an integral perspective on the drug phenomenon and an ability to address the problem in a wide-ranging way. As the cornerstone of the policy of integrality, CENDRO is responsible for coordinating and bringing together all national efforts against the drug trade. Its executive council, headed by the commissioner of the National Institute to Combat Drugs, includes representatives from all public agencies involved in antidrug efforts—the Ministries of the Interior, Foreign Affairs, Defense, Treasury and Public Credit, Social Development, Agriculture and Water Resources, Communication and Transportation, Public Education, and Health, as well as the Navy and the Office of the Attorney General. The executive council is responsible for implementing the National Program for Drug Control.

---

[2] Editors' note: Technically, "decentralized" (*desconcentrado*) means that an agency delegates operational authority to the state and local levels while maintaining policy control at the national level.

The National Program for Drug Control has been implemented differently at the various levels of Mexico's public administration (federal, state, and municipal), depending upon each level's relative independence. While federal authorities are obliged to implement federal programs, state and local officials retain greater independence and must be induced or persuaded to do so, a process referred to as "coordination." Nongovernmental organizations have even greater independence, and thus their cooperation depends on "consensus building."

International Aspects of the Drug Problem

As mentioned above, the various manifestations of the drug phenomenon—production, consumption, trafficking, and other related crimes—are present in practically every country. In certain countries the drug industry has achieved dangerous levels of social and economic infiltration, and in some it has even penetrated the political system, with alarming consequences.

The countries that have been most attentive to these dangers have responded in various ways, depending on their respective traditions and circumstances. All of these responses, however, share certain hallmarks. These include the prevention of drug use and the treatment of drug addicts through programs designed to encourage educational opportunity and social participation; the interdiction of illicit drugs in transit; and the arrest and prosecution of those involved in drug- and gunrunning, especially the leaders of criminal organizations.

In designing policies, strategies, and other mechanisms to fight the drug trade, countries that entered the struggle relatively late have benefited greatly from the experience of those countries that preceded them. The latecomers have drawn lessons from both the successes and the missteps—conceptual, legal, functional, and administrative—of the pioneers. This learning process has been compressed into the five short years that followed the adoption in Vienna in December 1988 of the United Nations Convention Against Illicit Traffic in Narcotic Drugs and Psychotropic Substances.

Countries have tended to adopt one of three basic organizational models for fighting the drug war. Some have established a system of government-wide policy coordination under presidential supervision, with specific public agencies directly responsible for designing and implementing programs for preventing and treating drug abuse and for prosecuting drug-related criminal activities. Other countries have tried to improve their drug control efforts in a general way, but without establishing a special agency for coordinating policies and strategies at a government-wide level. In these cases, the absence of such an agency has resulted in a lack of coordination and efficiency. Still other countries have failed entirely to apply the decisions taken in Vienna regarding the prevention and treatment of drug abuse. They have strengthened only their prosecutorial abilities while neglecting the social, economic, and health aspects of the drug problem.

As we have seen, no single organizational model is appropriate for every country that faces a problem of such gravity and complexity. Mexico's own approach to the drug control problem rests upon a conceptual, organizational, and strategic framework clearly defined and characterized by the vision of integrality.

Evolution of Antidrug Structures in Mexico

The Mexican government has worked steadily to modernize the public agencies responsible for antidrug operations and improve their efficiency and adherence to legality. To this end, on August 9, 1985, the government amended the law governing the Office of the Attorney General in order to create the General Supervisory Board of Technical and Criminological Services, charged with coordinating, supervising, and directing Mexico's ongoing campaign against the drug trade.

By the end of the 1980s, the Mexican government had focused its modernizing efforts on three aspects of the antidrug struggle: the legal and penal systems, social participation in antidrug efforts, and regional development and eradication of drug production and trafficking. During the early years of the Salinas presidency, these efforts resulted in better coordination among the different levels of government and between government and civil society for the purpose of creating a "national front" against drugs.

Additional institutional changes to improve the government's antidrug efforts included the establishment in December 1988 of the Office of the Assistant Attorney General for Research and Operations against Drug Trafficking. The government redirected its efforts in 1990, establishing within the Office of the Attorney General the General Coordinating Committee for Attention to Crimes against Health. This new office was responsible for policy coordination on matters of drug abuse, production, and trafficking, as well as prevention, education, medical care, and criminal prosecution. The General Coordinating Committee also assumed the duty of helping the Federal Public Ministry investigate drug-related criminal activities.

As noted above, President Salinas decreed the establishment of CENDRO, in June 1992, as a new organization responsible for planning effective antidrug operations. CENDRO has fostered an integral understanding of the drug phenomenon and encouraged antidrug programs and activities through various coordinating mechanisms at the federal, state, and local levels. These mechanisms have been both public and private, domestic and international.

On June 16, 1993, the government created the National Institute to Combat Drugs to serve as a decentralized organization under the authority of the attorney general. The institute's goals included the planning, execution, supervision, and evaluation of national-level actions to fight the drug problem. It was jointly responsible with other relevant public agencies for protecting the health of the Mexican people, within the policies and guidelines established by the attorney general.

The new institute was to design and develop the most effective strategies and actions for prosecuting crimes against public health (including such related crimes as gunrunning and money laundering) and the criminal enterprises that engage in such activities. It would gather intelligence by means of aerial, maritime, and land-based interception activities, and assist the Federal Public Ministry in investigating and prosecuting drug-related crimes. It would operate the Statistical System for Drug Control, strengthen mechanisms for cooperation and coordination at all levels of government, and foster interinstitutional co-responsibility in fighting drugs. Finally, it received authorization from the Federal Public Ministry to participate in antidrug police operations, especially the detection, arrest, and prosecution of criminal individuals and organizations.

The institute would take part in specialized agencies of the United Nations and the Organization of American States, as well as other multilateral organizations engaged in drug-related work. It would also work with Mexico's Foreign Ministry to advocate the adoption and implementation of bilateral, multilateral, or regional cooperation agreements.

In all of these different ways, the Mexican government has shown constant readiness to modernize, professionalize, and make more efficient the governmental structures responsible for controlling drugs.

Drug Control in Mexican–U.S. Relations

Mexico and the United States are collaborating actively in the antidrug fight, as shown by their joint adherence—along with the other Western Hemisphere countries—to the concept of hemispheric information. One consequence of this multilateral cooperation has been the establishment of the Hemispheric Information System for Drug Control (SHICOD), which serves as a hemisphere-level intelligence network for fighting drug trafficking. The United States has shown its cooperation mainly by exchanging experiences with the Mexican government and supporting its wide-ranging drug prevention activities.

The cooperative spirit that today characterizes Mexican–U.S. relations also animates the joint efforts of these two countries to fight the drug trade. Speaking on June 21, 1993, Mexican foreign minister Fernando Solana described these relations as follows:

> Mexico is convinced that the new relationship between our two countries, under the leadership of Presidents Carlos Salinas de Gortari and Bill Clinton, is achieving exceptionally high levels of cooperation. Together we are building new bridges of understanding in order to resolve our problems and differences through negotiation, in a context of mutual respect and taking advantage of the great potential for economic and cultural complementarity.

For his part, President Clinton remarked on the same date to a Mexican delegation attending the Tenth Binational Mexico–United States Meeting that relations between Mexico and the United States are closer than those between any other two nations.

U.S.–Mexican cooperation in the antidrug struggle rests upon an institutional foundation that is solid, objective, and freighted with enormous positive potential. An important step forward was the Mexican–U.S. Agreement on Cooperation in Fighting Drug Trafficking and Drug Dependency, signed on February 22, 1989. This agreement set forth the basic concepts and aspirations of both nations regarding drug control. An integral scope informs this agreement's perspective on the drug problem, just as it characterizes Mexico's domestic policies regarding drugs and the numerous drug-related initiatives that Mexico has advanced in international forums.

This agreement illustrates most clearly the recognition that the drug problem demands an integral solution. One provision emphasizes the values of security, cooperation, self-determination, nonintervention, legal equality, and respect for the territorial integrity of states. Additionally, another states that the agreement

> does not give the authorities of one of the countries the right to undertake, within the territorial jurisdiction of the other, the exercise and discharge of those functions the jurisdiction or competence for which are reserved by national laws or rules exclusively to the authorities of that other country.

The accord emphasizes the joint responsibility of both countries to carry out specific programs to fight drug trafficking and addiction.

Mexico has held that the drug-trafficking problem is driven mainly by mounting levels of drug consumption. Empirical evidence indicates that the United States has the fastest growing internal demand for drugs.[3] The binational agreement thus emphasizes programs of prevention, treatment, and public awareness intended to reduce demand for illicit narcotics and psychotropic substances. On the supply side, the accord recommends programs to eradicate illicit drug crops and foster alternative crop development. The document reflects the spirit of good neighborliness and cooperation, as shown in the expressed determination of both countries to consult in advance regarding any activity by one of them that might negatively affect the interests of the other, thereby undermining the agreement's objective and purpose.

Drugs and U.S.–Mexican National Security

Mexicans regard national security as a fundamental precondition for peace, freedom, and social justice. The government and civil society secure these values within the framework of law, guaranteeing the viability of the national project. The defense of Mexico's national security implies a dynamic equilibrium among national objectives, one that preserves the nation's territorial integrity and the full exercise of sovereignty and independence.

Mexico views national security as an indispensable precondition for the preservation of sovereign order both within national borders and in the sphere of international relations. In the internal sphere, preservation of national security demands strict adherence to the state of law and to specific constitutional laws, with constant attention to concertation, consensus, and full respect for human rights. Mexico preserves its national security in the external sphere by acting in accordance with its most basic constitutional principles, especially the self-determination of peoples, nonintervention in the internal affairs of other countries, peaceful resolution of conflicts, the legal equality of all states, international cooperation for development, prohibition of the threat or use of force, and the struggle for peace and international security.

Drug traffickers assault the health of the inhabitants of countries they use as transit points by fostering drug production and consumption there. They undermine the territorial integrity and national security of these countries by illegally shipping drugs through them by

---

[3] See the *International Narcotics Control Strategy Report*, U.S. Department of State, April 1994.

air, sea, and land routes. Drug traffickers also promote destabilization, weaken societal ethics, and gravely violate national laws by conducting money laundering operations, trading illegally in weapons and precursor chemicals, and using their abundant drug proceeds to foment corruption in various social spheres. In sum, drug traffickers assault national security in a variety of ways.

For Mexico, the fight against the drug trade is a top national security priority. Drug trafficking has occasionally complicated Mexico's external relations by generating frictions with other countries in ways that can degrade mutual understanding and cooperation. The practice of the U.S. Congress of linking foreign assistance to annual certification by the U.S. State Department of each recipient country's antidrug commitment has prompted numerous complaints in Mexico. Although Mexico recognizes the sovereign right of the United States to issue opinions on domestic matters, it believes that the annual certification procedure has damaged international cooperation by serving as a prominent forum for criticizing other governments.

Although the trafficking in drugs poses a clear threat to international harmony and cooperation, Mexico and the United States enjoy a special advantage in overcoming the difficulties posed by the huge illicit drug-trafficking industry. That advantage rests on their shared conviction that coordinated action can cut through the snares of the drug trade and neutralize its threats.

The Future of International Control Operations

Recent experience has shown that no single country, acting alone, can neutralize the drug trade. Only a perfectly concerted, multinational, and many-sided effort can successfully confront the criminal drug-trafficking organizations which together constitute a transnational business empire worth some $500 billion annually.[4]

For the same reason, no government can risk postponing the development and improvement of its drug-fighting strategies. Participants in several recent international meetings on the topic have called for greater creativity in developing new antidrug strategies that respond directly to the challenges posed by drug traffickers. In order to confront these challenges effectively, governments should maintain existing antidrug legislation and improve the professionalism and effectiveness of judicial proceedings. National governments should implement the drug control recommendations of international organi-

[4] This estimate is based on information contained in the annual statistical report of the U.S. National Narcotics Intelligence Consumers Committee (NNICC).

zations in a consensual and coordinated way, taking care to respect the sovereignty of states and national laws.

An objective analysis of the drug control policies of Mexico and the United States indicates that both countries are moving steadily closer in their perception of the problem and their choice of methods to address it. Mexican–U.S. cooperation in confronting a problem of such transnational magnitude will constitute one of the most powerful fronts that has ever been established for fighting the drug menace.

This binational cooperation rests on the solid conviction, shared by the peoples and governments of both countries, that there is an urgent, inescapable need to defend themselves against an aggressor that endangers such fundamental values as life, health, development, national security, and human excellence. Virtually all countries of the world share these attitudes and priorities. Mexican–U.S. cooperation can help to stimulate similar collaboration at the global level, which would sound the death knell of the drug scourge.

The experience and understanding that countries such as Mexico and the United States have acquired in fighting the drug trade constitute the most effective instruments for waging this struggle at the global level. Their effectiveness depends upon international solidarity and cooperation, and upon the use of creativity and imagination.

Drug traffickers have tremendous economic clout, which allows them constantly to improve their methods and equipment. The defensive efforts of society must outpace, not lag behind, the aggressive actions of the drug barons. Success in this struggle, which embraces complex causes and damaging results, hinges largely upon intelligence gathering. Thus a thoughtful public discussion of the role of intelligence in law enforcement is of fundamental importance.

8

Intelligence Services and the Transition to Democracy in Mexico

Sergio Aguayo Quezada

We know little—almost nothing—about the Mexican intelligence services. This ignorance is not only absurd but dangerous, since what the intelligence services do or fail to do has tremendous importance. With this consideration in mind I will discuss the role of Mexico's intelligence services in the country's democratic transition, taking as my point of departure the following premise: if Mexico is to establish an authentic democratic system, its institutions and laws must be nourished by a democratic culture. Consequently, Mexico's intelligence services must "democratize themselves."

What Are the Intelligence Services?

The intelligence services of any country have close ties to the security apparatus. Both find their raison d'être in the possible rise of domestic or external threats to national security. To confront these threats, governments—which monopolize the legitimate use of violence—establish institutions with the special mission of defending national security. Some of these institutions—such as the army—specialize in the use of force, while others engage in what is known as "intelligence gathering." I use this rather schematic separation of functions for purely analytical purposes, since in reality the line of demarcation is not sharp: the armed forces have their own intelligence services, and some intelligence services have operational functions.

The research for this chapter was funded by a "research and writing" grant from the John D. and Catherine T. MacArthur Foundation.

The intelligence services have the mission of gathering huge amounts of information. Once processed, this information allows governments to anticipate and understand the magnitude, characteristics, and origins of national security threats. Government officials who must make decisions—especially regarding the use of violence by the security apparatus—rely heavily on the documents containing this information (that is, "intelligence").

The goals, working materials, and procedures of intelligence services present society with a very serious dilemma: these agencies are necessary to defend national security, but in accumulating power they can become extremely dangerous security threats (see Twentieth Century Fund 1992). To be effective, these agencies must operate in the shadows. Their secrecy affords them a wide margin of discretion that is subject to abuse, especially in view of the privileged information to which these agencies have access. Information is power, and its uncontrolled use can harm either individuals or society as a whole. That risk increases when the intelligence services have operational capability (that is, when they include units with expertise in using violence to answer threats).

That risk is higher still under totalitarian or authoritarian regimes in which the governmental apparatus can act with considerable impunity and in which security and intelligence agencies are responsible for controlling the population. In these cases the intelligence services render obedience and loyalty to the rulers, who in return provide them with often excessive power and perquisites. Although these intelligence agencies might serve the ruler effectively, they also degrade themselves by becoming little more than protectors of the interests of a tiny elite that violates the rights of citizens—especially those who dare to disagree.

These risks are also present in modern political democracies but not nearly to the same extent, since intelligence services are organized and carry out their activities in accordance with increasingly clear legal and administrative rules. The experience of recent decades testifies that these democracies have come close to striking a balance between efficiency, on the one hand, and checks on the potential abuse of power on the other. This achievement has helped to strengthen (or in some cases to restore) the social legitimacy of these institutions.

Tensions between efficiency and control tend to arise when governments establish criteria for identifying threats to national security, the actors that perpetrate those threats, and the methods for fighting them. The definition of such criteria is neither easy nor straightforward. One must ask difficult questions: Under what circumstances, for instance, can one legitimately spy on a political party or an opposition leader? Where does one draw the line between licit monitoring and illicit spying? How much ought society to know about the intelligence services? Since it is not easy to establish clear criteria, rulers tend to keep intentionally vague the terms of reference governing the activities of their intelligence services.

With these potential dangers in mind I have reviewed the literature on the intelligence services in various countries (Canada, the United States, Germany, Spain, Italy, Britain, and Israel, among others) and identified six requirements that these services should satisfy in order to reconcile efficiency with respect for human rights. Some of the following observations also apply to the security apparatus.

First and most important, social mechanisms of supervision and control must be established. As society's representative, the legislative and judicial branches of government are responsible for designing, approving, and implementing these mechanisms. Experience shows that this supervision and control are most needed at two highly sensitive moments: when these agencies seek congressional authorization of their budgets, and when they request the necessary legislative approval of operations affecting the rights of citizens or the sovereignty of other countries (such as telephone eavesdropping or covert actions that promote destabilization).

Second, the intelligence-gathering and operational functions of these agencies must be kept separate. The institution that produces intelligence must not also be responsible for confronting security threats in practice.

Third, the agencies responsible for foreign and domestic intelligence must be kept distinct in order to limit the concentration of power and promote specialization.

Fourth, mechanisms and coordinating agencies must be established to limit the search for independence so characteristic of the intelligence (and security) institutions. The tendency of these agencies to amass unchecked power often undermines their efficiency.

Fifth, the intelligence services should have career personnel. Specialization and professionalism improve the quality of intelligence and strengthen the principle that these agencies serve the state and nation rather than the incumbent government or ruler. (Obviously this distinction is meaningful only if the possibility of alternation in power exists.)

Finally, it will always be possible for intelligence services to abuse their power and violate citizens' rights. When such abuses occur, the victims must have access to the necessary institutions and legal means for self-defense.

Although these criteria are clearly insufficient for resolving every problem that might arise, I believe they provide a framework for guaranteeing that intelligence services fulfill the difficult task of being both effective and respectful of citizen rights. They constitute an ideal for all countries that have an intelligence apparatus.

Intelligence Services at the Moment of Transition

The movement of totalitarian or authoritarian regimes toward democracy provides the most common reference point for discussions of political transitions. This assumption is not quite valid when applied to the intelligence services, as will be shown by a review of some countries that are formally democratic according to the criteria set forth at the end of the previous section.

I shall begin with the United States, which has always been regarded as democratic and boasts some of the world's most famous and closely studied intelligence services. The history of the Central Intelligence Agency (CIA) illustrates how inadequately these services have satisfied the aforementioned criteria.[1] Between 1947 (when the CIA was established) and the early 1970s, neither the U.S. Congress, nor the news media, nor society in general made serious efforts to monitor the CIA's activities. The cold war atmosphere encouraged these actors to give the executive a "blank check" to manage the powerful intelligence services at its discretion, thereby violating a key requirement for the operation of such services under democratic auspices. The CIA took advantage of this discretion to abuse its mandate.

As CIA-related scandals mounted during the 1960s, both Congress and society began to reconsider their indifference. In 1975 and 1976 they subjected the CIA to minute examination—society did so through the news media and Congress by means of the famous Senate select committee headed by Senator Frank Church. These investigations led to the imposition of controls on the CIA and other intelligence agencies. Supervision of the CIA by Congress and society during the ensuing twenty years has confirmed the compatibility of efficiency with controls to prevent abuses of power. In fact, the CIA's evolution shows that the efficiency of intelligence services depends less upon the impunity that they have heretofore enjoyed than on other factors, especially the skills and professionalism of their personnel. Recruitment of the best minds depends largely upon the legitimacy and prestige that these institutions command.

During these same years the United States enriched the world's political lexicon with the suffix "gate" (deriving from "Watergate," the famous U.S. case of political espionage), which has since become synonymous with espionage against opposition political parties. Although the CIA was not formally involved in the break-in by officials of President Nixon's re-election committee at Democratic Party headquarters in the Watergate Hotel, that building became emblematic of the excesses to which intelligence services are prone.

---

[1] Two works that were especially useful were Ranelagh 1987 and Smist 1990.

The U.S. experience is not unique. Most industrialized countries have imposed restrictions on their intelligence services, sometimes in the wake of similar political espionage scandals. Legislatures in Germany, Spain, and Italy have established committees or commissions to supervise their respective intelligence services. Great Britain has provided a widely noted model in its Security Service Commission, which reports annually to the prime minister, who in turn reports to Parliament. This commission is complemented by a parallel tribunal of three to five lawyers named by the Crown to hear complaints from citizens who believe that they have been victimized by the intelligence services (this tribunal acts as a sort of specialized ombudsman).

Canada has one of the most extensively monitored intelligence services of any developed country. The Canadian Security and Intelligence Service is supervised by the Security Intelligence Review Committee, composed of members of the Queen's Council, who report to the legislature although they are not members of it (see CSIS 1992). Among Western democracies Israel is an exception—its intelligence agencies are subject to no parliamentary oversight whatsoever, due to the militarization of Israeli society.

These industrialized countries have "democratized" their intelligence services in the sense in which I have used the term. Unfortunately, we lack sufficient information about the possible role of intelligence services in the democratic transitions of totalitarian or authoritarian countries. One finds in the relevant scholarly literature only passing and inadequate references to the role played by the intelligence apparatus; the role of the armed forces tends to receive far more attention.[2]

This omission must be remedied, since the intelligence forces are highly relevant to the democratization process. If we apply the above-mentioned criteria to the Southern Cone, for instance, the available information indicates that recent democratic transitions there have been incomplete. Although the Southern Cone countries have held credible elections and established alternation in power, their intelligence services—and their security apparatuses—face no supervision or control.

Although the armed forces of Argentina, Uruguay, and Chile handed over power to civilian successors, they retained control over the intelligence services. Perhaps this sort of concession was inevitable due to pragmatic considerations and to the fact—let us not for-

[2]With the help of Marisa Studer, I searched the U.S. Library of Congress and several specialized documentation centers and found that little has been written about the role of intelligence services in democratic transitions. For example, one article on democratic transitions mentions these agencies only in passing (Stepan 1990). On the role of intelligence services in the Eastern European transitions, see Kinzer 1992; Sturdza 1991; Oltay 1991. For the Chilean case, see Programa 1992.

get—that the armed forces controlled the intelligence services of these countries even before the coups d'état that brought them to power in the 1960s and 1970s. This situation leaves open the possibility of a return to authoritarianism, as we have been reminded by the threats sent by the head of the Chilean armed forces, General Augusto Pinochet, on July 24, 1995.[3]

Every military institution has its own intelligence service, the social supervision of which should be discussed within the framework of civil-military relations. Consequently, my discussion will focus on the civilian intelligence services.

Of the three Southern Cone countries mentioned above, Chile is the only one that has tried to assert civilian control over its intelligence services. Small armed insurgent groups remained active in Chile following the election in 1990 of Patricio Aylwin as the country's first freely chosen president in twenty years. At that time, discussion of the intelligence services centered on how these agencies could more effectively repress the insurgents. The focus of discussion shifted in 1991, however, when it was learned that a Chilean intelligence agency was spying upon an opposition political party, the Independent Democrat Union (UDI).

As in other countries that experienced similar abuses, Chileans began to discuss the need to oversee the intelligence agencies. At the center of debate was a proposal by President Aylwin to establish a Subministry for Public Security and Information within the Interior Ministry that would coordinate the various services and establish a relationship with the legislature.[4] Aylwin's proposal made sense in view of General Augusto Pinochet's influence over the army, which constituted an ongoing challenge to Chilean democracy. The attempt to subject the intelligence services to Interior Ministry control indicated that Chile was still struggling to become a modern political democracy.

Similar patterns have emerged in some Eastern European countries. Even after the fall of communism in Hungary, the former regime's intelligence agencies remained virtually intact. Effective civilian controls began to be imposed only after it was revealed that the State Security Service (AVSZ) was spying on opposition political groups (the so-called Dunagate scandal). In Romania the former communist regime's feared Securitate agency transformed itself into the Romanian Intelligence Service (RIS) but continued to employ some of its traditional methods and even personnel. In May 1991 a group of journalists from *Romania Libera* discovered tons of docu-

---

[3]Pinochet said to the defense minister in relation to the conviction of General Manuel Contreras: "Minister, you know we don't want to stage another coup d'état, so don't force us to do so" (quoted in Rosenberg 1995).

[4]Particularly useful in examining the Chilean case is Rojas Aravena 1992.

ments hidden in the Berevoesti forest that implicated the RIS in espionage against political parties. The resulting scandal touched the highest levels of the RIS leadership and forced a fundamental restructuring of the security service (Oltay 1991; Sturdza 1991).

Thus the intelligence services of former totalitarian and authoritarian regimes in several countries have remained active following transitions to democracy, conducting political espionage against opponents with impunity. These activities were formally forbidden following the establishment of democracy, but they were not necessarily stopped.

These cases show two other common features. First, the independent news media play a central role in each case, which is entirely logical given the importance of independent communications media in a democracy. Second, as democratization extends and deepens itself, it becomes more possible to establish controls on the intelligence services. In my opinion the degree to which society oversees these agencies provides an objective measure of the extent of democracy in societies emerging from authoritarian rule. Free and fair elections are an indispensable but insufficient ingredient of democracy.

These observations provide the context for discussing Mexico's intelligence services. This discussion rests upon the assumption that the country's history is projected in the evolution of these agencies. That is, during Mexico's most authoritarian years the intelligence services were nothing more than a political police that spied on and repressed any group or individual that dared to oppose the regime or even act in an independent manner. Once Mexico's political system began to change, the intelligence agencies also began a transformation that has not yet ended. Although it is hard to establish a precise chronology (since the country's transition has not yet concluded), 1985 can be taken as the watershed year.

Civilian Intelligence Services in Mexico before 1985

The closest thing to a civilian intelligence service in Mexico is the Federal Security Directorate (DFS), established in 1947 by President Miguel Alemán. In its creation and functioning the DFS reflects the presidentialism and authoritarianism of the Mexican political system. President Alemán decreed its creation without consulting Congress. Moreover, although the DFS comes under the formal jurisdiction of the Interior Ministry, in reality—and in accordance with the logic of presidentialism—it has obeyed and reported directly to the president.

From its creation until its dissolution in 1985 the DFS never reported to or received oversight from Congress or society. Its main activities have involved operations rather than the processing of intelligence. Violence was one of its favorite methods, and its main hiring criterion was personal loyalty to the chief, which in the absence of clear guidelines encouraged illegality and abuse of authority.

The DFS was never a proper "intelligence" service. Instead, it served as an instrument for controlling the population. In fulfilling its mandate it flouted legality and legitimacy, as became clear during the counterinsurgency campaigns of the late 1960s and early 1970s when the regime strove without legal or ethical compunction to annihilate the urban guerrillas. (The armed forces waged war against the rural guerrillas.) I maintain that the freedom granted the DFS to operate against the guerrillas with impunity contributed to the agency's degradation. There follow some examples that illustrate this relationship between impunity and degradation.

When antigovernment guerrilla movements arose during the early 1970s in the Mexican state of Jalisco, the federal government relied mainly on the DFS to suppress the insurgents. To carry out this mission the DFS made use of student "shock troops" that were already active in Guadalajara (the capital of Jalisco), transforming them into paramilitary organizations responsible for extra-judicially pursuing, capturing, and executing the guerrillas. Although the term was rarely used, these groups were in fact death squads that acted with impunity.

At the same time, although for different reasons, drug traffickers began to expand both their drug production in Mexico and their delivery of drugs through that country. Following the Mexican army's launching of Operation Condor against drug trafficking in northern Mexico and the U.S. government's decision to clamp down on Caribbean transshipments of Colombian cocaine, international and domestic drug traffickers chose Guadalajara as their main operational base in Mexico. This city offered a temperate climate, an excellent geographic location, the necessary police protection, and a long-standing culture of violence that guaranteed a constant flow of recruits into the drug traffickers' armies.

The death squads mentioned above—along with other social and governmental groups—became involved in the restructuring of Jalisco's economic life, combining their counterinsurgency activities with participation in the state's flourishing drug industry. Recovered legal documents and interviews with well-informed sources indicate a growing association among these groups, the security forces, and the drug traffickers. The role of the DFS in this triangular structure was to protect leading drug traffickers and garner economic benefits while sponsoring death squad activity and liquidating the guerrillas, whose military preparation was highly deficient despite their high morale. In this way, the behavior of Mexico's main civilian intelligence service facilitated the arrival of the international drug trade to Guadalajara.

This complicity between the DFS and drug traffickers grew to unprecedented levels after the counterinsurgency campaign ended. The problem festered until 1985, when it reached crisis proportions. In February of that year, Mexican drug traffickers in Guadalajara kidnapped and killed Enrique Camarena Salazar, a U.S. Drug Enforcement Administration agent, and his Mexican pilot. Soon thereafter it became known that the DFS and other Mexican police forces were protecting the drug lords. Anger in Washington rose to unprecedented heights, and diplomatic relations between the two countries were severely strained. Consequently, in late 1985 President Miguel de la Madrid ordered the abolition of the DFS in order both to free his government from a liability and to signal his intent to reform the intelligence organization. Two years later, in 1987, de la Madrid cited drug production and trafficking as the main threat to Mexico's national security, a position maintained by his two successors, Carlos Salinas de Gortari and Ernesto Zedillo.

An organization established to protect national security thus helped to foster the main threat to that very security. DFS directors believed that their agency should be free to act with impunity in order to defend the president and the nation against the guerrillas and other enemies. They believed that the risks they incurred (and their low salaries) fully justified the economic benefits that accrued to them in the line of duty. Knowing the attitude of these officials, we can better understand both the abuses they committed and their failure to generate the intelligence needed to anticipate the potential risks involved in drug trafficking. This way of thinking gave rise to several problems related to the "intelligence culture" and the way in which rulers and society understand intelligence (which in turn influences how intelligence is handled).

Throughout its existence the DFS was seen by successive presidents as an instrument for doing dirty work and gathering raw information, which the presidents or their advisers then processed. In other words, they kept very tight and personalized control over the DFS and other key organs of power, arguing that only they possessed a comprehensive understanding of security matters.

Mexico's presidents succeeded in keeping this power because the congress had renounced its right to oversee the intelligence services, thereby showing its political irrelevance. (It is indeed surprising that not one congressman asked the president in 1985 to explain why he had ordered the abolition of the DFS.) Most media either kept quiet or distorted all news about the armed movement and the governmental institutions that fought it, and they showed dangerous indifference to the gradual increase in drug trafficking and violence. By failing to monitor the activities of the intelligence services, the media and congress facilitated their abuse of power and the perversion of their true mission.

In sum, the state lacked societal controls, which is one of the hallmarks of authoritarianism. After 1985 the country and its intelligence services entered a period of transition in which their character and mission began to be reconsidered.

An Unfinished and Peculiar Transition

In order to understand the current condition of Mexico's intelligence services, we must recall that the country is undergoing a transformation characterized by three interacting variables. First, the liberalization and opening of the Mexican economy have unleashed dynamics that undermine political authoritarianism. Investors, for instance, demand the certainty that results from adherence to law. Internationalization of the political sphere has likewise accelerated. Various Mexican actors have begun to seek allies in other countries. Conversely, foreign actors have shown increasing interest in domestic Mexican affairs, especially with regard to human rights and democracy.

Second, the use of state violence by an authoritarian regime fosters fear, which facilitates control. The Mexican regime's use of coercion has been losing viability for several reasons, one of which is generational change within the ruling elite. (Although the new elite is not democratic, it recognizes pragmatically that Mexico's opening to the world has imposed limits on the use of state violence.) The regime's use of force is also inhibited by the metamorphosis that the Mexican military has undergone: although they have improved their professionalism and the quantity and quality of their weapons and technical equipment, they have also shown greater reluctance to use force against social groups that assert their independence from the regime.

Finally, the above-mentioned developments have facilitated the rise of new actors and strengthened existing ones. Despite their heterogeneity, these groups share the desire to assert their independence from the regime, strengthen democratic procedures, and broaden respect for human rights (Skocpol 1979).

These developments have changed Mexico, provoking a growing intolerance of state violence that has restricted the maneuvering room of the security and intelligence institutions. I will support this argument with some vignettes from the experience of Mexico's main intelligence service since 1985.

The killing of Camarena, U.S. pressures, and the abolition of the Federal Security Directorate combined to spark an intense debate within the Interior Ministry, with some officials urging the creation of a truly professional intelligence service. Although this proposal failed to win support from other political actors, who saw no need to change old habits that had served them well, it was partially adopted because the culture of intelligence had undergone a fundamental change. As problems facing the country increased exponentially in complexity, President Miguel de la Madrid decided to restructure the intelligence apparatus.

As frequently happens in bureaucratic battles, this one ended in a draw. At the end of 1985 the government announced the creation of the General Directorate of Investigation and National Security (DISEN), which combined in one agency the remnants of the DFS along with the General Directorate of Political and Social Investigation—a body which had previously been advanced as a possible nucleus for a new intelligence service within the Interior Ministry. This combination does not seem to have worked, due both to the shortcomings of the new agency's director, Pedro Vásquez Colmenares, and to the admixture of operational and intelligence functions within a single agency. Its unworkability became apparent in 1988 when, according to well-informed sources, the DISEN failed to anticipate or explain the impressive showing of the leftist opposition in that year's presidential election.

Subsequent developments have confirmed this judgment. One of the first acts of President Salinas was to abolish the DISEN and replace it with the Center for Investigation and National Security (CISEN). The president decreed that the CISEN would be the federal agency responsible for "establishing and operating an investigative and information system for the country's security" (*Diario Oficial*, December 8, 1988).

The CISEN represented the Mexican government's first serious attempt to create a genuine intelligence service, as became evident when the organization eliminated part of its operational capacity and began a systematic program of professionalization. Indications of the CISEN's commitment to professionalism included the high status of its first director, Jorge Carrillo Olea, and the formation of a National Security Cabinet (with the CISEN director serving as its technical secretary). This cabinet had only limited success in coordinating the various institutions that together constituted a "community" characterized by divisions and disputes over areas of responsibility.

Two years later, in 1992, President Salinas removed Carrillo Olea from the directorship of the CISEN in order to put him in charge of federal antidrug policy. The director's transfer can be interpreted as a change in priorities: in his eagerness to fight the drug trade, the president deprived the CISEN of an effective and proven leader, thus weakening an institution that had not yet consolidated. The weakening of the CISEN became even more clear with the nomination of its second director, Fernando del Villar, who lacked the needed skills for directing an intelligence service. In naming a blindly loyal subordinate rather than a competent professional, Salinas demonstrated his failure to understand the central feature of an intelligence agency: it must serve the state rather than the government.

Information about the intelligence services of authoritarian regimes is usually scarce. Nevertheless, there is reliable evidence that by 1993 the CISEN had deteriorated. On June 13, 1993, Francisco Rodríguez published in the magazine *Siempre!* an internal CISEN memorandum that was highly critical of the organization. (Well-informed sources have confirmed the document's authenticity.) I present below the most relevant observations contained in this unusual document.

- Regarding the CISEN's organization, the document states that "some progress was made between 1989 and 1990, but now we see considerable backsliding due to ignorance of defined methods and norms, giving way once again to disorder and improvisation. General activity is now ruled by a disorderly conjunction of empiricism, improvisation, customs, and even prejudices, especially in the area of investigation."

- Regarding the CISEN's reporting, the document asserts that "the coverage of the investigatory apparatus is superficial. . . . It does not produce enough information to permit predictions of where events are likely to lead. In most cases, information is obtained mainly from the open communications media: written press, radio, and television. . . . Basic weaknesses of the primary reports include irrelevance, incomplete and insufficient information, poor editing, and lateness."

- Regarding the CISEN's activities, the document adds that "the Center for Investigation and National Security inherited some operational functions from the Federal Security Directorate." CISEN was also given responsibility for "the surveillance of mail and individuals, and the identification of foreign intelligence services and agents in Mexico," as well as for intercepting "telephone communications."

- Regarding the CISEN's use of resources, the document notes that "budgetary controls assigned to the state delegations are applied selectively, with the most important resources going to delegates who have the best political connections to the leadership."

This description of the CISEN does not reflect the efficiency that one expects from an intelligence service. Moreover, it illustrates the violation of principles that govern democratic societies. As of mid-1993 the CISEN was beset by disorganization, superficiality, and low morale, and some of its operational activities were illegal and prejudicial of the rights of Mexican citizens. The CISEN had come to resemble the typical intelligence service of an authoritarian regime.

Among the first victims of the indigenous rebellion that erupted in Chiapas on January 1, 1994, were the interior minister and the director of the CISEN, both of whom the president dismissed and replaced with officials having rather different career profiles. Jorge Carpizo, the new interior minister, assumed his duties with the intention of undertaking political reform. Carpizo named as the new CISEN director an intelligence professional who again took up the task of creating a professional service.

During the first months of 1994, some commentators suggested repeatedly that the intelligence systems had failed in Chiapas. This judgment would be correct if the standard for measuring success were the CISEN's ability to anticipate the rebellion. From the standpoint of society's long-term interests, however, the CISEN's real failure consisted in the absence of close supervision of it by the news media, the legislature, and social groups. Taking that perspective, we should not bemoan the CISEN's failure but instead be grateful for its inefficiency. The admixture of impunity and efficiency could have devastating consequences for Mexico's democratic transition.

Indifference and an inability to understand the real social dilemma posed by the CISEN and other security and intelligence agencies become especially worrisome when we consider the opposition parties. In previous pages I made reference to some countries in which political espionage unleashed scandals that resulted in the imposition of more extensive controls on the intelligence services. Nothing of the sort has taken place in Mexico. Despite the country's emerging pro-democratic consensus, the opposition political parties have not thought it necessary to include the intelligence services on their reform agendas.

"Morelia-gate" provides the clearest and most recent example of this indifference. In March 1992 the national leadership of the National Action Party (PAN) discovered that the party had become the victim of political espionage in Morelia, for which it correctly blamed the CISEN.[5] In the wake of the ensuing public scandal, some congressmen vowed that Congress would pass legislation on this subject. More than two years later, however, the situation remained unre-

[5]My affirmation that members of CISEN were responsible for the espionage relies on the internal CISEN document cited above, which states that the "infiltration of the sources has been greatly reduced since the incident with National Action in Morelia."

solved. The material authors of the espionage had been fined the equivalent of less than one U.S. dollar, and the congress had yet to pass any legislation directed specifically toward the intelligence services.

Why did "Morelia-gate" not provoke in Mexico a reaction similar to those that arose in response to espionage scandals in the United States, Chile, Hungary, or Romania? There are several possible explanations. In the first place, Mexico's rulers have used force more selectively than have other governments, and thus the CISEN and Mexico's other intelligence and security services lacked the visibility of similar organizations in other countries (Romania's Securitate, for example). Another reason had to do with the ignorance and impotence of most of the nation's congressmen, who lacked technical knowledge of the real functions of an intelligence service and seem to have assumed and interiorized their own irrelevance and submission to the president's dictates.

In gradual transitions—those in which the old regime does not collapse suddenly—priority is given to the establishment of alternation in power. The opposition appears to assume that its victory will inevitably be followed by systemic reforms that at some point will touch the intelligence services. In holding this expectation, the pragmatic aspirants to political office evade a problem that they find particularly difficult and complicated. Such contenders fail to understand that in leaving these services free of restraints, they leave the democratic transition unfinished and vulnerable.

A final consideration involves what the intelligence and security services have both done and failed to do during 1994, one of the most tumultuous and important years in Mexican history. During that year the CISEN fulfilled its responsibility to provide intelligence to the president and the interior minister. Nevertheless, there is no evidence that it harassed pro-democratic activists in the context of the Chiapas rebellion. The agency's circumspect stance was in large measure voluntary and responded in part to the constraints posed by the tremendous changes that have transformed Mexican society. That is, the transformation of bureaucratic institutions, the impact of international actors, and the rise of new social forces have all undermined the viability of violence and coercion as instruments of policy. The interaction of these variables also makes democratization in Mexico possible, although many challenges and uncertainties remain.

Conclusion

At the time of this writing (October 1995), President Zedillo had already changed his initial choice for interior minister. The fact that the mandates of the CISEN's directors have been renewed despite this change, together with the other important transformations already described, allows us to make some moderately and cautiously optimistic final observations about the possibility of further "democratizing" of the intelligence services.

The state needs professional intelligence services. Recent profound changes in Mexico's society and environment have enormously complicated the country's security agenda. It is essential for the country—not the ruling party—to have the ability to *interpret* these changes correctly and *anticipate* threats. To the extent that the nation sees itself reflected in the government (that is, to the extent that Mexico undergoes democratization), it will require increasingly sophisticated intelligence analysis, which in turn depends upon scarce and highly specialized human resources. The CISEN's ability to obtain these human resources does not hinge entirely on its financial means, which it has in abundance—its employees are among the best paid in the federal bureaucracy.

The experience of other countries testifies that the attractiveness of an intelligence career depends upon the perceived legitimacy, legality, and (relative) transparency of the agency's work. For example, the CIA's positive public image helps to explain its ongoing ability to attract promising university graduates. When the legality and legitimacy of its actions came into question during the 1970s, it had to suspend its traditional recruitment campaigns on college campuses.

A prevailing impression is that those who are aware of the CISEN's existence regard it as a police entity involved mainly in political espionage. Public opinion surveys indicate that the police are among the least trusted institutions in Mexico. (According to one such survey, only 12 percent of Mexicans trust the police [Basáñez 1991: 5].) If the CISEN is to win popular trust and professionalize itself, it must strengthen its legitimacy through a process of "democratization."

Another equally important development—and one that allows us to advance some observations from another angle—has to do with a silent revolution within the security and intelligence services. These organizations have changed, but society has not yet realized it. A very clear example is provided by the armed forces, which have abjured their former role of repressing popular demonstrations. Since the early 1980s they have engaged in dialogue with civilians and officials from other public agencies. This interaction has broken the armed forces' isolation and moved them to resist any effort to use them for illegal purposes. So far, they have the weapons, but they have not the will to use them.

This liberalization coincided with the entry into these agencies of new employees with less authoritarian outlooks, which should not be surprising since it is consistent with society's slow parallel evolution. Various conversations have led me to conclude that some intelligence and security personnel have improved their understanding of independent and opposition sectors and of themselves and their mission in a democratic Mexico. Possibly as a result of these transformations, the Mexican security and intelligence agencies have adopted a relatively open attitude toward the Chiapas insurrection and the national elections of 1994, at least when compared with earlier periods.

These dynamics—which I have merely sketched in outline—could become stronger and accelerate if the opposition parties, media, and society come to understand the character and objectives of the security and intelligence institutions. The ability to advocate and exert pressure for the imposition of societal controls on these institutions depends upon such knowledge. That advocacy and pressure must now be directed toward the country's new legislature, which has to increase its interest in these issues. It would be absurd and dangerous to remain indifferent to institutions that are so central to the success of Mexico's democratization, which is the best foundation for real security. In the consolidation of these trends lies one of the key variables of Mexico's transition to democracy.

References

Basáñez, Miguel. 1991. "Encuesta Electoral 1991: en los laberintos por la democracia," *Este País* 5 (August): 2–6.

CSIS (Canadian Security Intelligence Service). 1992. *The Canadian Security Intelligence Service, Public Report 1991*. Ottawa.

Kinzer, Stephen. 1992. "East Germans Face Their Accusers," *New York Times Magazine*, April 12.

Oltay, Edith. 1991. "Hungary: Intelligence Services Burdened by Communist Legacy," *Report on Eastern Europe* 2 (19): 11–14.

Programa de Análisis Legislativo. 1992. "Tareas de Inteligencia para la Seguridad Interior," *Análisis de Actualidad*. Santiago de Chile.

Ranelagh, John. 1987. *The Agency: The Rise and Decline of the CIA*. New York: Simon and Schuster.

Rojas Aravena, Francisco. 1992. "El debate sobre la seguridad interna: las tareas de inteligencia y su control democrático." Santiago de Chile. Manuscript.

Rosenberg, Tina. 1995. "Force Is Forever," *New York Times Magazine*, September 24.

Skocpol, Theda. 1979. *States and Social Revolutions*. New York: Cambridge University Press.

Smist, Frank J., Jr. 1990. *Congress Oversees the United States Intelligence Community, 1947–1989*. Knoxville: University of Tennessee Press.

Stepan, Alfred. 1990. "On the Tasks of a Democratic Opposition," *Journal of Democracy* 1 (2): 41–49.

Sturdza, Mihai. 1991. "Romania: The Files of the State Security Police," *Report on Eastern Europe* 2 (37): 22–31.

Twentieth Century Fund. 1992. *The Need to Know: The Report of the Twentieth Century Fund Task Force on Covert Action and American Democracy*. New York: Twentieth Century Fund Press.

9

Law Enforcement and Intelligence in the Bilateral Security Context: U.S. Bureaucratic Dynamics

John Bailey

This chapter focuses on bureaucratic dynamics of U.S. agencies engaged in law enforcement and intelligence in U.S.–Mexican bilateral security relations. Especially important are organizational structures and cultures and the ways in which U.S. federal government agencies adapt their missions and reorient their behavior in radically new contexts. This subject is especially elusive at the time of this writing (winter 1996), due both to uncertainty following the historic watershed of the 1980s and to the Clinton administration's difficulties in formulating and implementing coherent policies in the areas of law enforcement and foreign affairs.

The notion of bureaucratic structure is straightforward: how does the internal organization of public agencies affect their implementation of policy? That is, the definition and distribution of tasks within and among agencies affect organizational behavior, including patterns of cooperation and conflict. Beyond structure, organizational culture is taken to mean "a persistent, patterned way of thinking about the central tasks of and human relationships within an organization" (Wilson 1989: 91). Structural and cultural factors in bureaucratic politics, which are given freer play by the decentralized, pluralistic nature of U.S. politics, require that government agencies cultivate clienteles, along with favorable public opinion and legislative support, in order to carry out their tasks. The significance of bureaucratic politics for U.S.–Mexican relations, including bilateral security relations, is too easily underestimated. Agencies often behave in ways that both Mexicans and Americans find difficult to comprehend. Misunderstanding, in turn, complicates ordinary problems of bilateral conflict.[1]

Bureaucratic politics is important to the overall U.S.–Mexican bilateral relationship due to a mix of institutional and conjunctural factors. First, the Clinton presidency has been especially weak, due to structural reasons (continuing party dealignment, end of cold war discipline, fiscal constraints, and pressures to downsize government and decentralize government programs) and performance (the perception of drift and indecision, recurring setbacks in policy-level personnel appointments). Second, the Republican resurgence in the Congress after November 1994 weakened presidential control over the executive branch and further politicized defense and law enforcement issues (Dobbs 1995). This has given the career bureaucracy more policy space in which to maneuver. But rather than independence or innovation, most career bureaucrats tend to adopt more cautious strategies in such a conflictive setting (see Lipmann 1995). Third, relations with Mexico (and Canada) are more intermestic than is the case with other countries; that is, they more closely touch on U.S. domestic issues and policy jurisdictions (such as environment, law enforcement, migration, interstate commerce, and the like). Thus Mexico-related issues are drawn into mainstream domestic policy debates and thence more deeply into bureaucratic maneuvering. Fourth, along with economic insecurity, U.S. public opinion is most preoccupied with crime and violence. The intermestic nature of the U.S.–Mexican relationship means that this preoccupation with personal security will influence, perhaps even dominate, the agenda with Mexico. Also, while trends in U.S. public opinion point toward a declining interest in foreign affairs, the most salient external concerns (including drugs, migration, employment, energy, trade) involve Mexico (Reilly 1995).

In this broad context, I shall briefly sketch the ways in which certain bureaucracies—particularly the Departments of State, Justice, and Defense, and the Central Intelligence Agency—appear to be redefining their missions in the bilateral relationship in the post–cold war context. The first section examines aspects of bureaucratic structure and behavior, especially the ways in which organizational structures and cultures affect interagency conflict and cooperation. The subsequent section describes the Clinton administration's efforts to link national security to broader concerns about law enforcement, democracy, and human rights, and the likely implications of this link-

---

[1] See, for example, Jorge Castañeda's fascinating discussion of the propensity of some well-informed Mexicans—even those who understand the complexity of U.S. bureaucracy and society—to construct conspiracy theories about U.S. actions (Pastor and Castañeda 1988: 60–72).

age for organizational dynamics in the bilateral relationship. The concluding section emphasizes that some aspects of bureaucratic politics will continue into the future because they reflect underlying institutional features (congressional oversight and problems of control and coordination, for example). On the other hand, some significant bureaucratic changes should be expected as the defense and intelligence communities shift from their cold war orientation toward greater attention to issues of law enforcement. Also, the downsizing of the federal government and the shift of functions to state and local levels would imply even greater challenges for bureaucratic coordination.

U.S. Agencies in Law Enforcement and Intelligence

As one might expect, bureaucratic involvement in U.S.–Mexican security relations is especially dense as a result of the two countries' extreme interdependence. In the area of drug control, the White House Office of National Drug Control Policy (ONDCP) attempts to coordinate some thirty federal agencies, each having its own legal mandate, constituency, and methods. Further, the experience of the last decade teaches that large, complex federal agencies are poorly suited in structural terms to oppose unconventional types of transnational crime.[2] It is also noteworthy that organizational culture, in the sense of patterned ways of thinking about tasks and human relationships, takes on meaning at the agency or even program level rather than at the departmental level. This cultural locus results largely from patterns of personnel recruitment and socialization. Unlike some continental systems, which promote government-wide mobility, career paths in U.S. federal agencies are more deeply rooted within specific agencies.[3]

---

[2] By unconventional, I mean crime that is more complex and sophisticated, and often more violent (such as large-scale narcotics trafficking, terrorism).

[3] For example, the Federal Bureau of Investigation and the Drug Enforcement Administration are separate agencies "within" the Justice Department; they compete and cooperate under rather loose oversight by the attorney general. The Border Patrol is a constituent agency of the Immigration and Naturalization Service, which in turn is an agency of the Justice Department. Agents are recruited and socialized by the agency; their career tracks are set by the agency, not the parent department. Apart from agencies, cultures typically vary across bureaus within the same department. With regard to networks, the State Department's consular officers, for example, typically develop their closest ties among themselves and feel distant from political officers, who in turn tend to see themselves as closer to the Department's main mission of diplomacy. An implication that cannot be developed here is that similar agencies in the United States and Mexico sometimes form working alliances against other cross-national coalitions; for example, DEA and Mexico's Federal Judicial Police may coop-

With regard to intelligence, drug control, and law enforcement, the agencies noted in table 1 are most significant at the federal level in U.S.–Mexican relations. The most important bureaucratic tensions in a structural sense are those that divide conventional defense and intelligence agencies from general-purpose law enforcement agencies, and these, in turn, from drug-specific units. The theme that emerges in the subsequent discussion is how defense and intelligence agencies are reorienting themselves to deal with new security challenges, primarily law enforcement, and how law enforcement agencies are accommodating themselves to this new setting.

Of the various actors identified in table 1, I shall briefly characterize the organizational structure and bureaucratic culture of State, Justice, Defense, and the CIA. I will also examine the ways in which the rethinking of U.S. security interests may affect the definition of ongoing agency tasks, as well as the implications of that redefinition for patterns of cooperation and conflict among agencies. These agencies have different but overlapping goals; they are thus organized in diverse ways and define tasks in different, often incompatible, ways. Furthermore, they face constraints of tight, even shrinking, budgets and heightened uncertainty.

Charged with the conduct of diplomacy, the State Department is a "coping" agency in the sense that it generates few concrete products but rather manages relations with other countries (Wilson 1989: 168–71). The Department's organizational logic divides tasks among various functional and geographic bureaus, each headed by an assistant secretary. The Department, and especially the "P" bureau headed by the undersecretary for political affairs (to which the geographic bureaus report), is the keeper of the "Big Picture" in foreign affairs. The Department's elite typically are career foreign service officers with trajectories through political assignments (although economic jobs might count too) primarily in the geographic bureaus (which control job assignments in the field and thus career mobility), and especially those concerned with Europe, the former Soviet Union, and East Asia. With respect to organizational culture, State recruits generalists and rewards skills of effective writing, speaking, and negotiation.

State's Bureau of International Narcotics Matters (INM) is the lead agency in formulating U.S. anti-narcotics policy overseas. As a functional (as opposed to geographic) bureau, INM provides police training and support services—especially air support—for anti-narcotics

---

erate against the State Department and Mexico's Foreign Ministry (SRE). Moreover, although State Department officials sometimes complain about SRE's assertive nationalism, SRE's insistence that Mexico's agencies must act through it can actually strengthen the State Department's hand in dealing with U.S. agencies. Finally, savvy Mexican officials typically manipulate to their advantage conflicts among U.S. agencies.

TABLE 1
U.S. FEDERAL LAW ENFORCEMENT AND INTELLIGENCE AGENCIES INVOLVED WITH MEXICO

Executive Office of President

National Security Council (NSC): General policy coordination in international security and foreign affairs

Office of National Drug Control Policy (ONDCP): General (domestic and foreign) coordination of antidrug programs

Department of State

Bureau of Political Affairs (P): Overall political analysis and coordination of diplomatic activities

Bureau of Inter-American Affairs (ARA): Political analysis and coordination of diplomacy in Latin America and the Caribbean

Consular Service: Visa services, citizen welfare, initial screening of visa applicants for criminal records or security concerns

International Narcotics Matters (INM): Foreign dimension of antidrug policy, support services (training, transportation)

Department of Justice

Drug Enforcement Administration (DEA): Foreign and domestic antidrug law enforcement

Federal Bureau of Investigation (FBI): Federal law enforcement, antiterrorism, counterespionage

Immigration and Naturalization Service (INS): Regulation of aliens at points of entry and within the United States

Border Patrol (within INS): Illegal migration, unlawful entry of criminals

Criminal Division: Prosecution of organized crime, extradition proceedings

Department of Treasury

Bureau of Alcohol, Tobacco, and Firearms (ATF): Priority to arms smuggling

Internal Revenue Service (IRS): Tax administration, money laundering

Secret Service: Currency counterfeiting, antiterrorism

U.S. Customs: Generic smuggling, illegal currency transfers at points of entry along U.S. borders

Financial Crimes Enforcement Center (FinCEN): Tracking of money laundering associated with drug trafficking

Department of Defense

Office of the Secretary of Defense: Undersecretary of Defense for Policy, Assistant Secretaries for International Security Affairs, Reserve Affairs; Coordinator for Drug Enforcement Policy and Support

Joint Chiefs of Staff: J3 (Operations), J5 (Policy), Defense Intelligence Agency

Unified commands: FORCESCOM (Continental United States), SOUTHCOM (Latin America from Panama south), LANTCOM (Atlantic Basin), PACCOM (Pacific Basin)

continued

<u>*Department of Transportation*</u>
U.S. Coast Guard: Coastal patrol, antismuggling, illegal migration

<u>*Central Intelligence Agency*</u>
Deputy Director for Intelligence: General intelligence analysis
Deputy Director for Operations: Active measures, espionage, counterespionage
Counter Narcotics Center: Interagency coordination of anti-narcotics intelligence and operations
Counter Terrorism Center: Interagency coordination of antiterrorist intelligence and operations

programs. Created in 1978, the Bureau inherited its police training functions from the Agency for International Development (AID) in the early 1970s, largely due to controversial charges that AID police training contributed to serious human rights abuses in various countries. INM inherited most of the U.S. trainers in the reorganization. The Bureau is a relatively small actor, employing 124 direct hires and operating with a budget of $110 million in fiscal year 1994.

As a functional bureau, INM is typically not the first choice of fast-track younger officers.[4] On the other hand, mid-career officers find the Bureau's anti-narcotics training and support programs attractive for providing the management experience they need in order to squeeze through the bottlenecks that restrict entry to upper ranks. In interagency negotiations, State typically labors to place anti-narcotics programs in the context of broader U.S. foreign policy goals. Its focus on cultivating good overall relations with specific governments sometimes opens it to charges of "clientitis," in which State may be seen to defend foreign interests. The issue of antidrug cooperation with Mexico frequently creates tensions within State between INM and the Bureau of Inter-American Affairs, and pits State (often with a reluctant INM) against other U.S. government agencies in the broader bureaucratic struggle. Thus the head of INM usually takes a harder line with respect to dealing with Mexico on antidrug issues than does the Office of Mexican Affairs, but the two entities work to show a united front in State's negotiations with other agencies.

The Justice Department is larger and more complicated than State and deals with matters that have put it at the center of more foreign and domestic controversies in recent years, among them the civil

[4] "Death by functional bureau" is how one interviewee put it, although INM assistant secretary Melvyn Levitsky apparently raised the bureau's visibility and prestige (author interview, May 1993). Robert Gelbard, Levitsky's successor, also has proved effective as INM chief in the Clinton administration.

rights struggles of the 1960s, Watergate in the 1970s, and Iran-Contra in the 1980s. Although trivial in comparison, the Clinton administration's initial setbacks in confirming nominees for high-level Justice posts and the criticisms leveled at former FBI director William Sessions fit long-standing patterns of controversy.[5] Structurally, the Justice Department contains both agencies and divisions, the latter operating under closer oversight from the attorney general. The agencies most involved in bilateral issues (DEA, FBI, Border Patrol) act with considerable internal freedom, even with respect to the Department's Criminal Division, which is one of eleven such divisions.[6]

Since its primary mission is law enforcement, Justice's elite officers are lawyers. Although they readily grasp the broader implications of antidrug programs for U.S. foreign policy goals, their mission and deep instinct by training is to build cases that can be successfully prosecuted in U.S. courts, where standards of evidence are especially precise and exacting. In interagency negotiations, Justice attorneys focus rigorously on legal interpretations and specific cases, and their adversarial style leads them less to negotiate with other agencies than to debate, particularly on specific points of law (author interviews, May 1993).

The Drug Enforcement Administration (DEA) was created in 1973, primarily from elements of its forerunners: the Bureau of Narcotics and Dangerous Drugs (in Justice), agents from the Customs Service (Treasury), and two lesser entities. DEA is organized internally by drug (heroin, cocaine, and so on), not by country or region, in order to combat transnational crime more effectively from source to sale. The agents in charge of regional and overseas DEA offices operate with considerable independence and power.[7] An obvious implication is that DEA agents do not focus on state-to-state political relations. Rather, DEA's "product" is arrests and drug seizures, which bring career status and rewards. DEA recruits primarily from "street cops" of proven ability and veterans of military service. There is something of a "macho" culture encouraged among the officers. Agents volun-

---

[5] Although the charges against former FBI director William Sessions seem inconsequential—for example, his alleged misuse of government services—it is significant that some senior career officers in the FBI appeared to oppose their political overseer.

[6] The FBI performs critical roles in law enforcement overseas and has long maintained an extensive presence in Mexico (see Ungar 1976: chap. 6, especially p. 234). The Border Patrol, which plays a central role in anti-narcotics matters, cannot be discussed due to space constraints.

[7] While the State Department's regional bureaus monitor U.S. ambassadors fairly closely, DEA agents in charge can and do dispute directives from Washington. "Think of these regional offices as McDonald's franchises. They operate pretty independently" (author interview, May 1993). Wilson (1978) emphasizes the gaps and conflicts between DEA agents, who live by their wits on the streets, and the political executives who manage the agency.

teer for foreign assignments, which provide no particular boost to their careers and for which they receive no extended training. Overseas, they work within rules established by host governments, operating by their wits and luck. Their success depends critically upon cultivating informants, whose identity the agents guard zealously. Operating in a dangerous and uncertain world, agents develop fierce loyalties to their colleagues and a deep wariness of outsiders.[8]

As a consequence of DEA's structural independence and its career incentive system, its various districts and overseas offices apparently do not coordinate their internal efforts very well, and the DEA's cooperation with other agencies is still more complicated. On the ground, everyone wants primary credit for "the bust." DEA's intelligence division has experienced related problems in effectively tracking transnational organized crime, although DEA agents insist that such efforts have improved in recent years. On the other hand, while DEA agents have no particular interest in the bigger diplomatic picture, their experience as law enforcement officers tends to make them less rigid in interagency negotiations than Justice Department lawyers.[9]

With the collapse of the Soviet Union and the shift to domestic priorities, the mission of the Department of Defense has become a prime topic of macropolicy debate. Does the United States face a global military threat? If so, what strategic response, force structure, and resource levels are required to meet that threat? The uniformed services have fiercely—and largely successfully—resisted efforts, first attempted in 1948, to restructure the armed forces and eliminate redundancies.[10] Various interests look to the Defense budget for money

---

[8] The best general discussions are Wilson 1978 and Nadelmann 1993. Even these little bits of structure and culture help one to understand the ferocity of DEA's commitment to avenge the February 1985 murder of Enrique Camarena. Dr. Humberto Alvarez Machain, alleged to have participated in the crime, was abducted from Mexico in April 1990 to stand trial in a Los Angeles federal district court. The kidnapping produced outrage in Mexico and ignited heated interagency battles in Washington. State had a bilateral relationship to protect, DEA a score to settle, and the Criminal Division a case to make. Interviewees (April–May 1993) insisted that DEA could not walk away from the Camarena case; it needed to send a very strong signal both to its own agents and to drug traffickers that an attack on an agent would be costly. In the event, the Alvarez Machain case was subsequently dismissed for insufficient evidence. It remains unclear whether the kidnapping was authorized by policy-level officials or was the work of rogue agents.

[9] Author interviews, Washington, D.C., May 1993; Monterrey, Mexico, July 1993; Alexandria, Virginia, August 1993; see also Wilson 1978: 147–58. As police officers, DEA agents have a reputation for impatience with intelligence analysts within their own agency and even more so with those from other agencies, although agents interviewed denied such a bias.

[10] The 1948 "Key West" agreement on roles and missions allowed the services considerable autonomy and redundancy. The inability of the services to resist reopen-

to fund domestic programs, which naturally leads the Pentagon to protect its resources. While conventional military matters have been relatively unimportant in the U.S.–Mexican relationship since World War II, the current debates—which have been complicated by staffing problems at the policy levels—might significantly affect the bilateral security relationship.

Structurally, the Department of Defense dwarfs the other agencies discussed here in both size and complexity. Much simplified, one might view the anti-narcotics programs of the Defense Department in terms of four "worlds" and three dimensions (author interview, June 1993). The structural worlds are (1) the Office of the Secretary of Defense, (2) the Joint Chiefs of Staff, (3) the uniformed services, and (4) the unified commands. The three dimensions are intradepartmental dynamics, coordination with other federal agencies, and operations of the country teams in the embassies. The Office of the Secretary exercises political functions, such as promoting defense interests in broader policy arenas and exercising civilian control; the Joint Chiefs advise policy makers and coordinate interservice policy and operations; the uniformed services tend to specific administrative matters and advocate their particular interests; and the unified commands carry out joint service operations in geographic regions.[11]

As is appropriate for a war-fighting organization, the military's prestige branches are the combat arms, such as the army's infantry, artillery, and cavalry branches (although engineers enjoy prestige as well). Navy elites include carrier pilots and officers of surface warships and submarines. Military officers are trained to define clear objectives, develop detailed plans and thorough training, and organize extensive support trains for combat forces. They are accustomed to multilayered bureaucracies and complex operations guided by detailed manuals and extensive written communications.

Some defense officials have responded to the specter of budget cuts by seeking to expand military functions beyond war fighting nar-

---

ing old battles "was demonstrated most recently by conflict within the Pentagon over the [February 1993] report of Chairman of the Joint Chiefs of Staff Colin Powell on roles, missions, and functions. While the final report recommends several important reforms in the activities of the armed services, the service chiefs compelled General Powell to remove or water down some of the more far-reaching measures that had been proposed by the chairman in an earlier draft" (Blechman et al. 1993: 1–2).

[11] This discussion stops short of another immense world of complexities linking the Department of Defense with state and local law enforcement. Problems related to antidrug enforcement include "common nomenclature, common grids, timely tactical intelligence, unambiguous target designation, correlated track data, interagency interoperability of hardware and software, configuration control, and mutually compatible [standard operating procedures]—to name a few. Overshadowing all of these is the necessity for effective command and control of tactical operations, end-to-end, despite the existing organizational, institutional, and political pitfalls" (Ault 1989: 52).

rowly conceived. These efforts at role expansion coincided with White House and congressional interest during the late 1980s in committing military assets to the war on drugs, which both branches of government defined as a threat to U.S. national security.[12] The Congressional Defense Authorization of 1989 designated the Department of Defense as the lead agency in detecting and monitoring illegal drugs entering the United States, and it required the Department to integrate the command, control, communications, and technical intelligence assets of federal agencies into an effective communications network. The act further required the Department of Defense to review and fund state governors' plans for using National Guard units in drug interdiction (Ault 1989: 50).

Although some military officers may have welcomed the new role for the armed forces, most seem to have viewed role expansion with ambivalence or reluctance. The debates, however, have remained largely within the bureaucracy to this point. Most officers do not view service in anti-narcotics programs as a career-enhancing, mainstream assignment unless one is serving in an area such as SOUTHCOM (Panama Canal Zone) where anti-narcotics programs carry high priority.[13] Military resources assigned to anti-narcotics programs, moreover, tend to be viewed as losses in a fixed-sum game, that is, as a subtraction from the military's primary mission of war fighting. Furthermore, clashing organizational cultures can frustrate joint planning by the military and DEA. The military thinks in terms of multiyear plans and complex training and logistical support for tactical operations, while the DEA mind-set is more direct: "Just send some agents and do it!" (author interview, Washington, D.C., May 1993).

Recent arguments for military role expansion, however, go considerably beyond antidrug efforts. Admiral Paul David Miller, while commander in chief of the U.S. Atlantic Command, offered a two-part argument for role expansion. First, military forces must become more adept at providing support services to a variety of civilian agencies involved in complex security-related activities. Second, the military can gain this ability by identifying its "core competencies" (such as combat engineering, medical support, logistics, operational planning,

---

[12] For example, Senator Sam Nunn, an authority on defense matters, perceived a diminished global threat that implied lower levels of strategic arms, fewer active duty personnel, and greater reliance on reserve forces. He viewed Europe, the Middle East, the Persian Gulf, and Korea as regions of strategic priority, and economic instability and drug trafficking as the most important threats posed by Latin America. U.S. armed forces, in his view, have a significant detection and monitoring role, in cooperation with federal and local law enforcement, in interdicting drug traffic (Nunn 1990: 38).

[13] SOUTHCOM has been substantially downsized since 1993, and its headquarters are to be transferred to Miami in 1998.

reconnaissance and intelligence assessment) and linking them flexibly to "roles and missions" (for example, crisis response, counter-narcotics) in various interagency "tasks" (including counter-narcotics detection and monitoring, humanitarian relief missions, and so on) (Miller 1993: 1–12, passim). Miller's vision called for the creation of various interagency action groups according to particular objectives. This arrangement would give the United States the long-term security benefit of highly trained, deployable military forces that could be mobilized for combat on short notice. Examples of military support to interagency action groups go beyond counter-drug programs to include humanitarian assistance (like water pipelines and medical facilities in Grenada), disaster relief, and migrant issues (interdiction of Haitian migrants on the high seas, for example). Miller's reasoning was echoed by then-commander in chief of SOUTHCOM, General George Joulwan (1992).

Military role expansion is bound to be controversial. For example, involvement in antidrug programs carries the risk of both corrupting and politicizing military forces. Most obviously, when drug trafficking is enmeshed with guerrilla activities, military forces must take sides in politics as well as law enforcement. Military planners seek clearly defined goals, decisive commitments, reliable allies, identifiable enemies. Antidrug programs offer none of these (see, for example, Bagley and Tokatlian 1992; Sharpe 1992). Furthermore, involvement of military forces in law enforcement–related activities risks undermining civilian support for the armed forces. Finally, but equally important, military forces engaged in nonmilitary missions such as anti-narcotics or disaster relief programs still tend to think as warriors and to prepare for their primary defense roles. For example, with regard to humanitarian assistance, Admiral Miller suggested:

> It makes practical sense to convert existing assistance programs to emerging security priorities by reallocating security assistance, exercise-related construction, and combined exercise funds to such efforts as preparing Caribbean island nations to participate in CARICOM, OAS, or UN peacekeeping operations (Miller 1993: 32).

Thus role expansion serves several ends: protection of the military's resources, training and preparedness, and preparation for longer-term military alliance building. Some have argued that it might also strengthen the U.S.–Mexican defense relationship (CSIS 1992). At first blush, role expansion would seem to promote the long-standing U.S. interest in a more robust inter-American security regime. The effectiveness and durability of such a regime, however, must ultimately rest on a solid political consensus.

As Cope (this volume) shows, the U.S.–Mexican military relationship is distinctive in the hemispheric context in both political and organizational terms. Mexico is not part of SOUTHCOM's jurisdiction, but rather is directly handled at the Joint Chiefs of Staff level. The goals of enhanced military cooperation are being pursued at higher levels of bureaucratic interaction and with greater political sensitivity.

Created in 1947, the Central Intelligence Agency provides analysis and intelligence to policy makers and mounts active measures of espionage, while protecting its own assets and resources through counterintelligence work. Like Justice, since the early 1960s the CIA has operated at the center of controversy. Although their precise labels have changed over time, the Agency's principal functional divisions remain those of analysis (intelligence), operations (espionage and counterespionage), and science and technology. The director of central intelligence both heads the CIA and coordinates the broader intelligence community. Like the uniformed military services, however, the various intelligence agencies have resisted effective coordination or oversight.

More than forty years of cold war forged an organizational culture within the CIA that emphasized penetration of virtual police states and thus prized operations over analysis. Furthermore, the operations branch provided a flexible arm that activist presidents could employ with relatively few constraints. From the late 1940s until the mid-1970s, directors of central intelligence were drawn from the covert side of the Agency. In the post-Watergate period, however, the size and importance of the operations division were significantly reduced.

> The Iran-contra affair [of 1986–1987] was probably the last heave of a slain dragon. Within the CIA, by all accounts, the directorate of intelligence more than pulled abreast of the directorate of operations. Centers that focused on terrorism and counter-narcotics made analysts and operators into colleagues. As director, William Webster put analysts into key managerial posts, and his successor, Robert Gates, himself [came] from the analytical side of the agency (May 1992: 67–68).

Policy makers and experts are actively debating the future role of the CIA in the post–cold war context.[14] The central issues concern the range of matters the Agency should address, the role of covert operations, and the most suitable structures to carry out intelligence work. Although most observers agree that secret intelligence is essential for addressing threats of weapons proliferation, regional conflict, terror-

[14] A blue-ribbon panel of experts was appointed in March 1994 to undertake a fundamental inquiry into the future of the intelligence community.

ism, and narcotics trafficking, they disagree about its relevance to issues such as migration, environment, and trade. Economic tensions and trade competition, however, have pushed the Agency toward greater involvement in these areas (see, for example, Smith 1993a). Disagreements about the operational roles of the Agency run deeper, with some preferring that operations be handled by the Defense Department.

Given our focus on U.S.–Mexican relations, the CIA's potential for increased involvement in fighting drug trafficking and organized crime is especially interesting. U.S. elite opinion, both conservative and liberal, has long been profoundly suspicious of CIA involvement in domestic operations. Further, the Agency's founding charter, experience, and skills have all steered it away from law enforcement activities. Moreover, its bias toward intelligence gathering has been ill suited to law enforcement, as demonstrated by allegations that the Agency withheld information from the Justice Department in 1992 in an Iraq-related criminal investigation. The CIA's purposes in gathering intelligence were quite different from those of a standard law enforcement agency.

> When asked about the CIA's handling of BNL [Banca Nazionale del Lavoro]-related information during his confirmation hearing . . . CIA Director R. James Woolsey observed: "If someone involved in intelligence, with respect to an overseas party, let's say, learns of activity that is against the interests of the United States, there is, I think, in the intelligence community often an inclination to watch and wait and to understand, because the next time . . . one might learn something more. And that next thing one learns might be something that is truly vital to the interests of the country. . . . And the mindset of those who are involved in prosecuting crimes on behalf of the United States is, of course, quite different," Woolsey said. "They both are legitimate interests" (Smith 1993b: A22).

Partly in response to the BNL case, a report by the Agency's inspector general subsequently opened the way for closer cooperation between CIA and Justice in law enforcement. The reforms authorized federal prosecutors to direct the Agency to gather evidence needed to bring indictments against foreign individuals or organizations for violating U.S. laws. Criminal prosecutors could also gain access to CIA files and testimony from Agency analysts. Influential members of Congress apparently support this direction (Smith 1993c). In short, the CIA—like the Defense Department—is also experiencing role expansion.

The CIA's recent evolution raises at least three significant issues. First, new functional units within the CIA, such as counter-narcotics and counterterrorism, bring together analysis and operations (as noted by May [1992]). Some observers view this evolution as natural and desirable, since it better connects the kinds of analysis needed with the kinds of active measures indicated, while others maintain that joining the two functions typically distorts intelligence in ways that justify activities and products of operations.[15] Second, CIA involvement in law enforcement raises the possibility of biasing criminal investigations to suit security preferences. For example, the CIA might steer U.S. law enforcement efforts away from a particular criminal activity that might have broader intelligence value; or (less likely) it might bias—even fabricate—criminal cases to address perceived security problems. A related problem is the inevitable spillover of Agency investigations into U.S. domestic matters, which directly violates the CIA's present charter. Third, although the CIA appears better suited organizationally than DEA (or FBI) for overseas operations and global monitoring, an expanded covert role in counternarcotics activities could raise new problems. Such an expanded role might prove useful if it is limited to penetrating criminal gangs for intelligence gathering and prosecution within the United States. If, however, its broader role encompasses wide-ranging paramilitary operations against drug traffickers, it is likely to face political problems similar to those that might confront the Defense Department.

This sketch barely scratches the surface of structural and cultural features that affect behavior of bureaucracies involved in the bilateral security relationship. It may serve, however, to set the stage for an understanding of continuity and change in bureaucratic politics in the Clinton administration.

Clinton and Security: Drift and Controversy

Arkansas governor Bill Clinton based his 1992 presidential campaign primarily on the theme of sustainable domestic economic recovery. Although his foreign policy ideas essentially echoed those of the Bush administration, he spoke more aggressively about linking international trade to domestic economic restructuring, modernizing U.S. military forces, and promoting human rights and democracy. His campaign statements portrayed democracy promotion as a high na-

---

[15] This argument assumes that operations officers who have invested their prestige in various activities will naturally want analytical officers to produce findings that justify those activities. Aguayo (this volume) discusses the relationships between analysis and operations in comparative perspective.

tional security priority (see, for example, Clinton and Gore 1992: 136–37).

Elected with only a 43 percent plurality in a three-person race, Clinton subsequently focused largely on domestic affairs, enjoying the good luck of a business cycle that brought low interest rates and a strong economic recovery. His administration encountered recurring delays and setbacks in filling policy-level posts in Justice, State, Defense, and CIA. Four initial points are in order here. First, deficit reduction and tight budgets have driven security policy. Second, the administration has been preoccupied with domestic issues, with foreign policy largely left to crisis coping. Third, the administration has proposed and implemented unprecedented reductions in the size of the federal bureaucracy, with potential consequences for bureaucratic morale and performance. Fourth, the administration's initial weakness and the severe setback suffered in the midterm elections of November 1994 have meant that the Republican-dominated Congress and alliances of bureaucracies and interest groups can act increasingly independently of the White House.

This said, democracy promotion has clearly been a central theme in Clinton's foreign policy. It also appears that U.S. strategy to counter drug trafficking abroad has shifted away from aggressive interdiction and toward bolstering other nations' law-enforcement capabilities.[16] The administration has not yet enunciated clear policies with respect to migration, organized crime, and terrorism, but the shift to the right in public opinion has prompted the administration to adopt harder-line positions, which has been reflected in U.S.–Mexican relations. For example, the Clinton administration substantially beefed up law enforcement along the southwestern border in January 1996, in part to show tough deterrent measures against illegal immigration and drug smuggling to prepare for the re-election campaign. The new border control program is aimed at knitting together special operations in the San Diego and Tucson sectors, respectively called "Gatekeeper" and "Safeguard," into a single coherent regional strategy that also includes antidrug efforts (Branigin 1996).

While the Clinton administration has received mixed reviews of its domestic policy performance, general opinion about its foreign policy record was negative until late 1995 when apparent successes in the Middle East and a clearer stance on Bosnia appeared to help the president's image. For the most part, Clinton invested little time or

---

[16] While reiterating that illicit drugs continue to be a national security threat, the shift aimed to redirect Pentagon resources away from interdiction and toward more military assistance for operations against cocaine laboratories and trafficking organizations in South America. The proposed shift brought strong protests from the Customs Service and Coast Guard, which relied on military assets to block drug entry into the United States (Isikoff 1993a, 1993b).

interest in foreign affairs, his core policy team was viewed as weak and inarticulate, and the administration's tendency to let U.S. actions fall short of rhetoric created a serious credibility gap. It was the administration's good fortune that a major foreign policy crisis did not erupt during its first months. Core national interests were not at stake in Somalia, Haiti, or even Bosnia.[17]

U.S.–Mexican relations ranked near the top of the administration's rather short list of foreign policy successes. Its last-minute scramble in November 1993 to win congressional approval for the North American Free Trade Agreement (NAFTA) marked a major victory. Despite the anxiety about fraud and possible violence, Mexico's August 1994 presidential election was widely viewed as much cleaner than previous elections. And the administration showed unusual decisiveness in responding to the severe financial crisis that erupted in Mexico in December 1994.

Antidrug policy offers a useful perspective on bureaucratic dynamics in the Clinton administration. Although it is too soon to judge, the FBI appeared to be emerging as a stronger actor in interagency dynamics as a result of new and effective leadership, the new domestic policy context, and problems afflicting other antidrug programs and agencies. Louis J. Freeh brought strong credentials and considerable skill to the FBI directorship. A former FBI special agent and prosecuting attorney in New York, Freeh won considerable acclaim (and favorable press attention) for his role in successfully prosecuting cases against the Mafia. Also important, two other top Justice Department officials were recruited from New York State: Tom Constantine was appointed to head the DEA, and Lee P. Brown was brought in to direct the Office of National Drug Control Policy. Freeh had worked closely with both officials in New York.

The FBI has also benefited from the administration's focus on domestic problems, and it took advantage of the resurgence of congressional interest in anticrime legislation and willingness to spend more on domestic law enforcement. On another front, the Commission on Reinventing Government, headed by Vice President Al Gore, proposed merging the DEA and FBI to improve coordination and efficiency. Although Attorney General Janet Reno ultimately blocked this initiative, the FBI strengthened its influence over DEA as a result of a

---

[17] Elizabeth Drew reports the president-elect's attitude toward foreign policy: "Clinton finally settled on [Warren] Christopher, whose role was to be to not let foreign policy get in the President's way as he focused on domestic policy. Clinton felt he could trust Christopher on this score. . . . [National security advisor Anthony Lake] had the same assignment as Christopher: keep foreign policy from distracting the President from his domestic agenda" (Drew 1994: 28). But the foreign policy team performed poorly, and well into 1994 speculation continued that Christopher would be replaced (Devroy and Williams 1994).

Justice Department internal order and close personal cooperation between the two new agency directors.[18] Also, while congressional hearings on the Justice Department's handling of armed encounters in Waco, Texas, and Ruby Ridge, Idaho, damaged the Bureau of Alcohol, Tobacco, and Firearms, Freeh was able partially to deflect attacks on the FBI by dismissing the official in charge of the Waco operation. Even so, the Bureau's record in antidrug programs has been criticized, and the agency suffers from an image of aloofness and opportunism.[19]

Problems of varying degrees of seriousness afflicted other antidrug agencies. The ONDCP was targeted for the deepest personnel cuts in order to help President Clinton fulfill his campaign promise to reduce the White House staff by 25 percent. Republican legislators subsequently proposed the agency's elimination as an economy measure. The State Department created a Bureau of Global Affairs in order to improve policy coordination with respect to environmental, law enforcement, and anti-narcotics and antiterrorism issues. The new agency, however, suffered important setbacks and drifted toward apparent irrelevance.[20] Also, the broader fiscal squeeze hurt the State Department generally and antidrug programs specifically: recent budget submissions by the Bureau of International Narcotics Matters came under strong attack both within the administration and in Congress.

Across the Potomac, the Defense Department suffered first from delays in filling top-level policy jobs, then from the forced resignation in December 1993 of Secretary Les Aspin, and finally from the abortive designation of retired Admiral Bobby Ray Inman to replace Aspin. Not until February 1994 was Defense Undersecretary William J. Perry appointed to replace Aspin. The consequent delays and con-

[18] An anecdote conveys the image. Constantine reportedly instructed his staff to inquire with the FBI about the protocol for his swearing-in ceremony. An aide replied that DEA doesn't take its cues from FBI, to which Constantine allegedly suggested that maybe that was how things worked in the past but that it wouldn't work that way in the future (author interview, Washington, D.C., April 1994).

[19] The FBI's antidrug performance in the Organized Crime Drug Enforcement Task Force was strongly criticized by the Justice Department's Office of Inspector General. The Bureau received the lowest rating of the various federal, state, and local agencies. According to the inspector general's report, "The FBI was the focus of most complaints from Task Force members [who] cited problems with exchanging intelligence information, operational control, and strained relationships with other federal and local agencies" (quoted in McGee 1995). As one interviewee (a DEA officer) put it to me, "Look, no one likes the FBI" (author interview, Washington, D.C., May 1993).

[20] Jessica Matthews, a noted expert on global environmental matters, resigned as deputy to the undersecretary for global affairs in November 1993, and Congressman Benjamin A. Gilman subsequently blocked the inclusion of antiterrorism programs in the new bureau's portfolio. Not until April 1994 did Congress agree to create the position of undersecretary for global affairs, to head the new bureau (Lipmann 1994).

fusion helped the uniformed services survive what might have been a thorough review and reallocation of resources. The priority at Defense remained protecting its budget, and it benefited substantially with the resurgence of Republican strength in the Congress.

At both State and Defense, anti-narcotics programs remained largely within the contours set by the Bush administration, and there was substantial continuity of approach at the assistant secretary and deputy assistant secretary levels in both departments. The first Clinton antidrug policy review (Presidential Decision Directive 14 of November 1993) shifted emphasis somewhat from law enforcement–oriented approaches toward treatment and prevention, and from interdiction of drugs toward assistance to antidrug forces in drug-producing countries, primarily Peru and Colombia. In May 1994 a high-profile dispute emerged between State and Defense over policy toward third nation (Peru and Colombia) efforts to interdict flights suspected of drug smuggling. The dispute resulted in cutting these countries off "from access to U.S. counter-drug intelligence, [and] blinded all three nations to many drug-smuggling flights and threatened to fracture a brittle alliance against the northward flow of heroin and cocaine" (Gellman 1994).[21] The interdepartmental conflict persisted for most of 1994.

President Clinton's strategy proved, however, no more successful than previous policies. In an unusually frank public statement in January 1996, Lt. General Barry McCaffrey, commander of the U.S. Southern Command, noted that the availability and price of cocaine in the United States remained unaffected more than two years after the new strategy was implemented. The central problems continued to be lack of an international antidrug coalition and lack of effective cooperation among the many U.S. agencies responsible for counter-drug activities. The military commander concluded that the antidrug struggle was not like fighting a war, but more like combating cancer or the Mafia (Smith 1996).

In terms of bureaucratic politics, both the Pentagon and FBI benefited more directly from the series of disasters that beset the CIA. In February 1994 came the sensational exposure of a traitor, Aldrich Ames, who had formerly headed the CIA's Soviet counterintelligence unit, one of the Agency's most sensitive posts. The FBI charged that it had not been notified in a timely manner about Ames's difficulty in passing lie detector tests. CIA director R. James Woolsey was forced on the defensive before Congress over the issue and resigned in December 1994, and executive regulations were rewritten to strengthen the FBI's counterintelligence role (Smith 1994; Smith and Thomas

---

[21] Oversimplified, Defense strongly opposed the use of lethal force against suspected flights, while State was less concerned.

1994; Thomas 1994). Another controversy involved the case of an alleged CIA cover-up of agency payments to a Guatemalan army officer accused of having caused the deaths of a U.S. citizen and a Guatemalan guerrilla leader.[22] Even more serious were revelations that the Agency had provided information to policy makers that it knew came from unreliable sources.

As with the State Department, however, the CIA's high-level problems did not necessarily weaken its counter-narcotics program, although the FBI gained ground at the Agency's expense in delicate day-to-day interagency negotiations. Also, the Bureau quietly expanded its overseas role in international law enforcement programs and was seen to threaten the CIA's foreign role in espionage matters.

> The agency [CIA], still reeling from the Aldrich H. Ames debacle, is in no position to fend off the FBI encroachment on its turf and budget.
>
> Freeh and the bureau also are moving into the nuclear anti-proliferation battle. Traditionally, stopping the proliferation would have been seen as part of the Arms Control and Disarmament Agency's mission. But with the Cold War over and the commies largely de-nuked, the action really shifts to enforcing non-proliferation. That's police work that the FBI can do. ACDA, also weakened by a political war in which the agency itself was almost nuked, can only watch as Freeh moves in (Kamen 1994).

None of this is to suggest that the FBI was necessarily poised to mount an aggressive campaign to replace the CIA or other law enforcement and intelligence agencies in overseas operations. An agency will not automatically seek advantage in a policy context in order to gain additional resources or policy turf. In fact, for many years under Director J. Edgar Hoover, the FBI avoided jurisdiction over antidrug law enforcement. Much depends upon how Freeh and other top officials interpret the agency's interests and the likely shape of the future bureaucratic context. But two points are in order: First, the FBI historically has staked a claim to a strong presence in Mexico. Second, the Bureau's culture and experience emphasize domestic law enforcement and put little stress on broader international trends (as does the CIA). One possible implication is that the Bureau's narrower focus on law enforcement may complicate bilateral relations.

---

[22] The scandal was based on the CIA's 1992 decision to keep paying an informant in the Guatemalan military who had been linked to the murder of a U.S. citizen and to the disappearance and presumed murder of a Guatemalan guerrilla leader, who was the husband of U.S. lawyer Jennifer Harbury. Lesser but still significant negative publicity for the CIA came with allegations that the Agency discriminated against women in its personnel practices (see Smith 1995; Pincus 1995).

Conclusions: Inertia and Adaptation

Some aspects of bureaucratic politics described here will continue indefinitely into the future due to agency structure and culture. That is, barring changes in the constitutional framework, one should expect the invitation to bureaucratic struggle to continue as a fundamental feature. Also, institutional tensions inherent to bureaucratic organization will persist. For example, interagency coordination will prove even more difficult to achieve as functions are shifted to state and local levels; there will continue to be tensions between functional versus geographical organization within agencies. Much of the dynamic that complicates the implementation of antidrug programs will go on suffering due to institutional-organizational reasons. Beyond these, however, policy implementation will be limited because the core solutions to drug abuse ultimately lie in demand reduction. Even in the unlikely event that sufficient resources are mounted to attack consumption, results will require several years—even decades—to show up. In the meantime, much of the antidrug effort remains in the realm of symbolic politics: activities are generated and products are publicized in order to promote an illusion that the problem is being attacked.

An area of important change in bureaucratic behavior, however, concerns the ways in which the leadership in the defense and intelligence communities will reorient their agencies' missions to play a larger role in combating a different array of threats that have succeeded the cold war. Equally important will be how an agency with strong domestic law enforcement capability (the FBI) learns to play broader roles in international politics. In this sense, especially significant in U.S.–Mexican relations will be the changed roles of these agencies in dealing with transnational criminal activities.

References

Ault, Frank W. 1989. "DoD Wades into Drug War," *Armed Forces Journal International*, July, pp. 50–53.

Bagley, Bruce M., and Juan Tokatlian. 1992. "Dope and Dogma: Explaining the Failure of U.S.–Latin American Drug Policies." In *The United States and Latin America in the 1990s: Beyond the Cold War*, edited by Jonathan Hartlyn, Lars Schoultz, and Augusto Varas. Chapel Hill: University of North Carolina Press.

Blechman, Barry, et al. 1993. "Key West Revisited: Roles and Missions of the US Armed Forces in the Twenty-first Century." Report No. 8. Washington, D.C.: Henry L. Stimson Center.

Branigin, William. 1996. "U.S. Beefing Up Forces on Southwestern Border," *Washington Post*, January 12.

Clinton, Bill, and Al Gore. 1992. *Putting People First: How We Can All Change America*. New York: Times Books.

CSIS (Center for Strategic and International Studies). 1992. *Intensifying North American Relationships: Implications for Defense*. Report prepared by the Americas Program, December.

Devroy, Ann, and David Williams. 1994. "Christopher Remains in Limbo," *Washington Post*, October 9.

Dobbs, Michael. 1995. "Domestic Politics Intrudes on Foreign Policy," *Washington Post*, June 26.

Drew, Elizabeth. 1994. *On the Edge: The Clinton Presidency*. New York: Simon and Schuster.

Gellman, Barton. 1994. "Feud Hurts Bid to Stop Drug Flow," *Washington Post*, May 24.

Isikoff, Michael. 1993a. "U.S. Considers Shift in Drug War," *Washington Post*, September 16.

———. 1993b. "White House Shifts Anti-Drug Focus, but Not Funds," *Washington Post*, October 19.

Joulwan, George. 1992. Keynote address at the conference "Warriors in Peacetime: The Military and Democracy in Latin America, New Directions for U.S. Policy," Washington, D.C., Inter-American Defense College, December 11.

Kamen, Al. 1994. "The Bureau Branches Out," *Washington Post*, July 11.

Lipmann, Thomas W. 1994. "One Year after Starting Work, Wirth Close to Getting Job," *Washington Post*, April 26.

———. 1995. "GOP-Controlled Foreign Policy Panels Would Reverse Several Clinton Stands," *Washington Post*, May 21.

May, Ernest R. 1992. "Intelligence: Backing into the Future," *Foreign Affairs* 71 (3): 63–72.

McGee, Jim. 1995. "FBI Drug Role Faces Renewed Challenge," *Washington Post*, December 28.

Miller, Paul David. 1993. *The Interagency Process: Engaging America's Full National Security Capabilities*. National Security Paper No. 11. Cambridge, Mass.: Institute for Foreign Policy Analysis.

Nadelmann, Ethan A. 1993. *Cops across Borders: The Internationalization of U.S. Criminal Law Enforcement*. University Park: Pennsylvania State University Press.

Nunn, Sam. 1990. *Nunn 1990: A New Military Strategy*. Washington, D.C.: Center for Strategic and International Studies.

Pastor, Robert A., and Jorge G. Castañeda. 1988. *Limits to Friendship: The United States and Mexico*. New York: Alfred A. Knopf.

Pincus, Walter. 1995. "CIA Director Adds 4 Deputies," *Washington Post*, August 1.

Reilly, John E., ed. 1995. *American Public Opinion and U.S. Foreign Policy 1995*. Chicago: Chicago Council on Foreign Relations.

Sharpe, Kenneth E. 1992. "The Military, the Drug War and Democracy in Latin America: What Would Clausewitz Tell Us?" Paper prepared for the conference "Warriors in Peacetime: The Military and Democracy in Latin America, New Directions for U.S. Policy," Washington, D.C., Inter-American Defense College, December 11–12.

Smith, R. Jeffrey. 1993a. "Administration to Consider Giving Spy Data to Business," *Washington Post,* February 3.

———. 1993b. "Change at CIA Will Give Agency Wider Role in Law Enforcement," *Washington Post,* February 10.

———. 1993c. "CIA Knew of British Iraq Deal," *Washington Post,* February 15.

———. 1994. "As Woolsey Struggles, CIA Suffers," *Washington Post,* May 10.

———. 1995. "CIA Director Pledges Swift Reform," *Washington Post,* May 10.

———. 1996. "Cocaine Flow Not Slowed, General Says," *Washington Post,* January 12.

Smith, R. Jeffrey, and Pierre Thomas. 1994. "Plan Shifts CIA Tasks to FBI Staff," *Washington Post,* April 26.

Thomas, Pierre. 1994. "Inter-Agency FBI-CIA Tensions Defy Decades of Efforts to Resolve Them," *Washington Post.*

Ungar, Sanford J. 1976. *FBI.* Boston, Mass.: Little, Brown and Company.

Wilson, James Q. 1978. *The Investigators: Managing FBI and Narcotics Agents.* New York: Basic Books.

———. 1989. *Bureaucracy: What Government Agencies Do and Why They Do It.* New York: Basic Books.

10

In Search of Convergence: U.S.–Mexican Military Relations into the Twenty-first Century

John A. Cope

While the landmark North American Free Trade Agreement (NAFTA) governs economic relations among the United States, Mexico, and Canada, its influence has not been confined to the commercial realm. During its formative years, the free trade agreement stimulated efforts in other policy areas to define common interests, encourage openness and closer collaboration, and, in the process, work to improve confidence among neighbors. One area where the cooperative spirit of NAFTA has given impetus to tentative bilateral initiatives is in the traditionally circumscribed and limited realm of relations between the armed forces of the United States and Mexico.

This long-standing but distant relationship has attracted little scholarly interest in either country over the last forty years. Poorly understood in government circles, it is generally taken for granted as an inflexible and therefore not significant association. Circumstances are changing within and between both countries, however. Mexico, in particular, is having to adjust not only to NAFTA but also to a simmering rebellion in Chiapas, worsening domestic economic and political turmoil, and increasing U.S. pressure to collaborate more aggressively and effectively against narcotics trafficking. The current

The author wishes to thank Tim Goodman of the Latin American Studies program at Georgetown University for his invaluable assistance in drafting this chapter. The views expressed are those of the author and do not reflect the official policy or position of the National Defense University, the Department of Defense, or the U.S. government.

state and future potential of the bilateral military association is far more important for an emerging security partnership than it has seemed in the past. This chapter seeks to dispel some of the mystery surrounding U.S.–Mexican military relations in order to take a step toward better mutual awareness and increased professional cooperation similar to that which animates the new commercial partnership. The story begins with a brief review of each country's historically different approaches to national security and a short discussion of the pressures today for greater multilateral collaboration. The focus shifts first to introduce five ways in which the United States and Mexico traditionally interact, then to explain how aspects of the relationship have begun to change and discuss policy concerns that stem from this association, and, finally, to provide a brief epilogue bringing the story up to date as of December 1995.

The presentation is unavoidably skewed toward a U.S. perspective. Deep Mexican aversion to outside scrutiny and the absence of transparency in their domestic policy making make Mexicans' views on improving military-to-military relations difficult to determine. In addition, a cultural veil of secrecy traditionally conceals the thinking of both the Mexican armed forces and Foreign Ministry (SRE) on issues related to national security. Actions in this case must substitute for words. It is not clear, therefore, where this new trend toward improving cross-border contact will go nor what the implications for security policy and resources will be.

Understanding the various ways in which U.S. and Mexican armed forces interact provides several important benefits:

- The frame of reference within which military dialogue and cooperation occur provides a rare analytic window through which to observe aspects of Mexican strategic thinking about national defense and cooperative security.

- The traditional structure for contact continues to be a medium for military diplomacy, providing a means for signaling government positions or intentions. Actions taken by both sides within the formal context of military relations have often either anticipated more significant substantive shifts in official security policy, confirmed the status quo, or hinted how one neighbor or the other might respond to a specific overture. The structure also offers a way to take rough measurements of the effectiveness of international and bilateral security- and confidence-building programs.

- The military association provides a case study of how change can occur within corresponding national institutions in neighboring countries when both are affected by a common compelling influence, such as the development of a free trade agreement. The experiences of the U.S. and Mexican defense establishments stemming from NAFTA may hold lessons from which other government institutions may benefit.

The Setting

Exactly when and how bilateral military relations began to improve and which side took the first step are debatable issues, but by the turn of the decade, ever warmer economic and diplomatic relations unquestionably provided an opportune context for this course of development to take shape. When pro-NAFTA presidents George Bush and Carlos Salinas de Gortari commenced their regimes in 1989 by openly encouraging closer and more cordial relations,[1] U.S. defense officials had already been looking informally for signs of possible openings with their southern counterparts in order to give life to one of the Defense Department's least developed military-to-military relationships anywhere. The U.S. catalyst was a 1988 internal government review of policies toward its southern neighbor. Somewhat unexpectedly, the Department of Defense found indications of modest, rather reluctant, parallel interests in improving bilateral military relations. Mexico also had been cautiously trying to increase contacts with U.S. officers in the United States, and routine meetings there had become much more congenial.[2] By the end of the decade, as diplomatic relations improved and a modernizing mind-set favoring economic reform and international integration gained influence in Washington and Mexico City, it became less difficult for military leaders in both countries to discuss energizing dormant institutional relations. Circumstances improved again in late 1993 when formal U.S. acceptance of NAFTA was assured.

The U.S. military response to signs of interest at senior levels wisely avoided immediate pressure for more active bilateral military contacts. The Department of Defense nurtured its opening with care, patience, and no fanfare. And it has continued to do so, mindful of the strong nationalist culture within the Mexican armed forces, the sui generis complexity of the nation's political-military relations, and the fragility that has characterized past attempts to animate cross-border military-to-military contact. Due to potential opposition within the

---

[1] "The Bush administration . . . was characterized by an unusually high number of top officials who had lived and worked in Texas, including Bush himself. These individuals understood Mexico's importance to the United States and were comfortable working with Mexican leaders" (Purcell 1994: 44).

[2] Interviews with Defense Department staff officers from the army, navy, air force, and Joint Staff.

U.S. government and Congress, the Defense Department has tried not to create expectations for the sale of military arms and equipment that it cannot sell with assurance. The causes of concern stem from such sources as past failures by Mexico's army and police personnel to respect human rights, exacerbated by incidents early in the Zapatista uprising; instances of corruption involving law enforcement, antidrug, and military officials; and overall poor national performance in counter-narcotics activities.

Mexican military authorities have been circumspect for their own reasons. The institutional position on this fundamental issue of national security, cross-border military relations, is not easily modified, especially when shrouded in a heritage of suspicion. That the subject was considered at all in the late 1980s suggests that Mexico's military leadership is not homogeneous in its traditionally conservative viewpoint and that a forward-looking, modernizing element within the institution's leadership has emerged. Today's senior officers apparently intend to expand the association in a slow and incremental way, keeping the scope of renewed contact at a level consistent with Mexico's traditional distrust of U.S. intentions, the civilian government's evolving security priorities, and the changing professional needs of the armed forces. Both defense establishments have made progress over the last eight years, particularly among top military leaders.

Neighboring National Security Policies

The asymmetry of power, differences of history, and changing national security interests have shaped the nature of U.S. and Mexican military relations and their evolution over the last fifty years. The armed forces in both countries have responded to civilian direction in this matter. Strategic considerations and foreign policy issues rather than professional motivation and institutional interests, which have never been keen, have shaped the evolution of bilateral military interaction. Nonmilitary considerations moved interservice contact from relatively close collaboration in the 1940s, through near complete estrangement during most of the cold war (although both sides kept channels for communication open), to recent efforts to find convergence in the era of an unprecedented NAFTA. U.S.–Mexican defense relations have followed different rules and procedures than those between Washington and Ottawa, or between Washington and the rest of Latin America. A review of two very different North American approaches to national security provides the context for military-to-military interaction since World War II.

The United States

Washington has traditionally seen U.S. security tied to stability in the Caribbean Basin and then South America. The emergence of a hostile or politically unstable Mexico has not been a serious, recurring security concern, although that country's size, proximity, history of northerly migration, nationalism, and even anti-Americanism have made unavoidable bilateral relations difficult at times, and always important.

In the early 1940s, a positive spirit of collaboration dominated the association as the United States and Mexico worked together to defend against the fascist threat to North America. They developed a comprehensive plan for mutual defense, including participation in the lend-lease program, an early form of today's security assistance. A relatively warm relationship, culminating in early 1945 with a deployment of Mexican aviation to the Pacific theater, gradually cooled after the war as respective national security interests and fundamental principles of foreign policy increasingly came in conflict.

Since the end of World War II, Washington's strategic priorities in the Western Hemisphere have not focused on Mexico. They have included protecting access to and transit across the region, with unrestricted use of the Panama Canal; maintaining a small military presence at several bases in the Caribbean Basin; preserving the ability to obtain essential raw materials, particularly bauxite and petroleum; and realizing solidarity within the region for U.S. positions in international forums. Above all, the United States wanted to avoid having a Latin American or Caribbean country align itself with the Soviet Union, providing this hostile power with a position of strength in the region. And after Cuba's revolution gave substance to these fears in the early 1960s, the United States sought to keep other American governments from allying themselves with Castro, as Nicaragua and Grenada ultimately did twenty years later.

To this end, President Kennedy initiated the Alliance for Progress, a $20 billion social and economic development program to promote peaceful domestic reform in the hemisphere, and expanded counterinsurgency programs to assist American governments in their efforts to defeat leftist guerrilla movements. Mexico turned down direct economic and military aid because of the implicit support for U.S. policies symbolized by such assistance. By the late 1960s, after fervent but often unsound U.S. engagement to promote social and political reform had produced largely inconsequential results, Washington's interest waned. Strategic planners in the nation's capital, responding to higher priority agendas in other regions, relegated the Americas to the margins of U.S. international concerns.

Despite the noble sentiments of the Alliance for Progress, economic integration and security cooperation in the hemisphere have never been dominant aspects of U.S. strategic thought. Its central aim, with deep roots back to the 1823 Monroe Doctrine, has been the exclusion of rival powers from the region. In practice, the nature of U.S. regional policy has been characterized by long periods of routine attention but general indifference punctuated by occasional crises when Washington, caught poorly prepared for events closer to home, found its interests were advanced only by some form of U.S. intervention—diplomatic, economic, or military—or by a serious threat to intervene. Even in the 1990s, U.S. officials have felt strategically and historically compelled to take action to control events in the circum-Caribbean rather than remain passive as political instability threatens its security interests and those of several other states in the region.[3]

By the early 1990s, the focus of U.S. security policy in the Americas had shifted noticeably in several ways. The five Central American presidents had successfully pressured the Reagan administration to alter its strategy in their subregion. This led, ultimately, to Washington embracing the United Nations for the first time as a prime participant in efforts to bring peace and stability to the hemisphere, and it led to a trend of increased regional diplomatic cooperation. The end of the cold war, the emergence of a challenging global security environment without peer competitors, and the increasing competitiveness of the international economic system reinforced for the United States the importance of forging partnerships with its Latin American neighbors around shared interests, rather than unilaterally trying to assert its undisputed dominance. The United States began collaborating harmoniously in multilateral efforts to fight environmental degradation and illegal drug trafficking, promote democratization and peace operations, and strengthen hemispheric security mechanisms. The North American Free Trade Agreement is both a symptom and cause of this change in strategic thinking.

Mexico

The specter of the United States on its northern frontier has long dominated Mexican foreign policy and strategic thinking, and with

[3]While Operation "Uphold Democracy" in Haiti, launched in September 1994, fits this model, it also reflects changing U.S. attitudes. This use of U.S. military power was the first in the Western Hemisphere ever authorized by U.N. resolution. It came almost a year after the Governors Island Accord failed, and it followed more than six months of intense consultations with Latin American neighbors, unusually transparent U.S. military contingency planning, and relatively broad hemispheric participation of law enforcement officers and military units.

good cause. The United States repeatedly violated Mexico's sovereignty in the nineteenth and early twentieth centuries, both for territorial gain and to promote a U.S. vision of how to bring about domestic stability. The experience has made Mexico justifiably suspicious of U.S. intentions and led it to view its neighbor as the only serious threat to its national security. These perceptions of U.S. designs have shaped Mexico's different approach to defense planning and have figured prominently in its military's mind-set—a potent mix of nationalism, patriotism, and discipline. The ceremonial changing of the guard each day at Chapultepec Castle captures well this lingering hostility toward the United States—the "Orders of the Day" in essence instruct the new relief to "kill every *gringo* in sight."

As mentioned previously, World War II marked a historic opportunity in bilateral security relations. The war not only encouraged extensive professional collaboration for the first time and helped Mexico modernize its armed forces, but, of more lasting importance, it also changed the fundamental economic relationship between the neighbors. World War II spurred rapid industrialization in Mexico. The country's export sector changed from raw materials exclusively to an emphasis on industrial goods, largely to exploit the wartime void in the U.S. domestic market. This initial, limited opening of Mexico's economy marked a shift in the country's long practice of maintaining independence in every sector affecting national security by avoiding reliance on foreigners, their markets, and their capital. NAFTA is only the most recent milestone along the path of economic partnership that Mexico and the United States have tried to follow since the early 1940s.

Wartime collaboration with the United States strengthened Mexico's military establishment. A small, modern air force came into existence; the navy's capabilities improved; and the need for extensive combined planning encouraged the professionalization of the officer corps. In early 1942, the two governments formed a Joint Mexican–United States Defense Commission (labeled JMUSDC) to prepare an "Integral Defense Plan" that would coordinate the activities of the U.S. Army and the Mexican Defense Command. The commission also administered a $40 million lend-lease program that helped finance the modernization of Mexico's armed forces, leading ultimately to the deployment of a Mexican air squadron to the Philippines in 1945. This event, in particular, symbolized change in Mexico. Not only had the military institution improved as a professional force, but Mexico had also ended its self-imposed isolation from world events.

The nascent military association never solidified, and by the mid-1950s the partnership had withered to insignificance, even though some of its World War II manifestations of normalcy persisted, such as the JMUSDC and the exchange of military attachés. Presidential control over the Mexican armed forces, the strong influence of the Foreign Ministry, and the military's own deep internal sense of nationalism ensured that closer professional relations did not fully develop between Mexico and its neighbor during the 1940s.

Mexico City's foreign and defense policies went their own way with the advent of the cold war. For Mexicans, U.S. diplomatic behavior in Latin America—particularly in the 1954 overthrow of the Arbenz government in Guatemala, the confrontational reaction to the Cuban Revolution, and efforts to enlist Latin American countries in the struggle against international communism—was consistent with the historical view of the United States as "the bully—the abusive neighbor whose power, size, and proximity warrant Mexico's continuous watch" (Aguilar Zinser 1990: 225). Washington was violating basic principles that shaped Mexican thinking about national security.

With vivid memories of past foreign interventions in Mexico's affairs, the country's fundamental national security interest has been to prevent their recurrence. After the Mexican Revolution, succeeding governments realized that it would not be possible or practical to mobilize sufficient force to defeat U.S. military aggression if it ever happened again. Even determined resistance by a nation in arms would only slow a new invasion from the north. Mexican foreign policy and strategic thinking, therefore, evolved in a nonmilitary direction. National leaders chose to use world opinion as a rampart to hold back the United States. They decided to base national security not on standing military capabilities or even on physical force that could be quickly mobilized, but on internationally accepted principles—national self-determination, sovereignty, territorial integrity, respect for international law, and opposition to all forms of state intervention. Mexican leaders refuse to project force abroad to promote their country's interests or even to participate in international peace operations.[4]

Mexico's principles and its lingering fear of U.S. regional domination were important factors in its official opposition to the United States on numerous international issues during the cold war. For example, Mexico condemned the 1962 Bay of Pigs invasion and the Reagan administration's Central American policy on anti-interventionist grounds. Some U.S. officials wrongly interpreted this criticism as proof of Mexico's communist sympathies, when in fact it indicated little more than Mexico's traditional suspicion of U.S. hegemonic proclivities.

In its strategic doctrine, the role played by the Mexican armed forces is circumscribed and focused primarily on internal security.

[4]Mexico is not unique in relying on principles rather than physical force for its deterrent authority; an international organization, the Conference on Security and Cooperation in Europe (CSCE), does so as well.

Mexico's historic shield has two components: the Ministry of the Navy and the dominant Ministry of National Defense (with jurisdiction over the army and air force), both headed by active-duty officers. The military has no direct involvement in domestic politics nor national policy making other than security issues. On matters that touch on international relations, such as military-to-military relations, the Foreign Ministry plays a controlling role. Senior officers and military attachés rarely comment officially without receiving prior clearance from the Foreign Ministry, reflecting the strength of civilian control in Mexican culture.

The Mexican armed forces, particularly the army, play three important roles:

- They are responsible for the surveillance and control of the nation's territory, airspace, and a claimed 200–mile maritime exclusion zone. Demands on the military remained small and manageable until the 1980s, when Central American turmoil produced a migration explosion that spilled over Mexico's southern border. Since then, the swell in migration, a quantum jump in narcotics trafficking through and over sovereign territory to the United States, and a significant increase in the transit of stolen property and illegal aliens have complicated the external security situation.

- Army resources are used to detect and monitor potentially harmful domestic activities and to reinforce or supplement, as necessary, the limited capabilities of civilian law enforcement agencies at the federal level. The government's counter-drug strategy, for instance, involves the army in crop eradication. If a domestic crisis turns violent, the army, with the president's consent, can be called upon to deploy its riot control capacity and restore public order.

- Most significantly, the army supports the activities of other government agencies when civilian resources are insufficient to meet national requirements. The army, stationed across the country in major barracks and numerous small detachments, stays in close contact with the population to bring it the benefits of the "revolution." It fulfills an extensive civic action campaign that provides health care, road building, literacy programs, and disaster assistance, primarily in rural areas. The army also supports other government agencies by protecting strategic and economically vital sites such as oil refineries, airports, hydroelectric plants, and petrochemical complexes.

Until recently, the internal focus of national security has resulted in a significant degree of stability. Today Mexico is in transition to a new condition, yet to be defined, under the conflicting pressures of NAFTA, the uprising in Chiapas, domestic economic and political turmoil, and transnational threats such as drug trafficking and international crime.

Pressures for Improved Collaboration

The post–cold war frame of reference has introduced two new pressures on both governments to improve the current state of their cooperation: the transnational nature of today's security problems, and movement within the hemisphere toward the creation of a regional system of cooperative security, an initiative being championed by the Organization of American States (OAS).

The most serious challenges to national stability across North America in 1995 stemmed from domestic violence and common crime, intertwined with international drug trafficking, ethnic violence, hunger, disease, environmental degradation, trade protectionism, and illegal immigration. Unlike most traditional national security concerns, addressing these transnational problems demands more than unilateral action; such threats cannot be eliminated without the cooperation of neighboring states. And within national regimes there also must be greater collaboration among concerned governmental agencies. The line between domestic and international policy is now harder to define, as is the line at home between the responsible ministry's ability to meet a challenge itself and its need to draw upon the armed forces and the resources of other national institutions. These trends present a situation in which neighboring military institutions must become more comfortable working together if common transnational security threats are going to be met successfully. Pressure is growing, with national budgetary constraints high among them, to improve cross-border cooperation.[5]

The second source of pressure on the United States and Mexico comes from the Organization of American States, which has been working to preserve peace and improve security by boldly advancing the concept of inter-American cooperative security. In general terms,

---

[5]International narcotics trafficking provides a useful example of this trend. The United States and Mexico began working together to counter illegal drug activities during the early 1970s. The defense establishments in both countries now support federal drug law enforcement ministries and their subordinate agencies. In Mexico's case, the army has been supporting the Attorney General's Office for over thirty years by conducting eradication operations (against marijuana and poppies) in rural areas as a part of its national civic action role. The Defense Department's support officially began in late 1989. There are numerous ways in which neighboring defense forces can cooperate better in pursuit of this shared goal, such as a common system to detect and monitor air and maritime narcotics trafficking.

this concept asks nations to accept that their security—broadly defined to include economic, social, and political dimensions, as well as defense—is greatly enhanced if they can count on the support and cooperation of their neighbors. The OAS has taken several steps in this direction. Key among them are the establishment of a permanent committee to focus on hemispheric security issues and the aggressive promotion of confidence- and security-building measures capable of preventing unwanted conflict while increasing mutual confidence. The OAS recognizes that, on a practical level, subregional cooperation in confronting the new transnational challenges has proven to be workable, as between Argentina and Chile. The achievement of effective collaboration between the NAFTA states on a range of security issues would provide the OAS with a highly visible subregional model with which to encourage other groups of neighboring states toward cooperative security arrangements.

The Structure of Bilateral Military Relations

Traditionally, U.S.–Mexican military-to-military contact has taken place in five well-established ways. These include the presence of military attachés in each country's diplomatic mission; the Joint Mexican–United States Defense Commission (JMUSDC); service-to-service interactions (between national armies, for example); an assistance relationship that allows Mexico to purchase U.S. military material and services; and professional contact through institutions in the Inter-American defense system. Except for JMUSDC, these are normal avenues for military interaction in the Western Hemisphere. Even JMUSDC is not unique. The United States has maintained similar bilateral organizations for dialogue and cooperation with Canada and Brazil since World War II.

One form of routine contact does not exist between the United States and Mexico. The U.S. organization of its military resources includes five geographically oriented unified commands that exercise command authority over forces deployed around the world. These headquarters work closely with U.S. diplomatic missions in their areas of responsibility, support U.S. regional policies with defense resources at hand, and often develop mutually beneficial relationships with other military establishments. In the Western Hemisphere, Mexico and Canada have remained "unassigned" beyond the Joint Chiefs of Staff in Washington for over forty years, reflecting their importance to the core defense of the United States. The orientation of U.S. Southern Command, located in Panama, encompasses Central and South America. Mexico traditionally has been unwilling to interact with this headquarters, which symbolizes for Mexico City U.S. military intervention in the Americas.[6]

The Diplomatic Dimension

An exchange of military attachés is the traditional way countries interact formally on a military-to-military level. The three military departments within the Department of Defense (army, navy, and air force) regularly detail a small, select group of trained officers for assignment to U.S. diplomatic missions in most foreign capitals. The senior officer is usually designated the defense attaché, representing the chairman of the Joint Chiefs of Staff. The size of this military presence is limited by the host country's willingness to accredit nominated officers as members of the foreign diplomatic mission and to grant them the traditional protection accorded to official representatives of foreign governments. The U.S. military mission in Mexico normally consists of six or seven attachés, supported by a staff of five military and civilian personnel. The army attaché traditionally has been designated the senior defense representative, acknowledging the singular importance of the army in the structure of the Mexican armed forces.[7]

The mission of the military attachés is to gather and report (normally by fully overt methods) information on topics of either professional or diplomatic interest to the United States. These officers work closely with other members of the U.S. ambassador's team, sharing raw information and providing preliminary analysis about defense capabilities and political-military developments in the host country. These data are sent to the Defense Intelligence Agency in Washington. Additional duties of attachés include providing professional information to help counterparts better understand the U.S. defense establishment or buy military equipment, and fulfilling a representational or liaison role—from attending functions in dress uniform to arranging military visits to the United States.

The effectiveness of attachés depends heavily on their freedom to travel without restriction outside the capital city and to make personal contacts with national military officers and civilian officials. The movements of U.S. military attachés in Mexico are more tightly con-

---

[6]U.S. Southern Command provides the management support in the Defense Security Assistance Agency's system to the military liaison office in Mexico City. In this sense it is no different than the other security assistance offices in Latin America. Counter-drug support to Mexico's federal police, including material, services, and information sharing, is handled by U.S. Forces Command, a major army headquarters located in Atlanta, Georgia.

[7]There are occasional exceptions when seniority becomes an issue or service reassignment instructions create gaps in continuity.

trolled than in any other Latin American or Caribbean state. Officers request permission from the government to visit specific military locations; this frequently is delayed and frequently denied. Travel restrictions hinder the ability of the United States to gather even basic or timely information about the Mexican armed forces. For instance, the United States did not learn until two years ago where the Mexican Air Force conducts gunnery training for the F-5 aircraft purchased from the United States in 1981, and they found out then only because the Ministry of National Defense chose for its own reasons to reveal this information.[8] While the privileges enjoyed by each country's attachés are reciprocal, Mexican military attachés in the United States enjoy a more liberal approach to their freedom of movement and extensive access to U.S. defense officials and military personnel, if they choose to take advantage of it.

Ever sensitive to the potential security threat posed by the United States, the Mexican military carefully controls personal contact between its officers and U.S. military attachés, going so far as to require formal authorization for social contacts with U.S. officers. The Mexican government has occasionally expelled U.S. attachés for gathering information too aggressively and has imposed early retirement on senior Mexican officers who had become too friendly with the U.S. mission. Strong suspicion of U.S. motives is ingrained in the Mexican military's thinking. In this environment, the attaché's role as an overt collector has made this traditional form of bilateral contact largely ineffective.

The Joint Mexican–United States Defense Commission

Within three months of Pearl Harbor, the presidents of the United States and Mexico established an unprecedented defense commission, which continues to provide a forum for dialogue to the extent that national military leaders are willing to use it. With the outcome of World War II still very much in doubt in February 1942, JMUSDC functioned in Washington as a staff to administer lend-lease assistance going to Mexico, as well as to coordinate planning in both countries for joint defense against enemy attacks, particularly on the West Coast.[9] As mentioned earlier, the commission formulated an

---

[8] Conversation with members of the U.S. Military Liaison Office in early 1994.

[9] The Mexican government's willingness to participate in the commission eliminated any chance of a second wartime confrontation with the United States. During World War I, Germany sought to exploit Mexico's poor relationship with the United States: the famous Zimmermann telegram, intercepted by British intelligence and released to the press, was a message from the German foreign minister to the Mexicans encouraging them to go to war with the United States to recover their lost territories, in alliance with Germany. Publication of the telegram before Mexico could respond in-

"Integral Defense Plan" to repel attacks by Axis or Japanese submarines and aircraft, foil efforts to mine U.S. harbors, and defeat covert aggression. Implementation of the plan was Mexico's first military collaboration with the United States, and the government approached it carefully. Mexican authorities limited the U.S. presence south of the border, managing the number and size of U.S. technical assistance and liaison teams deployed there and controlling their ability to travel around the country.

After the war, the need for traditional joint defense planning diminished, and Mexico City slowly lost interest in working closely with a neighbor that had begun violating Mexico's core principles of nonintervention and self-determination. The commission remained active during the early years of the cold war and issued its last updated combined defense plan in 1955. As diplomatic relations turned increasingly sour, both governments continued to see value in retaining JMUSDC, a symbol of a successful military partnership, as a channel of communication between defense establishments. Its meetings became annual social events; substantive discussion was lost until the late 1980s.

The mission and organization of JMUSDC have stayed the same for over fifty years. The commission exists "to study problems and propose measures to be adopted relating to the common defense." With differing concepts of national security, the delegations do not agree about how to interpret this mission. This has been a point of frequent discussion since 1989. The U.S. delegation, led on a rotating basis by armed services representatives and responsible to the Joint Chiefs of Staff,[10] believes that the mission is still valid and can be useful in responding to such transnational threats to mutual security as drug trafficking and arms smuggling. The U.S. side does not equate the concept of "common defense" with violating the concept of "sovereignty"—both concepts can coexist. The Mexican delegation, provided by the Office of the Mexican Defense Attaché and responsible to the Mexican National Defense Headquarters, wishes to maintain the status quo and avoid any semblance of operational cooperation.

Both members of the commission have a permanent secretariat in Washington. In the early 1990s they began to organize meetings every

---

flamed U.S. indignation, increased suspicion, and decreased U.S.–Mexican cooperation in other areas.

[10] The U.S. chief of delegation is a two-star general. Each service also provides a (one-star) flag officer to serve on it. At one point, the position of chief rotated among the armed services and the Joint Staff, providing no continuity and suggesting minimal U.S. interest. This practice was discontinued as part of an effort over the last five years to streamline and standardize how the United States is represented on *all* of its international military commissions, as well as to demonstrate the importance of the military relationship with Mexico.

quarter at the staff officer level and semi-annually for the delegation's principal (flag) officers. The United States presented, and the commission explored, several proposals for increased bilateral cooperation without success. This process continues today. With disagreements on fundamental issues, as well as little evidence of Mexico City's willingness to use their delegation or this channel for constructive and substantive dialogue, JMUSDC has been losing its potential as a forum for bilateral military relations since 1993. The commission is reverting to its previously dormant cold-war state.

Service-to-Service Contact

There is a tradition of professional interactions between U.S. and Mexican armies, navies, and air forces, and it is this form of bilateral military relations that has shown the most positive progress since 1988, particularly among general, or flag, officers. Low-key and low-visibility annual exchanges of a small number of officers have long been the principal method for making contacts and learning more about each other's institutions. Service academies began exchanging language (or culture) instructors in the 1950s. A substitution in the air force of instructor pilots started in the 1980s. Mexican officers have routinely studied and taught at the U.S. Army School of the Americas and attended all U.S. senior service (war) colleges. The Mexican Navy has had an officer in every U.S. Navy Command College class since 1960. The high quality of these naval officers can be seen in the fact that thirty-three graduates have risen to flag rank, and six have gone on to lead the navy. In Mexico, one or two U.S. Army officers regularly attend the Superior War College, which is actually the rough equivalent to a U.S. military command and staff college.[11] Additionally, senior U.S. flag officers and civilian defense officials are often invited to Mexico for the annual national celebration of "El Grito de Dolores," which commemorates Mexico's independence from Spain, and for bilateral discussions. The scope of the traditional U.S. military engagement is slowly beginning to expand by service. This is discussed in the next section, which looks at recent steps toward improving military relations.

The intent, size, and success of the original approaches to service-to-service relations need to be kept in perspective. The principal aim of these initiatives has always been to benefit the U.S. military. Estab-

[11] The U.S. and Mexican war colleges are not equivalent. The one-year U.S. senior service college experience is the apex of military education below flag officer rank. The Mexican Superior War College provides a three-year command and staff course, one professional step lower in curriculum and status. U.S. Army students only attend the second year.

lished international education programs conducted in the United States have been designed to contribute to the professional broadening of attending U.S. officers. Today's engagement also benefits U.S. personnel, but it is more proactive and supportive of bilateral and regional policies. All of the annual education programs are very small in size. In many instances, there are only one or two officers—too few to influence an institution unless graduates go on to positions of great responsibility and introduce changes based on their U.S. experience.

For U.S. officers, overseas exchange programs have focused on making personal professional contacts, becoming familiar with military institutions and operational doctrines, and, more broadly, learning about a different national culture and its values. The number of officers that participate annually in these exchanges has been very small, less than twenty. The success of the educational experience in Mexico for U.S. officers has been mixed. The Mexican military culture is very different, stressing conformity and institutional loyalty above independent thought and creativity. It is prone to becoming strongly antiforeigner at times and difficult for international students.

Military Assistance

Closely associated with service-to-service contact is a military assistance relationship. This form of bilateral contact began as a lend-lease agreement during World War II, but over the last fifty years Mexico City has preferred to purchase U.S. military systems and equipment instead of accepting grant assistance. The primary reason for this practice is fear that the United States might use its security assistance to gain a form of influence or leverage over Mexican defense or security policy, as the United States has attempted in other countries. The one exception is Mexico's acceptance of grant International Military Education and Training (IMET) funds. Between 1950 and 1993, the United States allocated $6.7 million for 2,061 students (primarily officers) to receive professional instruction or technical training in the United States; over 800 have attended courses during the last ten years, many of them at the U.S. Army School of the Americas or in programs tied to counter-narcotics operations.

Mexico's first major commercial purchase of a U.S. military system was the multipurpose F-5 "Freedom Fighter" aircraft in 1981. This acquisition was followed during that decade by C-130 cargo planes, T-33 pilot trainers, and maintenance and technical training services. The United States established a military liaison office (MLO) to manage the F-5 purchase. The MLO has always been staffed by U.S. Air Force officers. As Mexican military interests have expanded over the last five years, this office has had to coordinate navy purchases of U.S.

frigates and army purchases of U.S. night vision equipment. The uni-service MLO has found that its suggestions concerning possible army or navy acquisitions often are not considered credible. In practice, the Mexicans want to initiate all sales agreements: they request specific items, and the United States decides whether or not to sell them. The same process is used to purchase items of military equipment from France, Russia, Britain, and Mexico's other trading partners when the United States refuses or delays deciding on a request.

In U.S. experience elsewhere, military assistance has proven to be an effective way to nurture military-to-military contact, particularly through the technical training associated with major acquisitions. In Mexico's case, a sale of military hardware relies totally on Mexican decisions to make a major purchase and U.S. willingness to respond. Even if all goes well, the contact is often short-lived. The Defense Department must be careful in discussing specific items of equipment. There is no assurance that the State Department, and in some cases the U.S. Congress, will approve the sale, especially of lethal items such as helicopter gunships or bombs for air force aircraft. This has been the situation since the beginning of the Chiapas uprising in January 1994. The Mexican Army's actions during the initial days of the rebellion sparked criticism from numerous human rights groups. Mexican military leaders would prefer to purchase U.S. material, but as the 1994 Independence Day military parade demonstrated with new French-made armed personnel carriers and Russian MI-8 HIP helicopters (flown by Russian pilots and seen for the first time), if Mexico cannot acquire a capability from the United States, it will buy the equipment elsewhere.

The Inter-American Defense System

The inter-American defense system provides the final opportunity for interaction between U.S. and Mexican officers, but it is limited by Mexican suspicions and the basic nature of this approach. There are three venues in the inter-American defense system: the Inter-American Defense Board (IADB), the Inter-American Defense College (IADC), and traditional meetings of service chiefs from countries with military establishments, such as the Conference of American Armies. Mexico has restricted its involvement, reflecting a belief that this system continues to be a vehicle for U.S. intrusion into the internal affairs of American states. This mind-set was carried to an extreme in July 1995 when the Mexican delegation to the first Defense Ministerial of the Americas, hosted by U.S. Secretary of Defense Perry in Williamsburg, Virginia, included only the Mexican ambassador to the United States, the defense attaché, and several embassy officials.

When there is involvement, the number of Mexican officers is very small, providing a poor context for engagement. In practice, the Mexican delegation to the IADB is led by the defense attaché, and for the last three years, for the first time in recent memory, there has been an officer on the board's staff. There are always two officer students, one each from the army and navy, in residence at the College, and the Foreign Ministry recently has started sending a diplomat. Mexican chiefs of service rarely participate personally in the biennial Conference of American Armies or the naval and air force equivalents, preferring to be represented by an envoy such as the senior military attaché in the country hosting the conference. No attempt is made to join the topically focused working groups that meet during the intervening years and report their activities at the plenary session.

Recent Steps toward Improved Military Relations

The Defense Department's 1988 classified internal review of bilateral military relations resulted in the adoption of a straightforward solution to be implemented over an unspecified number of years by the Joint Staff and the armed services (including the U.S. Coast Guard). The original concept, which was reassessed as part of a policy review prior to President Zedillo's inauguration in December 1994, still appears to be guiding U.S. initiatives. Research suggests that the armed forces were directed to establish more normal military-to-military relationships with their Mexican counterparts and to do so in two open-ended phases. The guiding plan included a preliminary step in which Washington's efforts would provide, to the extent Mexico's government and military permitted, a better understanding of the U.S. armed forces—the institutions, approaches to professional education and training, and values. Once having achieved regular, nonthreatening, and amiable contacts on Mexican terms, the concept envisions an incremental movement to a second phase in which contact would expand, but on a reciprocal basis. The original guidance seems to have stressed patience and flexibility in working around policy differences with Mexico and within the U.S. government, and in adapting to unforeseeable events such as the Zapatista rebellion. After almost six years, U.S. practitioners believe that progress has been made, principally through service initiatives. They are quick to point out, however, that forward movement has been uneven across the armed forces and is not institutionalized.

The pattern of proactive U.S. proposals and reluctant Mexican responses appears now to be in the third of three stages since the 1988–1989 time frame, when both military establishments, anticipating the advent of political and economic changes, asked literally "what's in it for us" and came to somewhat similar conclusions about the inevitability of closer military contact. Initially, interaction with Mexico expanded very slowly, hampered throughout 1989 and 1990 by contentious events in Central America and Panama, and by inherent nationalism and traditional caution on the Mexican side. Military dialogue in the first stage, while encouraging in form and content compared to the preceding thirty years, did not stimulate much action on either side. The first stage gradually ended in 1990–1991.

The focal point of the second stage, roughly 1991 to 1994, was the Joint Mexican–United States Defense Commission (JMUSDC) which at the time seemed to embody great potential for progress. Both U.S. and Mexican sections had agreed in 1989 to increase the frequency of formal meetings from annual to semi-annual, and to hold lower-level working group sessions quarterly. Early in the JMUSDC stage, the two sections agreed to explore how to refocus the commission to meet the challenges of the 1990s. In seeking to define points of agreement and disagreement, they discussed concepts of security and the nature of transnational threats as well as more practical topics such as cooperation in confronting the mutual drug threat and U.S. ideas for strengthening bilateral service ties. A long-moribund institution seemed to be coming to life. In the commission, the United States thought it saw a reliable conduit to the Mexican senior military leadership and an acceptable forum for discussing mutual security interests in the post–cold war era. A new, more positive spirit animated the fiftieth anniversary of JMUSDC, celebrated in Washington in early 1992 and attended by General Colin Powell, Chairman of the Joint Chiefs of Staff. The Mexican government took the unprecedented additional step of hosting a plenary session in Mexico City in April 1992. Despite an excess of symbolism over substance, the meeting signaled the clear desire of the Mexican armed forces to improve military relations with the United States.

But JMUSDC has not lived up to expectations. It became increasingly apparent in 1993 and 1994 that Mexican military leaders did not want to broaden the commission's mandate and were particularly opposed to it assuming an operational role. Various U.S. proposals had envisioned JMUSDC being a facilitator, a coordinator, a source of national information leading to small-unit training and personnel exchanges, and the conduit to bringing about staff talks between the U.S. Joint Staff and an ad hoc Mexican equivalent. Mexico wanted to retain the status quo: military officials insisted that, by law, their armed forces could not participate in combined or coordinated operations or exercises with any other country. Army units could not leave Mexico to train in the United States. There was no desire for high-level staff talks. And, in addition, service-to-service contacts had matured during the JMUSDC stage; from a Mexican perspective, this form of interaction was more beneficial and easier to control. The commission's role, consequently, has been gradually to return to its more symbolic and less substantive nature.

The current (third) stage in the enhancement of bilateral military relations, with roots back to 1991, emphasizes interservice contacts, primarily involving the U.S. Coast Guard and the navy's Third Fleet, headquartered in San Diego, and General Gordon Sullivan, Chief of Staff, U.S. Army (1991 and 1995).[12] Visible improvements in internaval interaction can be seen in the frequency of U.S. port visits in Mexico. The trend has increased dramatically from two navy and seven Coast Guard vessels in 1991 to forty-one navy and five Coast Guard ships in 1992. Two years later, the number of U.S. vessels stopping in Mexico for fuel and other logistical services exceeded by one those visiting Canadian ports.

Progress began in mid-1991 on the West Coast, where 90 percent of port visits occur. The Mexican government started to show a marked increase in flexibility by approving requests more quickly and without asking the U.S. Navy to disclose the on-board presence of nuclear weapons. This question had been asked routinely prior to mid-1991.[13] On the U.S. side, the Third Fleet reviewed and adjusted its procedures to request diplomatic clearance for port visits, taking into consideration the processing times built into Mexico's system and the need to carefully manage how many U.S. Navy or Coast Guard ships are in Mexican ports at the same time—the limit is three warships in port per coast.

Genuine naval and Foreign Ministry cooperation on a range of issues, from port visits to smuggled Chinese refugees, has led to the assignment in June 1993 of a Mexican naval liaison officer at Headquarters, Third Fleet. This assignment ultimately required President Salinas's personal approval, and three months later was followed by the first of a series of direct talks between the U.S. Navy, U.S. Coast Guard, and the Mexican Navy. Progress occurred in the operational realm as well. "Coincidental" interaction at sea—passing information and sharing professional experiences—has often taken place between these three services over the last ten years, introducing a sense of positive collaboration into several different types of maritime operations of interest to both countries: search and rescue, counter-drug, antismuggling (against Chinese refugees), and environmental protection. Contact at sea by ship captains gradually has led to planned

---

[12] The U.S. Air Force and U.S. Marine Corps have made strides toward better relations with their Mexican counterparts, which are not independent services. They are subordinate respectively to the secretary of national defense—an army officer—and the minister of the navy.

[13] The Mexican government continues to maintain its policy that nuclear powered warships are not permitted to visit the country's ports.

events by higher headquarters, such as a Gulf of Mexico oil spill response exercise (U.S. Coast Guard and Mexican Navy) in the summer of 1993 and Mexican port calls in 1993 and 1994 during San Francisco's Fleetweek and Seattle's Sea Fair. Senior naval leaders have participated in counterpart visits, and junior officer and noncommissioned officer exchanges also have taken place. In sum, professional interaction has begun to take place at low, middle, and senior levels in Mexico's Ministry of the Navy. The U.S. Navy and Coast Guard have adopted a "slow and steady" approach in this effort, emphasizing dialogue and coordination. The common nature and tradition of naval service and its shared routine of maritime operations are an advantage. The relative ease with which forward movement has occurred suggests that both navies realized that internaval relations had to improve over the last three years in the face of common transnational problems, and that NAFTA was a convenient catalyst to begin the process.

The U.S. Army continues to face a different and a difficult challenge trying to approach and interact more broadly with a counterpart institution that works to preserve its independent and self-reliant image. One of the few U.S. defense scholars studying the Mexican Army in early 1994 described well its view of change:

> The army does not place a high value on change. Military leaders have relied heavily on traditional values and principles, rather than on innovative approaches to old problems. The Constitution of 1917 designated the armed forces as the protector of national sovereignty. The military will continue to perform that mission. In so doing, it will try to assure that there will always be a "safe distance" from the powerful neighbor to the North (Wager 1994: 18).

Without opportunities for coincidental low-level contact and bound by a law that conveniently forbids unit activities (combined training exercises, unit exchanges) outside of Mexico or with foreign countries, interarmy relations could expand only if, at the top, there was tacit agreement to proceed. It was important that the service chiefs meet. Mutual understanding would not result from indirect communication through attachés, JMUSDC, or military assistance channels—all held in low regard by the Mexican side. The mistrusted U.S. Army had to demonstrate the sincerity of its interest in contact. Through at least four trips to Mexico and by hosting his counterpart in the United States several times during a three-year period, General Sullivan more than passed a "test." He developed a constructive personal relationship with the head of the Mexican Army and Air Force, Secretary of National Defense General Riviello, and, after the Zapatista rebellion in Chiapas in January 1994, reaffirmed U.S. friendship and cooperation at a time when the Mexican military was awakening to the realities of its doctrinal insufficiencies, old equipment, and today's intrusive world of nongovernmental interest groups, the international media, and information technology.

Attendance at the annual Mexican independence celebration, "El Grito," has always provided an opportunity for constructive interservice, particularly army-to-army, contact. Its importance for the United States, however, increased markedly during General Sullivan's tenure. Substantial U.S. military and civilian defense delegations, including at least one three- or four-star army general (usually several), have represented the United States, honored the Mexican defense forces, and, more to the point, taken advantage of opportunities to discuss privately future technical (not operational) contacts, information sharing, and the purchase of U.S. equipment. The U.S. Army, anticipating Mexican interests, has tried over the last five years to include in its delegation senior officers who could address technical issues. This has worked successfully. High-level professional talks have often followed between officers who met for the first time at El Grito, and it is the genesis of several discrete army-to-army initiatives. The Mexican military's handling of the U.S. delegation at El Grito provides one of the few ways to gauge progress in U.S.–Mexican military relations. This can be accomplished by observing the protocol associated with the event, such as the quality of the guest facilities, balcony space assigned for watching the military parade, and seating arrangements at official functions. Using this system as a guide, the treatment given to U.S. delegations in recent years has been notable, exceeding the hospitality accorded to other visiting delegations.

New forms of interarmy interaction that accommodate Mexican sensitivities and legal restrictions emerged under General Sullivan's leadership. These include post-Chiapas information-gathering visits by Mexican general officers to army installations and schools in the United States, researching subjects such as public relations and military training. Earlier initiatives comprise the establishment of a permanent seat at the U.S. Army War College (an uncommon step), annual visits to Mexico by the students from the National Defense University's National War College and the Industrial College of the Armed Forces, and several technical army "subject matter expert exchanges" in such fields as medical evacuation and disaster response. Also, in the early 1990s the Defense Department's CAPSTONE program—the pinnacle of U.S. military education, reserved for general officers—began to send one-third of each year's class to visit Mexico, Canada, and several Latin American countries. Another example of the new military cooperation, finally, was an unprecedented joint training mission in Mexico. The United States and Mexico conducted three airborne exercises in 1992 in which U.S. aircraft served as jump platforms for Mexican paratroopers. The Mexican Army and Navy conducted these airborne exercises separately, since tradition dictates that army and navy troops never jump from the same plane.

General Sullivan's personal involvement ensured that U.S.–Mexican interarmy relations did not disappear as an army priority within a large service bureaucracy. His most enduring contributions, however, may be his personal interaction with Mexico's military leaders after the January 1, 1994, uprising in Chiapas and his efforts to make sure that interarmy progress would continue after his retirement in June 1995. What transpired in discussions with his counterpart after Chiapas is not clear, but General Sullivan and a small delegation visited General Riviello in Mexico twice in early 1994 and were given an unprecedented look at the Mexican Army in its counter-drug operations during one of these trips. Characteristically, the chief of staff's approach in similar circumstances has been to personify candor, openness, and military professionalism, sharing experiences rather than lecturing. For Sullivan, there would be no hidden agendas in his personal contacts with either the Mexicans or U.S. foreign and defense policy officials. His unpublicized meetings with General Riviello resulted in several previously mentioned information-gathering visits to the United States, support for the sale of several nonlethal items of U.S. army equipment, and advocacy in Washington for increases in Mexico's allocation of grant IMET funds for professional military education and training in 1994 and 1995, and projected for 1996. Acknowledgment that General Sullivan had helped the Mexican Army and improved U.S.–Mexican military relations was the unprecedented presence of Mexico's new secretary of national defense, General Enriques Cervantes, at the U.S. Army chief of staff's retirement. (General Riviello had retired in December 1994.)

General Sullivan took two steps toward ensuring that his progress in interarmy relations would not die when he stepped down as chief of staff. First, he ensured that the pivotal U.S. Fifth Army, located in San Antonio, Texas, would be led by someone who would maintain the momentum, at least in the short run. In early 1994, Lieutenant General Marc Cisneros, a dynamic Mexican American, assumed command. His experience in Latin America and strong presence have sent a positive signal to the Mexican leadership. Another indication of continuity occurred when the new army chief of staff, General Dennis Reimer, demonstrated his exclusive interest in Mexico by meeting only with General Cervantes, among many well-wishers, on his first day of command.

An earlier, institutionalizing step was taken when both countries recognized the wisdom of holding annual Border Commanders' Conferences. The initial meeting was hosted by the U.S. Fifth Army in

1990, when Sullivan was vice chief of staff. The venue for the conference has since rotated between the countries (a meeting did not take place in 1991). The roots of this initiative are to be found in the U.S. military's involvement in counter-drug activity along the U.S.–Mexican border. The Defense Department's decision to have Reserve and National Guard units supplement federal law enforcement agencies in border states raised suspicions in Mexico about the real purpose. To ensure transparency and diminish Mexican concerns, both countries agreed to start holding annual meetings of neighboring military commanders and to invite observers. These sessions have proven very successful in allaying Mexico's suspicions and serving as a confidence-building measure. The conference has provided an opportunity for Mexican and U.S. general officers to discuss a range of border-related issues as well as security topics of broader mutual interest. For example, the 1994 conference—cohosted in Albuquerque by Lieutenant General Cisneros and Major General Baca, New Mexico adjutant general, and conducted entirely in Spanish—included topics ranging from arms trafficking south across the border to an academic discussion of the security ramifications of NAFTA. This forum may ultimately provide the opportunity for the substantive dialogue the Defense Department sought unsuccessfully via JMUSDC in the early 1990s. The most recent meeting took place in Chihuahua, Mexico, in late October 1995.

Thoughts on the Future of Bilateral Military Relations

In the near term, the slow warming trend in traditionally distant cross-border military relations is expected to continue. Service associations should remain cordial and productive, losing standoffishness somewhat faster in the navies than in the armies. But internaval and interarmy achievements are fragile and reversible, responding to more than internal service pressures. Military-to-military relationships between democratic states are not independent variables. They are integral to larger and more complex political, economic, and security relationships, which are never quite as harmonious as observers may think. An experienced political analyst recently commented that:

> Despite substantial improvements, many of the old emotions and beliefs live on, just below the surface, in both countries. Good intentions on the part of the two governments can help maintain a cooperative bilateral relationship, but the variety of interests in both countries make

> future conflict, as well as some attitudinal backsliding, in-evitable (Purcell 1994: 45–46).

If the broader context for military contact begins to weaken, military relations may falter as well. In fact, Mexico City has traditionally used its armed forces to signal diplomatic displeasure with the United States by abruptly halting all or part of its military cooperation. At the moment, however, there are ample reasons to be optimistic. NAFTA has changed the fundamental political and economic relationship between three neighbors and sparked a desire to cooperate in solving a range of mutual problems.

Current U.S. efforts to enhance military interaction deliberately favor the Mexican armed forces. This lopsided arrangement, envisioned in the 1988 Defense Department strategy, only touches the periphery of the institution. This approach, however, needs to continue for the foreseeable future until greater mutual understanding and trust are realized. Careful U.S. efforts to offer only programs that address service needs, as they become apparent, and stay within Mexico's legal and political bounds have played a pivotal role so far. This course of action is frustrating to follow, but pushing too aggressively and without cultural sensitivity for closer, more substantive bilateral military relations promises to trigger negative responses. For many Mexican officers, particularly those in the army, their northern neighbor still remains the potential threat to their national security. Mexico's highly structured, traditional system of officer education and professional development by rote and its advocacy of the military institution's mission to loyally defend the political structure have not changed.

The complexity of the evolving relationship was underscored in early 1994. As the personal interaction between army chiefs was developing a sense of mutual trust and the United States was demonstrating its support, the Mexican Ministry of National Defense published five thousand copies of a highly inflammatory 1993 polemic, introduced by Lyndon LaRouche, that accuses the United States of plotting to destroy ("*aniquilar*") Latin American armed forces (Small et al. 1994). Copies were given to all army general officers. The cautionary message was clear.

This awkward situation does not mean that the U.S. armed forces should take no interest in improving specific aspects of the Mexican military institution, particularly its education system. Many lessons from the recent army and air force experiences in Chiapas can be traced to a need for fundamental doctrinal and educational changes within service institutions. The hope is that through exposure to the U.S. and other foreign professional military education and training programs, Mexican leaders will recognize the inadequacies of their approach, seek assistance, and institute reforms. In this regard, Washington has increased the amount of its grant IMET program to be offered to the Mexican government in fiscal year 1996 from $400,000 to $700,000.

The United States must take care not to challenge the delicate balance in Mexico's civil-military relations, which both civil and military leaders believe they have under control, and thereby contribute to domestic political instability. Difficulties could arise if U.S. government representatives should begin to tempt the Mexican armed forces with visions of high-cost, high-tech equipment or urge Mexican officials to reform their system of civil-military relations along more democratic Anglo-Saxon lines. Civilian officials in Mexico have carefully avoided expensive arms purchases, which the country can ill afford. But trying to solve internal problems with new equipment, buying the loyalty of the armed forces rather than addressing the more painful root deficiencies in structure, doctrine, and professional development, has been a Mexican military trait. Too much exposure to U.S. and European establishments could become a liability if it prompts military leaders to demand more sophisticated equipment, precipitating an internal confrontation at a time when the Chiapas uprising remains unresolved, the peso collapse has contributed to an increase in corruption and domestic violence, and political officials need strong military support.

The Mexican postrevolutionary model of civil-military relations, with its emphasis on unquestioned and unfettered civilian control, has worked well for the country. But as the degree of domestic economic and political liberalization increases, many of the old associated arrangements are changing as well, aided by additional outside pressure. Washington has begun to press Mexico City to democratize, fearing that Mexico's authoritarian political system, the long-standing guarantor of stability, now threatens both the success of NAFTA and political stability. How these trends will affect civil-military relations is not clear. One view considers the relationship too well established to change markedly even during a political transition away from one-party rule. An alternative, and more troubling, perspective presented in a recent U.S. academic study suggests that there is "pervasive uneasiness about the degree to which greater strength and 'professionalization' of the military, together with increased contact with foreign armed forces, might lead to evolution of the kind of powerful, prestigious and autonomous corporate entity (with ideas of its own), which populate the political landscape of so many other Latin American nations" (CSIS 1992: 25). In working with the Mexican military, the Defense Department must walk a fine line between what is good for U.S. security interests and what is good for Mexican democracy.

Finally, in expanding cross-border military contacts, the defense officials and diplomats must remain cognizant of U.S. civil-military relations and not take them for granted. Military communications with Mexican counterparts have to be coordinated thoroughly with State Department representatives in the United States and Mexico. There should be no Defense Department "surprises" that complicate parallel efforts by other U.S. government agencies. A solid framework for interagency coordination currently exists. For it to continue functioning properly, however, there must be a willingness among defense and diplomatic officers to communicate openly and often, setting the correct example for others. U.S. officials must ensure that the occasional frustrations attendant upon working with an elusive neighbor do not complicate civil-military relations in the United States.

Conclusion

Judging from the period of NAFTA negotiations and the first eighteen months after the agreement's implementation, it is clear that NAFTA has created a conducive environment for reshaping bilateral military relations and that both defense establishments have seized the opportunity. While from a U.S. perspective some progress has been made, the maturation process has only just begun. It will be a slow evolution, more so for the army than the navy. Despite the fact that relations between the United States and Mexico have changed in ways that no one would have thought possible fifty years ago, Mexico's army is closer to 1945 than to 1995 in its self-perception and view of relations with its northern neighbor. The institution and its culture intertwine to be a pillar of the political system that emerged from a national revolution over seventy years ago. The army remains the most effective, responsive, and loyal coercive power available to the state. It is an inheritance passed from one chief executive to the next. However, many of today's military leaders recognize that their institution cannot remain figuratively in the 1940s: it must adapt professionally to the new and unsettling demands of democracy, economic integration, and national security in the 1990s. A modern Mexican defense establishment cannot avoid an association with its U.S. counterpart, which is an important albeit uncomfortable ingredient in shaping the alternate future. But can the institution accept and adapt to U.S. influence while continuing to fulfill its traditional role in Mexican society? Will the nation's political-military partnership even allow the gradual modernization of the military's core—its organization and cultural mind-set—to accelerate, possibly introducing progressive U.S. ideas, while a turbulent political transition is taking place across the country? The answers to these pivotal questions remain hidden from foreign eyes behind the traditional veil of Mexican secrecy.

Epilogue, December 1995

The search for convergence in cross-border military relations entered a fourth stage in late October 1995 with the first visit to Mexico by a U.S. secretary of defense. The trip, arranged at General Cervantes's invitation, has been cast by Washington as a natural step after the signing of NAFTA and the July meeting of American defense ministers in Williamsburg, Virginia, which Secretary Perry's Mexican counterpart did not attend. The third stage, with its orientation on interservice contacts, appears to have been subsumed in this new, broader, and higher-level approach to defense diplomacy that emphasizes bilateral *security* instead of *military* relations. The principal aim of the secretary's visit was to produce increased military cooperation in combating transborder trafficking in narcotics, but Perry tried, in his words, to "set the stage for our nations to do more in the security area, and at both higher and deeper levels: more defense and military contacts and dialogue; more officer exchanges; more cooperation on disaster relief; and more openness and sharing of information, such as in the areas of our counter-narcotics and border operations. [Finally,] looking beyond our counter-narcotics work, we have the opportunity for cooperation in equipment modernization" (quoted in Fineman 1995: 6; see also DePalma 1995).

Secretary Perry's visit is a major milestone in the U.S. quest to overcome the long history of Mexican suspicion and move toward a new strategic relationship based on openness, trust, and cooperation. Building on the progress to date achieved through interservice contacts and U.S. assistance with foreign military education, the trip makes apparent in a demonstrable way and for the first time the Clinton administration's commitment to improving defense relations. Until this point, the official U.S. approach has been passive, letting the armed forces take the lead with low-profile initiatives. Perry's remarks in Mexico City establish a framework for future interaction in five areas. These cooperative "themes" include: air and sea coordination, counter-narcotics, disaster assistance, an expansion of IMET, and the opportunity for some military modernization—principally, advanced technology satellite radar systems.[14]

---

[14] There also was a discussion of increasing the size of the military helicopter fleet leased to the Mexican Attorney General's Office, which is considering the acquisition of about a dozen UH-1H Huey helicopters.

Mexico badly needs radars to improve its capability for air and sea surveillance. In raising the issue of radar systems, the U.S. government explicitly recognizes that the day-to-day role of the Mexican armed forces in combating both the flow of illegal drugs and the influence of the traffickers is expanding and that the military's importance is increasing. Aware that Mexico's sovereignty and the independence of its defense institution are traditionally sensitive, Washington has offered either to provide the radars or assist in acquiring them. Mexico City will make the final decision.

The extent to which Mexican political and military leaders share Secretary Perry's perspective remains to be seen over the next year. However, initial signs are encouraging. Predictably, there has been no visible response from Mexico's security officials, but in less than forty-five days after the visit, a high-level bilateral working group met to explore the possibilities and obstacles inherent in each of Secretary Perry's five themes. The delegation of Mexican army, air force, and naval senior officers, many of whom had attended professional schools in the United States, led by a high-ranking official from the Foreign Ministry, was substantively well prepared for the meeting, interested in solving mutual problems, and willing to move ahead at this new stage in U.S.–Mexican military relations. As a result of the meeting, each theme now has its own sub-working group of U.S. and Mexican officers. Several additional sessions were anticipated before General Cervantes and Secretary Perry would meet again, in spring 1996.

In effect, the new stage of defense interaction continues to leave Mexico City in control of the way ahead. Mexican officials have the initiative to accept or refuse all or part of what the United States offers, as well as to shape the general conditions under which the programs are developed and ultimately operate. While U.S. legislation that Mexico finds objectionable, such as the requirement for end-use monitoring of U.S. military equipment sold to a foreign country, cannot be changed, Mexico's military leaders control the extent to which U.S. counterparts get to examine their army, air force, and naval establishments to determine training and material needs. The Ministries of National Defense and the Navy should have no difficulty continuing to protect the core values of their institutions from outside influence while, at the same time, improving cross-border coordination of daily counter-narcotics operations and working to carefully modernize service equipment and doctrine. Mexican defense officials appear to be saying to their counterparts from north of the border: we are sincere in engaging you, but can the United States deliver on its initiatives?

How Washington intends to develop its expanding defense engagement for this new stage is not clear. Three immediate issues should provide an indication. How will the secretary's office, heretofore not an active player, tie together the various old and new Defense Department dimensions of a now expanded U.S. agenda, in coordination with the Department of State and others? How will established relationships between neighboring armies and navies proceed side by side with a new defense-to-defense relationship that involves the same Mexican military officials? And what role will three unified commands—U.S. Southern Command, Atlantic Command, and Space Command (counter-narcotics radar)—play when there are no Mexican counterparts? The recent bilateral working session suggests that the Defense Department will continue to go forward carefully step by step, nurturing its opening with enthusiasm, patience, and no fanfare. The secretary's staff and the Joint Staff will now take control of all initiatives, and the developing service contacts will be subsumed in the new activities insofar as possible.

At this point in the evolving relationship, the earlier conclusions retain their validity, but a potent, new, catalytic ingredient has been introduced. As a result, the continuing search for convergence on both sides of the border has just become more complicated to conduct with new and old actors and issues; more visible to the media and political observers outside the defense institutions, at least in the United States; and more likely to be politicized in both countries as the nature of the agenda changes and resource requirements increase. In this new era of apparent cooperation and potential progress, the U.S. side cannot lose sight of the fact that military convergence between neighbors, shrouded as it is in a heritage of suspicion, will never be perfect. For both sides, there has never been more than partial symmetry in U.S.–Mexican security interests, which continue to be defined in very different terms.

References

Aguilar Zinser, Adolfo. 1990. "Civil-Military Relations in Mexico." In *The Military and Democracy: The Future of Civil-Military Relations in Latin America*, edited by Louis W. Goodman, Johanna S.R. Mendelson, and Juan Rial. Lexington, Mass.: Lexington Books.

CSIS (Center for Strategic and International Studies). 1992. "Intensifying North American Relationships: Implications for Defense." A draft report prepared for the Department of Defense. Washington, D.C.: CSIS, December.

DePalma, Anthony. 1995. "U.S. Defense Chief Meets Mexican to Discuss Military Distrust," *New York Times*, October 24.

Fineman, Mark. 1995. "Perry Visit Opens Ties with Mexico's Isolationist Military," *Los Angeles Times*, October 25.

Purcell, Susan Kaufman. 1994. "NAFTA and U.S.–Mexican Relations," *North-South, the Magazine of the Americas* 4 (3): 42–47.

Small, Gretchen, et al. 1994. *El complot para aniquilar a las fuerzas armadas y a las naciones de Iberoamérica*. 2 vols. Exclusive edition for the Mexican Army. México, D.F.: Biblioteca del Oficial Mexicano.

Wager, Stephen J. 1994. "The Mexican Military Approaches the 21st Century: Coping with a New World Order." A Strategic Studies Institute Special Report. Carlisle, Penn.: U.S. Army War College, February 21.

Appendix

Study Group Members and Participants

(with affiliations at time of joining group)

Sergio Aguayo Quezada, El Colegio de México
Drew Arena, U.S. Department of Justice
Delal Baer, Center for Strategic and International Studies
John Bailey, Georgetown University
Raúl Benítez Manaut, Universidad Nacional Autónoma de México
Lilia Bermúdez, Centro de Investigación y Docencia Económicas
Jorge Carrillo Olea, Centro de Investigación y Seguridad Nacional
Manuel Carrillo Poblano, Secretaría de Gobernación
Jorge Chabat, Centro de Investigación y Docencia Económicas
John A. Cope, National Defense University
Oscar de Lasse, consultant, Mexico City
Gabriel Díaz, Universidad Americana
Michael Dziedzic, National Defense University
Mark Falcoff, American Enterprise Institute
Rafael Fernández de Castro, Instituto Tecnológico Autónomo de México
Aaron Friedberg, Princeton University
Roy Godson, Georgetown University
Guadalupe González González, Centro de Investigación y Docencia Económicas
Timothy Goodman, Georgetown University
Luis Herrera-Lasso, Secretaría de Relaciones Exteriores
Robert Lieber, Georgetown University
David R. Mares, University of California, San Diego
William Olson, National Strategy Information Center
William Perry, Center for Strategic and International Studies
Jesús Reyes Heroles, Grupo de Economistas Asociados

David Ronfeldt, RAND Corporation
Arturo Sarukhan, Secretaría de Relaciones Exteriores
Mónica Serrano, El Colegio de México
Sally Shelton-Colby, Georgetown University
Peter H. Smith, University of California, San Diego
William Sullivan, Department of State (retired)
Jorge Tello, CENDRO
Cathryn L. Thorup, University of California, San Diego
Celia Toro, El Colegio de México
Joseph Tulchin, Woodrow Wilson Center
Arturo Valenzuela, Georgetown University
Mónica Verea, Universidad Nacional Autónoma de México
Manuel Villa, Secretaría de Gobernación
Steven Wager, United States Military Academy

About the Contributors

Sergio Aguayo Quezada is a professor in the Center for International Studies of El Colegio de México. His research focuses on security, U.S. foreign policy, U.S.–Mexican relations, and human rights. Aguayo was a founding member, and now serves as president, of the Mexican Academy of Human Rights, founding member of the Civic Alliance (a coalition of pro-democracy groups), and a founder of *La Jornada*. He has written or contributed to over twenty books and writes a weekly newspaper column which appears in Mexico's major newspapers.

John Bailey is professor of government at Georgetown University. His main research interests are Mexican internal politics, with a current emphasis on center-periphery relations, and U.S.–Mexican relations. Along with colleagues from the Norman Patterson School of Carleton University and the International Studies Program of the Instituto Tecnológico Autónomo de México, he codirects the NAFTA Trilateral Initiative, a program of research and graduate training.

John A. Cope is a research professor specializing in hemispheric security affairs at the National Defense University's Institute for National Strategic Studies. He previously served as military adviser to the Assistant Secretary of State for Inter-American Affairs, as Deputy Chief of Staff of U.S. Southern Command, and as special assistant to the Commander in Chief and the Deputy Chief of Staff for Operations and Plans at U.S. Army South. He is the author of *International Military Education and Training: An Assessment.*

Michael J. Dziedzic is a colonel in the United States Air Force and Senior Military Fellow at the Institute for National Strategic Studies of the National Defense University. He is the author of *NAFTA and North American Security* and *Mexico: Converging Challenges.*

Guadalupe González González is professor of political science at the Centro de Investigación y Docencia Económicas (CIDE) in Mexico City and is completing her doctorate in political science at the University of California, San Diego.

Luis Herrera-Lasso is a career officer in Mexico's foreign service and currently serves as Consul General in San Diego. He recently completed service in the Center for Intelligence and National Security.

David R. Mares is associate professor of political science at the University of California, San Diego. His publications include *Penetrating the International Market* and numerous articles and chapters on Latin America. He is currently finishing a manuscript on managing conflict in a heterogeneous world and editing a comparative collection on civil-military relations in Latin America, Southern Asia, and Central Europe.

Jorge E. Tello Peón is director of the Center for Intelligence and National Security in Mexico City and former director of the National Anti-Narcotics Center in Mexico City.

Manuel Villa Aguilera is professor of political science at the Universidad Nacional Autónoma de México (UNAM). He has also taught at El Colegio de México, Brown University, and the University of Connecticut. A former official in Mexico's Interior Ministry, his publications include *¿A quién le interesa la democracia en México?* and *El archipiélago mexicano.*

Publication of important new research on Mexico and U.S.–Mexican relations is a major activity of the Center for U.S.–Mexican Studies. Statements of fact and opinion appearing in Center publications are the responsibility of the authors alone and do not imply endorsement by the Center for U.S.–Mexican Studies, the International Advisory Council, or the University of California.

For a complete list of Center publications and order information, please contact:

Publications Sales Office
Center for U.S.–Mexican Studies
University of California, San Diego
9500 Gilman Drive, DEPT 0510
La Jolla, CA 92093-0510
Phone (619) 534-1160 Fax (619) 534-6447
e-mail: usmpubs@weber.ucsd.edu